HISTORY OF THE UNITED PANJAB

Volume III

DR. BAKHSHISH SINGH NIJJAR
Ex-Director, Punjab State Archives, Patiala

ATLANTIC PUBLISHERS AND DISTRIBUTORS

Published by
ATLANTIC PUBLISHERS AND DISTRIBUTORS
B-2, Vishal Enclave, New Delhi-110 027
Phones 5413460, 5429987

Sales Office
4346/4C, Ansari Road, Darya Ganj,
New Delhi-110 002
Phones 3273880, 3285873
Fax 91-11-3285873

ISBN 81-7156-534-4 (Vol. I)
ISBN 81-7156-535-2 (Vol. II)
ISBN 81-7156-536-0 (Vol. III)
ISBN 81-7156-540-9 (Set)

Typeset at
APD Computer Graphics, Delhi

Printed in India at
Mehra Offset Press, New Delhi-110 002

FOREWORD

Dr. Bakhshish Singh Nijjar, M.A., Ph. D., has followed his history of *Panjab Under the Sultanate (1000-1526), Panjab Under the Great Mughals (1526-1707)* and *Panjab Under the Later Mughals (1707-1759)* now by his *History of the United Panjab*. It covers a period of almost a century from 1849-1947. Like his earlier works it is well written and authorities for the various statements in the text are almost invariably given. As such it can be easily recommended for reference and even for study to students of history of the Punjab under the British.

As his bibliography demonstrates, he has depended for the History of the United Panjab in the nineteenth century (1849-1934) mostly on official records or works, written by Anglo-Indian writers who were not very sympathetic to the Indian point of view. If this makes this study partial occasionally, it must be acknowledged that records of this type serve a useful purpose. One wishes, however, that Dr. Nijjar had not taken Thorburn as his guide as neither his facts nor his inferences were accepted even by the Government of the Panjab at that time.

Coming to the twentieth century Dr. Nijjar's account is more selective. He gives us all the information about the career of various Lieutenant Governors and Governors who governed the Panjab. He gives a story of the Ghadar Movement to its rapid collapse within a few months. Rather than describes the Martial Law regime in the Panjab, he concentrates on the events at Amritsar. Here, however, he presents General Dyer as a straightforward, truth telling soldier entirely unversed in the way of politicians on the authority of Trevasikis ignoring the findings of the Hunter Committee. But left to himself he rightly calls the Jallianwala Massacre "a calculated piece of inhumanity towards utterly innocent and unarmed men and unparalleled for its ferocity in the history of modern British administration." His account of the Gurdwara reform agitation is very full, covering some fiftynine pages. Again it is largely based on the statements issued by the Shiromani Gurdwara Parbandhak Committee. It is good to find the efforts of the Sikhs for securing their "rights" related in one place.

To one reader however it seems that he has made too much of the Hindu-Sikh, Muslim riots in the Panjab during the years 1924-1932 to which he devotes twentyone pages. Thirtytwo pages have been devoted to the Terrorist Movement (The Babar Akalis) in the twenties.

In the thirties he discusses the Communal Award at large emphasising however the special demands of the Sikhs. This is followed by an account of the Civil Disobedience Movement in the Panjab 1930-1934. Here however he could have laid more emphasis on what happened in the Panjab rather than on events of all India importance.

There is a very valuable chapter as the 'Canalization of the Panjab'. Story of the Panjab States 1849-1947 is told elsewhere covering some eighty pages. Here at times, depending upon the authorities used, Dr. Nijjar seems to be pro-Maharajas and elsewhere favouring the struggle of the people of the states which he describes at length.

Another very valuable feature of the work is the chapter on the Kisan and the Muzara Movement in States from 1935 onwards. The chapter on the Panjab Civil Code gives us information not usually found in historical works. Not being a lawyer himself, it is not surprising that Dr. Nijjar seems sometimes to adopt easily the view of the early Panjab administrators whose word was law which nobody – not even a lawyer – could ever anticipate. He forgets that those apostles of personal rule were apt to go astray. Lord Minto had estimated that in the Canal Colonies alone the Colony Administrators had realized in six years twenty lakhs from the cultivators by way of fines which they had no right to extract.

Dr. Nijjar traces the history of the demands of the Sikhs from separate representation with weightage – as the Muslims had got – to 'Khalistan Scheme' when a section of the Sikhs demanded three independent Sikh States, one from Jamuna to Jamrood, second, Nander State in Hyderabad, third, Patna State, he has described the Khaksar movement as well stressing the danger they represented to the peace of the Panjab. His description of the partition of the country and emergence of Pakistan touches the conditions in the Panjab as well. It is interesting to find that though he describes both the Sikh and Muslim preparation for a violent struggle early in 1947, he had not a word to say, probably roughly, about the alleged part that the Jan Sangh is said to have played at this time.

He brings his story to an end by citing a declaration of Master Tara Singh, on 4th March 1947 at Lahore "The time has come when the might of sword alone shall rule. One hundred years from today our yellow flags were flying on the fort of Lahore, the same flag shall fly again."

We recommend the study of this work to all interested in the history of the Panjab. They are likely to find that at places it adds to their knowledge, at other it refreshes the memory of those who lived through these strenuous times. In the end we must congratulate Dr. Nijjar for his laborious task in writing a detailed account of the British Panjab, not hitherto available in one place anywhere else.

SHRI RAM SHARMA

PREFACE

The book is primarily designed to fulfil a long-standing need of the Degree and the Post-graduate students of the Panjab History on the period from 1849-1947. They have always felt greatly handicapped for want of proper and comprehensive material put with a detached objectivity so essential for a historian. Keeping in view the dire need of the students and the teachers, this book has been brought out after many years of research. Almost all the contemporary sources have been consulted to make the book authentic.

This is for the first time that this period has been explored in detail and systematically. Emphasis has been laid to touch every aspect of this period. This book is divided into XIX chapters. The main contents of this work can be summarised as below :

Geography of the Panjab, Panjab at the advent of Britishers, Panjab Under Lawrences, Political history of the Panjab from 1849-1947, North-West Frontier and the British Government, Religious and Political Movements *e.g.* the Kukas, the Komagata Maru, Jallianwala Bagh, Nankana Holocaust, the Jaito Morcha, Guru-Ka-Bagh, Panja Sahib, and Babar Akalis, Riasti Parja Mandal, the Khaksars, Agrarian Agitations, the Legislation, the Civil Administration, Social and Economic life of the Panjab from time to time, the Singh Sabha, S.G.P.C., the revolutionaries of the Panjab, various riots, Canalisation of the Panjab, the Panjab States with the role of their rulers in the Panjab History, Muzara Movements, the Panjab Civil Code, the provincial autonomy, the Unionist-Ministry, and Partition of the Panjab.

Being a detailed study, it has become voluminous. Therefore, it has been thought proper to publish it in three Volumes. The author will welcome suggestions for further improvement of the work.

BAKHSHISH SINGH NIJJAR

CONTENTS

1

CANALISATION OF THE PANJAB 1849-1947

Opening of canals in the Panjab is the greatest achievement of the British rule, the magnificent system of irrigation canals which it has given to this province. Its great alluvial plain traversed by large rivers drawing an unfailing supply of water from the Himalayan snows afforded an ideal field for the labours of the canal engineer. The vastness of the arid areas which without irrigation yielded no crops at all or only cheap millets and pulses made his works of inestimable benefit to the people and source of income to the State.

THE WESTERN JAMANA CANAL

Early History

The Western Jamana Canal was an important perennial irrigation works in the Panjab, taking off from the west bank of the river Jamana. It irrigates Ambala, Karnal, Hissar, Rohtak, and Delhi districts, and parts of the erstwhile Patiala and Jind States. It is by far the oldest of the great canals in the Panjab, and irrigated the lands in 1357, when Feroze Tughlaq utilized the torrent-bed now known as Chautang to conduct water to the royal gardens at Hissar and Hansi. This was little more than a monsoon supply-channel, and after about a hundred years water ceased to flow farther than the lands of Kaithal.

Under the Mughals

In 1568, Emperor Akbar re-excavated the works of Feroze Tughlaq and brought a supply from the Jamana and the Somb into the Chautang, and so on to Hansi and Hissar.[1] This was undoubtedly a perennial canal, as is testified by the ancient bridges

1. The Wealth & Welfare of the Panjab-Calvert, p. 120.

at Karnal and Safidon, and the complete set of water-courses with which the canal was provided, besides the original sand or working plan of the canal which is still in existence.

Jamana was dammed up annually about 14 miles below the present headworks of the canal, and the water led along the drainage line at the foot of the highland through Panipat and Sonepat to Delhi. Drainages and escapes were fairly well provided for; and the Pulchaddar aqueduct, which took the canal across the Najafgarh lake drain near Delhi, was, for the time, a great engineering feat, and was retained, with slight modifications, when the branch was reopened in 1819. The net revenue from the canal was reckoned equal to the maintenance of 12,000 horses.

After Aurangzeb

With the decline of the Mughal empire the up-keep of this canal was no longer attended to. The water ceased to reach Hansi and Hissar in 1707, the flow on Feroze Tughlaq's line at Safidon ceased in 1720. The Delhi branch ceased to flow in 1753-60. The Delhi branch was re-opened in 1819 by the British and the Hansi branch in 1825. The alignment of the canal was, however, by no means satisfactory. As early as 1846 it was noticed that the concentrated irrigation, the defective drainage of the country, all contributed to the rapid deterioration of the soil and the decline in the health of the people. Saline efforescence was rapidly spreading, and the inhabitants of the waterlogged area were affected with chronic disorders of the liver and spleen.

Between 1870 and 1882 various remodelling schemes were sanctioned, with the object of securing increased control over the supply and its distribution. Greater facilities for navigation and improved drainage had resulted in the complete disappearance of the swamps and accumulations of water and a most marked improvement in the health of the people. The Sirsa branch was sanctioned in 1888, and this and subsequent minor extensions had largely increased the irrigation capacity of the canal. No less than 200,000 acres were rendered secure in 1896-97 by the Sirsa branch alone.[2]

---

2. Panjab Administration Report 1896-97, p. 198.

Tajewala Headworks

The head of the Jamana Western Canal is at Tajewala in Ambala District about one and a half miles from the point where the river emerges from the lower hills. The river is here crossed by a weir, 1,700 feet in length, flanked at each end by a scouring sluice and head regulator for the Eastern Jamana Canal on the right, the full capacities authorised being respectively 1,300 and 6,380 cubic feet per second.[3]

Maximum Discharge

The Western Jamana Canal has a maximum discharge. For the first 14 miles of its course the canal runs almost entirely to the old west branch of the Jamana river. It then affects a junction with the Somb river, a masonry dam across which holds up the combined streams and forces them into the canal head at Dadupur, which is provided with a regulator at a short distance below. After a farther course of about 38 miles, chiefly in natural channels, there is at Indri regulator with a lock and escape head, where the canal divides into the Sirsa branch and the new main line.[4]

Sirsa Branch

The Sirsa branch has a capacity of 2,000 cubic feet per second, and runs for 115 miles, watering the arid tract of the country between Indri and Sirsa. Some 31 miles farther on, the main line bifurcates into the Hansi and New Delhi branches. The Hansi branch has a length of 47 miles and a discharge of nearly 2,000 cubic feet a second, and the Butana branch with a capacity of 700 cubic feet a second taken off from it. The New Delhi branch has a capacity of 1,750 cubic feet a second and a length of 74 miles to the point where it meets the Okhla navigation canal at Delhi.

The total length of main canal and branches is 343 miles, of distributaries (major and minor) 1,797 miles; of drains 657 miles; of escapes 76 miles, and mill channels 9 miles. The total area commanded by the canal is 4,000 square miles, of which 3,300 square miles are cultivable. The average area of crops

3. Panjab Administration Report 1897-98, p. 226.
4. Ambala District Gazetteer, p. 12.

irrigated during the twenty years ending 1894-95 was 529 square miles, which rose in the four years ending 1903-04 to an average of 944 square miles; and the work was estimated to irrigate altogether 1,259 square miles. The capital outlay to the end of March, 1904 (excluding a contribution of eleven and a half lakhs from the Patiala State), was 172.7 lakhs. The gross revenue for the three years ending March, 1904, averaged 23 lakhs, and the net revenue, after paying all interest charges and working expenses, 7.6 lakhs, or 4.4 per cent on the capital outlay. The main line and the New Delhi branch are navigable from the headworks to Delhi.[5]

The Hansi Branch

The Hansi[6] branch is navigable to where it meets the Southern Panjab Railway at Hansi. The expenditure on the provision for navigation is estimated at 16 lakhs; and, although near Delhi there is a certain amount of boat traffic, and timber is largely rafted down the canal, this large expenditure had proved hitherto to financial loss, and the combination of navigation with irrigation a failure. There were flour-mills at several of the falls; but the flour and the other mills at Delhi, which at one time were worked advantageously.[7]

SIRHIND CANAL

The Sirhind Canal weir is at Rupar, where the Satluj emerges from the Shivalik Hills. It is a perennial canal, taking off from the Satluj, and irrigating the high land betweeen the Satluj on the north-west and the Patiala and Ghaggar streams on the south-east, and extending as far south as the borders of Rajasthan, Bahawalpur, and the Bikaner State. The canal was constructed by the British Government, in association with the erstwhile Patiala, Nabha and Jind States. The preliminary survey work was begun in 1867, and the canal was formally opened in 1882, though irrigation did not commence until 1883. The

5. Ambala District Gazetteer, p. 12.
6. Punjab Administration Report 1897-98, p. 223.
Hissar District Gazetteer, pp. 142-143.
7. Panjab Administration Report 1896-97, pp. 198-200.

area commanded by the canal was 8,320 square miles, of which 4,027 were in British territory, and the remainder in the erstwhile Patiala, Nabha, Jind, Faridkot and Kalsia States. The headworks are at the town of Rupar,[8] where the Satluj issues from the Shivalik Hills into the plains.[9]

A weir 2,370 feet long crosses the river from bank to bank, having 12 arched undersluices each of 20 feet span. Extending up-stream on the east bank is the canal head regulator, with 13 arched openings of 21 feet span. About 500 feet farther up the river there is the lock channel head, to admit of navigation between the river and canal. The crest of the weir is seven and a half feet higher than the canal-bed, and along it extends a line of 586 falling shutters 6 feet high. When these are raised and the undersluices closed, the whole of the river supply is turned into the canal, and this is usually the case from early in October to the end of April.

Area Irrigated

The main canal has for 30 miles a bed-width of 200 feet, with a depth of eleven and a half and could carry 8,000 cubic feet per second. At the 39th mile it is divided into two large branches, the combined branch on the west and the Patiala feeder on the east. The former, which had a bed-width of 136 feet and a capacity of 5,200 cubic feet per second, soon divided again into two branches. The northern of those, the Abohar branch, ran parallel to the Satluj through Ludhiana and Ferozepore Districts, terminating after a course of 126 miles at the town of Govindgarh. The southern of Bhatinda branch ran through Ludhiana District and Patiala territory, with a length of 100 miles.[10]

The irrigation from these two branches was mainly in British territory, and the administration was entirely under the British Government, which retained all the revenue derived from them. They received between them 64 per cent of the supply of the main line. The Patiala feeder the eastern of the

8. Panjab N.W.F.P. & Kashmir-Douie, p. 136.
9. Phulkian States Gazetteer, p. 105.
10. Phulkian States Gazetteer, pp. 106-107.
Panjab Administration Report 1897-1898, p. 225.

two large branches into which the main line bifurcated, ran to the town of Patiala, having a bed-width of 75 feet, and a capacity of 3,000 cubic feet per second. On its way it gave off to the south the three native State branches, the Kotla (94 miles long), the Ghaggar (54 miles), and the Choa (26 miles). Those three branches irrigated almost exclusively the non-British territory. The distributaries and irrigation arrangements were under the erstwhile Phulkian States; who received the whole of the canal revenue. But the Patiala feeder and the branches were maintained by an officer of the Canal Department as agent for the States, who distributed the water according to a fixed allotment, Patiala taking 83 per cent, Nabha 9 per cent and Jind 8 per cent.[11]

The Distributaries

The distributaries were constructed so as to penetrate the border of every irrigated village, and thus to save the people the expense of making long water-courses and the difficulty of taking them through the land of other villages. This system, though expensive to construct and maintain, had been repaid by the rapidity with which irrigation had spread over the Panjab. As during the cold season the whole of the river supply was turned into the canal, it was necessary to provide a substitute on the canal for the river navigation thus closed.

Accordingly the main line, the combined branch, and 48 miles of the Abohar branch were provided with locks at the falls; and from the 48th mile of the Abohar branch a special navigation canal to the Satluj near Ferozepore, 47 miles long, was constructed with a branch 4 miles long to Ferozepore. The Patiala feeder was also made navigational along the branches, though the main line from Ropar to the North-Western Railway was much used, and brought down a considerable amount of timber from the hills.[12]

Flour Mills

There were 25 flour-mills at different falls along the branches. The greater part of the main line and branches was bor-

---

11. Phulkian States Gazetteer, pp. 105-108.
12. Panjab Administration Reports 1896-97, pp. 202-203.

dered by rows of trees, and the strip of land (reserved for the spoil or borrow pits) was generally covered with plantations. A telegraph line extended from the canal head down the main line, the two British branches, the Patiala feeder, and part of the longer native States branches. Since 1896-97 the area irrigated had in only one year fallen below 1,560 square miles; the greatest area irrigated was 2,142 square miles in 1899-1900, of which 1,452 were in British territory. The total cost of construction to the end of 1903-04 had beeen 388.7 lakhs, of which 247.7 lakhs was paid by the Government, and 141 lakhs by the three Phulkian States. Of the cost of the headworks and main line, the Government paid 64 per cent, and the Phulkian States contributed 36 per cent. The Government defrayed the whole cost of the British branches, and the Native States that of their branches. The charges for annual maintenance were divided in the same way.[13]

The Revenue

The gross revenue on the British branches averaged about 28 lakhs, and the net revenue 20 lakhs. On the Native States branches the gross revenue averaged about 12.5 lakhs and the net revenue about 7 lakhs. The return on the British capital outlay was as high as 10.8 per cent, in 1897-98 and averaged 8 per cent during the six years ending 1902-03. On the Native States capital outlay the return for those six years averaged 5.3 per cent. This canal was then not only a successful commercial scheme paying a handsome profit, but its advantages in years of drought were incalculable. It saved from famine a large tract of the Panjab and also provided food for exportation. The tract of country irrigated was then traversed in all directions by several different lines of railway, some of which would not have been required if no canal was in existence.[14]

BARI DOAB CANAL

The Bari Doab Canal is a perennial irrigation canal in the Panjab, taking off from the left bank of the Ravi and watering

13. Phulkian States Gazetteer, pp. 106-108.
14. Panjab Administration Reports 1897-1898, pp. 226-227.

the districts of Gurdaspur, Amritsar, and Lahore in the Bari Doab or tract of country between the Beas and the Ravi. The present undertaking originated in a project for the improvement of an older work, the Hasli canal, constructed about the year 1633 by Ali Mardan Khan, the famous engineer of emperor Shahjahan.[15] After the occupation of Lahore in 1846, Major Napier turned his attention at once to this project, and set on foot for the necessary surveys.

Progress Interrupted

The progress of the work was interrupted by the outbreak of the second Anglo-Sikh War. After annexation of the province in 1849, the work was pressed on, because the immediate construction of the canal was regarded as almost a matter of political necessity to provide employment for the disbanded Sikh soldiers, who, having their homes in the centre of the tract, would otherwise had little encouragement to turn to agriculture. The alignment of the Hasli canal proved on examination to be so defective that the officers in charge decided upon the adoption of an entirely independent line, parts, only of the original channel being utilized as distributaries.

Irrigation Started

Irrigation began in 1860-61, but the present permanent weir and other regulating headworks were not completed till after 1875. The headworks were at the village of Madhopur in Gurdaspur district, where the river is crossed by a weir of 2,700 feet long. The canal was capable of carrying 6,500 cubic feet per second. The highest average supply in the hot season was 4,850, while in the cold season it varied from 1,270 to 2,170 cubic feet per second. The main line terminated at its 31st mile, there separating into the Kasur and main branches.

The Kasur branch 7 miles lower down gave off the Sobraon branch, and the main branch after 25 miles gave off the Lahore branch, the four branches following the crest of the ridge into which the tract was divided by the natural drainage. The total length of the main and branch canals was 369 miles, and there were 1,591 miles of distributaries from which water was

---

15. Gurdaspur District Gazetteer, p. 16.

brought upon the fields by means of water-courses constructed and maintained by the cultivators. The canal was not navigable. The rainfall was greatest in the upper part of the system, which had necessitated a special system of irrigation in Gurdaspur district and in the portion of Amritsar district north of the North-Western Railway on the Kasur and Sobraon branches.[16]

In that tract the distributaries were closed during the cold season after a watering had been given for showing the spring crops, the winter rains with some help from wells being sufficient to mature those crops. The water thus set free had been utilized in extending irrigation in the driest part of Lahore district, where bordered on Montgomery—a tract for which it would otherwise had been impossible to provide a perennial supply. The gross area commanded by the canal was 2,710 square miles in Gurdaspur, Amritsar, and Lahore Districts.

Area Irrigated

The lower portion of the Doab in Montgomery and Multan was not irrigated, as there was not sufficient water available in the Ravi during the winter. The area irrigated was 297 square miles in 1860, 677 square miles in 1880-81, 1,346 square miles in 1900-01, and 1,464 square miles in 1903-04. The total capital expenditure (exclusive of interest) up to the end of 1903-04 was 197 lakhs. The gross income for that year was about 33 lakhs, or, inclusive of the increase of land revenue due to irrigation (which was credited to the canal in the accounts), 36 lakhs. The working expenses amounted to 11 lakhs, leaving a net profit of 25 lakhs, or 12.68 per cent, on the capital outlay.[17]

The Lower Chenab Canal : Formerly A Desolate Region

The Lower Chenab Canal is a perennial canal in the Panjab, taking off from the left bank of the Chenab river and watering the tract between it and the Ravi. The greatest part of this area was before the introduction of irrigation a desolate region, unpeopled except for a race of pastoral nomads known as Janglis. The land was for the most part Government waste, and was thus adapted for colonization on a scale. The original work was

16. Panjab Administration Report 1887-1888, pp. 122-123.
17. Panjab Administration Report 1897-1898 p. 225.

designed as a small inundation canal and opened as such in 1887, but in 1889 it was decided to convert it into a perennial canal of the first magnitude.[18]

Khanki Headworks

The headworks of the canal are at Khanki, a village in Gujranwala district, 8 miles below Wazirabad. Here there is a weir across the river, by which the supply to the canal was regulated and controlled. The main line of the canal had a bed-width of 250 feet, and had been run with a depth of about 11 feet and a discharge of 11,000 cubic feet per second. This weir was commenced in 1890 and completed in 1892. The largest branch of the canal, the Gugera, carrying about one-half of the total supply, took off from the left bank of the main line at the 28th mile. It had a length of 55 miles and then bifurcated into two subsidiary branches, the Gugera Lower and the Buralla, with lengths of 77 and 45 miles respectively.

The Kot Nikka Branch

On the right bank, not far from the same off-take was the Kot Nikka branch with a length of 18 miles. The extreme length of the main line was 40 miles, and it then divided into the Jhang, Rakt, and Miani Ali branches. The Jhang was the second largest branch of the system, and carried about 3,000 cubic feet per second. Its length was about 62 miles, before it bifurcated into Jhang Lower (38 miles) and the Bhowana seven and a half miles long. The length of the Rakh and Mian Ali were 55 and 27 miles respectively. The total length of the main channels was 425 miles. For the distribution of the water-supply from the branches to the watercourses which directly irrigated the land there were, at the end of 1903-04, 2,323 miles of distributaries; and for the villages colonized by Government there had been constructed about 11,000 miles of water courses.[19]

Area Irrigated

The total area commanded by the canal at the end of 1903-04

---

18. Panjab Administration Report.
19. Panjab Administration Report 1901-1902, pp. 133-134.

was 5,255 square miles in Gujranwala, Lahore, Jhang, and Montgomery District, of which 3,098 square miles were irrigated, and area which was capable of substantial increase. The total area of Government waste in the Doab was about 3,817 square miles, of which 2,828 square miles of land commanded by the canal had been allotted by the end of 1903-04.[20]

Categories of the Grantees

The grantees were divided into three classes (1) Capitalists, (2) Yeoman, and (3) Peasants. The greatest part of the land had been distributed to peasants, who were by far the most satisfactory tenants. For the purpose of allotment the whole of the Government waste had been divided into squares, the side of each square being 1,100 feet and the area about 28 acres. A peasant's grant consisted of from one-half of three squares, a yeoman's of four or five and a capitalist's of any number from five to twenty or more. Each settler was practically granted water for the annual irrigation of a certain percentage of the holding.

Proprietory Rights Retained by the Government

The Government retained the proprietory rights in the land, and the colonists were its tenants, the peasants for a term of years, the yeomen with right of continued occupancy so long as they pay their assessment, while the capitalists had also the right to purchase proprietory rights in their tenancy after the lapse of a certain period. There were also tenures which carried the liability to provide a certain number of camels for military service. For the purpose of distributing the land and of settling the colonists in villages, a special Colonization Officer was appointed with head-quarters at Lyallpur. There were 1,423 villages in 1903-04, the average size being about 50 squares or 1,400 acres. The population of the colony at the Census of 1901 was 782,690, and ultimately reached two and a half millions. A railway for the transport for the produce was constructed, running the whole length of the Doab such as from Wazirabad to Khanewal, and several feeder-lines.

A Large Revenue

The canal earned a large revenue even while under cons-

20. Gujranwala District Gazetteer, pp. 117-118.

truction, while the profits in 1903-04 amounted to 21 per cent on the capital invested. The gross and net revenue derived therefrom in that year amounted to about 84 and 66 lakhs respectively. By 1913 the net revenue was considerably increased. The value of the crops raised in a year was estimated to rise to 650 lakhs. The canal had thus not only enormously relieved the pressure of population in the congested districts of the Panjab, but had proved a most remunerative investment, besides adding largely to the general wealth of the country. An extensive telegraph system ran from the head of the canal down its main line and branches, and along some of its larger distributaries, thus facilitating rapid regulation of supply.[21]

THE LOWER JHELUM CANAL

The Lower Jhelum Canal is a perennial irrigation work in the Panjab. It was opened on October 30, 1901. It was taken off from the left bank of the Jhelum and is supplying perennial irrigation to the whole of the country lying between the Jhelum and Chanab rivers, west of a line joining the town of Maini on the Jhelum with Pindi Bhattian on the Chanab. The head of the canal is near the village of Mong Rasul in Gujarat District. The river was dammed by a weir, 4,100 feet long, and a regulator across the head of the canal took the form of a bridge of 8 spans of twenty four and a half feet each. The main line had a bed-width of 140 feet and had running full a depth of 7.5 feet, and a discharge of 3,800 cubic feet per second.[22]

The Shahpur Branch

The Shahpur branch took off at about the 28th mile of the main line. This branch had been designed to take up the irrigation performed in Shahpur District by the Imperial, Provincial, and privately owned inundation canals. After a course of 39 miles, in which it gradually approached the centre of the highlands of the Doab, the canal bifurcated into two main branches,

21. Panjab Administration Report 1897-98 pp. 227-228.
Labour District Gazetteer, pp. 129-131.
Gujranwala District Gazetteer, p. 117.
22. Panjab Administration Report 1901-1902, p. 134.

watering the northern and southern portions of the Doab respectively. The total length of the main line and main branches was about 167 miles, and about 960 miles of distributing channels was constructed.[23]

Area Irrigated

The canal protected an area of 2,400 square miles, and irrigated annually about 1,200 square miles. Of 2,400 square miles protected, about 850 were Government waste, which it was intended to turn into an immense horse-breeding colony for the supply of remounts to the Indian Army. For this purpose the greatest portion had been leased out to colonists on the condition of their keeping an approved brood mare, and other areas had been reserved for public and private breeding establishments and horse runs. The work of colonization was under an Officer of the Indian Civil Service, who had his head-quarters at Sargodha then in Shahpur district. The land had been divided into squares of nearly 28 acres each, and one brood mare had to be maintained for every two and a half squares. A railway had been constructed from Malakwal on the Sind-Sagar line to Shorkot on the Lyallpur-Khanewal line, affording facilities for the immigration of colonists and the export of produce.[24]

Precautions Against Waterlogging

Elaborate precautions were taken to prevent water-logging of the soil by over-irrigation. The depth at which spring-water was found below the surface of the ground was carefully observed over the whole of the commanded area, and the country was divided into three zones according to those depths. Where the spring level was 40 feet or more below the surface, 50 per cent of the gross area commanded was irrigated; where the depth lay between 25 and 40 feet, 40 per cent of the area had been irrigated; and where the water was nearer to the surface than 25 feet, only 25 per cent was allowed perennial irrigation, and powers had been reserved to reduce those supplies if they could be found to be in excess of requirements. On the Shahpur

---

23. Shahpur District Gazetteer, pp. 192-193.
24. Shahpur District Gazetteer, pp. 194-195.

branch 50 per cent, of the area was irrigated.[25]

Shahpur Inundation Canals

The Shahpur inundation canals is a system of inundation canals, fed from the Jhelum river and mainly situated in Shahpur District. About sixteen of them were owned by private persons and six by Government. Of the latter three were classed as Imperial and two as Provincial, while one, the Pind Dadan Khan Canal in Jhelum district, had been made over to the Municipal Committee of Pind Dadan Khan for management. The three Imperial canals lay wholly in the Shahpur tahsil, and were developments of a canal dug in 1864 by Colonel Sir Willian Davies, to supply water to the civil station of Shahpur.[26]

In 1870 Government acquired this canal and added two new canals. The Imperial canals commanded an area of 105 square miles and irrigated fifty square miles a year on an average, yielding a net revenue of Rs. fifty thousand, or 24 per cent on the capital outlay. Of the two Provincial canals the largest was the Raniwah, and old native canals which had fallen into disuse and was reopened in 1870-71. It commanded 72 square miles in the Bhera tehsil and irrigated 30 square miles annually, yielding a net revenue of Rs. 11,000. It had extinguished its capital cost and yielded a net profit of 4.1 lakhs to Government. The Corbynwah, constructed in 1879,[27] irrigated about 4,500 acres, mostly grass lands, in the Kaushab tahsil on the right bank of the Jhelum.[28]

Area Irrigated

The Pind Dadan Khan Canal did not pay expenses, but it supplied the town with sweet water. It performed a small amount of irrigation as well, the area irrigated in 1904-05[29] having been 395 acres. The private canals had a total length of about 227 miles and irrigates 87 square miles. Many of them were old

25. Panjab Administration Report, 1919-1920, p. 99.
Jhelum District Gazetteer, pp. 171-172.
26. Panjab Administration Report 1869-1870, pp. 76-77.
27. Panjab Administration Report 1879-1880 pp. 123-124.
28. Panjab Administration Report 1901-1902, pp. 194-196.
Jhelum District Gazetteer, pp. 171-172.
29. Panjab Administration Report 1904-1905, pp. 34-35.

canals which had silted up and were re-excavated, under Sir Donalf McNabb and other Deputy Commissioners of the District, by owners and lessees to irrigate their own lands. They also irrigated the lands of other persons on payment of a water rate.[30]

THE UPPER SATLUJ CANALS

The Upper Satluj Canals comprised a group of Imperial system of four inundation canals in the Panjab, known as the Katora, Khanwah, Upper Sobag, and Lowar Sobag (or Lower Sobag and Para) Canals. They took off from the right bank of the river Satluj and irrigated the low-lying land bounded on the north by the old dry bed of the Beas, which separated it from the tracts commanded by the Hari Doab Canal. The tract commanded by the Katora Canal lay in Lahore District, and the remainder in Montgomery.

Area Irrigated

The canals existing at the end of 1903-04 aggregated[31] 325 miles in length with 394 miles of distributories, and carried an aggregate supply of 4,935 cubic feet per second. During the five years ending 1903-04 they irrigated an average annual area of 3.5 lakhs or, inclusive of the land revenue due to irrigation,[32] 5.4 lakhs per annum. The average annual working expenses during the same period were 3.6 lakhs. There was, therefore, an annual profit of 1.8 lakhs. No capital expenditure was recorded against the canals till 1894-95; upto the end of 1903-04, it had amounted to 17 lakhs.[33]

Lower Satluj Inundation Canals

It was an Imperial system of inundation canals, taking off from the right bank of the Satluj and irrigating part of Multan

30. Shahpur District Gazetteer, p. 193.
Panjab Administration Reports, 1897-98, p. 235; 1919-20, p. 100.
31. Lahore District Gazetteers, pp. 210-211.
Panjab Administration Report 1896-1897, p. 208.
32. Which was credited to the Canals in the accounts.
33. Panjab Administration Report 1897-98, pp. 232-234.
Lahore District Gazetteer, pp. 130-131.

District. They were for the most part constructed in the middle of the eighteenth century by the Daudputras, a powerful tribe who were in possession of this part of the country from the downfall of the Mughals to the rise of Maharaja Ranjit Singh, but one of the largest, the Diwanah, was excavated in 1831 by Diwan Sawan Mal, who also enlarged and improved several others. Excluding the Hajiwah canal, whose history is separate from that of the rest, there were in 1850 nineteen of these canals; those, however, had been gradually amalgamated, and in 1903 there were only three, the Mailsi, Muhammadwab-Sardarwah, and Bahawalwah. Lodhran canals of which the last two were later amalgamated.[34]

Cultivated Area

The gross cultivable area commanded by these canals was 1,414 square miles. The canals generally flowed from April to October; but since the Sirhind Canal had come into full operation the supply of water at the commencement and end of the flood season had been considerably reduced, and the actual area irrigated in the five years ending 1903-04 was only 263 square miles.

The Crops

The normal autumn crop was sown and matured with canal water alone; but for the spring harvest only the preliminary waterings required for ploughing and sowing were given from the canal, and further irrigation was supplied from wells. The maximum discharge was 5,000 cubic feet per second, and the total length of main canals was 394 miles and of distributaries 328 miles. Clearance was affected by the labour of the cultivators; the system was, however, finally abolished in 1903 and rates were then paid. No capital account was kept for these canals.

The Katora Canal

The Katora Canal had a bed-width of 55 feet, and an authorised discharge of 685 cubic feet per second. It was made in

34. Panjab Administration Report 1896-1897, pp. 209.
Multan District Gazetteer, pp. 147-150.

1870-71, and followed the bed of a mullah for 21 miles, when it separated into three channels called the Pakhoki, Atari, and Chunnian distributaries.[35] The Katora Canal takes of the river; Satluj at the village of Kassoki in the Kasur Tahsil about 9 miles above the Kaisar-i-Hind Railway Bridge over the river; from there it takes a westerly course irrigation from 5,000 to 8,000 acres of land in 49 villages of the Kasur Tahsil, before it reaches the town of Khudian, which is situated in the Chunian Tahsil near the Kasur border.

The Khanwah Canal

The Khanwah had a bed-width of 65 feet, and an authorised full supply of 1,290 cubic feet per second. The date of first opening is not known; it is, however, recorded that the canal was improved by Mirza Khan, a minister of emperor Akbar; but it was neglected by his successors, and silted up. In the time of Maharaja Ranjit Singh Diwan Radha Ram repaired the head and cleared the channel, and the canal flowed from 1807 to 1823: It was again neglected till 1841, when Fakir Chriagh-ud-din, under the orders of Maharaja Sher Singh, had the canal repaired, and it was in flow when taken over by the British Irrigation department on the annexation of the Panjab in 1849.[36]

The Upper Sohag Canal

The Upper Sohag Canal had a bed-width of 60 feet, and an authorized discharge of 1,540 cubic feet per second. It was first made in 1827, and worked till 1840, when it was neglected; and nothing further was done to it till 1855, when the canal having been taken over by the British Irrigation Department, the channel was again put into working order. Upper Suhag, which take off the river at the villages of Jalloke and Mokal in the Chunian Tahsil, about 35 & 40 miles respectively below the Kaisar-i-Hind Railway Bridge, are the other inundation canals. The total area irrigated in the third decade of the twentieth century by these canals, within the district was on the average 54,800 acres in 206 villages.

---

35. Lahore District Gazetteer, pp. 130-131.
36. Panjab Administration Report 1896-1897, pp. 207.

The Lower Sohag Canal

The Lower Sohag Canal had a bed-width of 90 feet, and an authorised discharge of 1,420 cubic feet per second. It may be said to date from 1816, when the first attempt to irrigate was made by means of a dam across the Sohag nallah, which caused it to overflow its banks. In 1831 another dam was made, and the water was led on to the lands of Jawand Singh at Depalpur, who was said to have obtained a large return from the water. After some fighting the dam was demolished in 1835; and from that date the canal existed only in name, irrigation being effected on only 3,000 acres by lifts by means of a narrow cut 200 feet wide. In 1885-86 the present regular canal was opend.[37] The canal follows nallah for 33 miles, till it gave off the Para Nallah.[38]

Two Branches

The canal continued in the form of two branches, one along the Para nallah and the other along the Sohag nallah. The Channel, however, was not formed in the bed, but consisted of an artificial cut, which was crossed and recrossed by the tortuous dry nallahs. The canal was constructed mainly for the purpose of bringing under cultivation 142 square miles of Government waste. This area was colonized by allotting parcels of land to chosen peasants from adjacent over-populated Districts. For the purpose of allotment the land was divided into squares, 27.7 acres in area, and each allotment consisted of 4 squares, or 111 acres. The canals being dry in the cold season the colonists were required to construct wells at least one well per holding being necessary.[39]

Grey Canals

Grey Canals was a system of inundation canals, taking off from the south bank of the Satluj and irrigating the low-lying tracts of Ferozepore Districts. They took their name from Colonal L. J. H. Grey, under whose orders, as Deputy Commissioner of the District, they were constructed.

The work had started in 1875-76, when 11 canals were

37. Lahore District Gazetteer, pp. 130-131.
38. Panjab Administration Report 1896-1897, p. 207.
39. Panjab Administration Report 1896-1897, p. 207.

made; the number was increased to 13 in 1883, and in 1885, after the incorporation of the Fazilka Tahsil-Ferozepore District, two of the canals were remodelled and extended so as to irrigate this Tahsil. In addition to those, a new canal, named Kingwah, had just been completed at a cost of 1.7 lakhs. The 14 canals varied to length from 28 to 107 miles, in bed-width from 30 to 80 feet, and in discharge from 283 to 640 cubic feet per second. Their total length in 1,034 miles, and their aggregate discharge 6,340 cubic feet per second. Being inundation canals they ran only when the Satluj was at a sufficient height. Up to and including 1905-06 the total cost on original works was 11.6 lakhs, and on repairs and establishment 23.4 lakhs.[40]

Area Irrigated

The average area irrigated was approximately more than 227 square miles. The canals were remarkable as being constructed and maintained on the co-operative system without any direct aid from Government, except a small grant towards the cost of establishment in Fazilka which had been stopped since the Settlement of 1902. The excavation work was performed by the agriculturists whose lands the canal was to benefit, supervised by the ordinary revenue staff of the District. Since 1881 the special establishment required for their up-keep was met by a charge of three to four annas per 'ghumao' and the annual silt clearance and other works had been carried out at the expense of the irrigation at the average rate of 8 to 10 annas per irrigated 'ghumao'. In addition to those charges for maintenance, a royalty of 12 annas per 'ghumao' of superior, and 6 annas per 'ghumao' of inferior, crops was taken by Government.[41]

Ghaggar Canals

The Ghaggar Canals was a group of an Imperial system of minor canals, taking off from the Ghaggar. Owing to the waste of water in the lakes and swamps of that river, and the insanitary condition to which the low-lying lands in the valley below Sirsa were reduced, it was agreed between the British Government and the State of Bikaner that the Dhanur Lake, about 8

40. Ferozepur District Gazetteer, pp. 184-185.
41. Ferozepur District Gazetteer, pp. 184-185.

miles from Sirsa, should be converted into a reservoir by the construction of a masonary weir at Otu, and that irrigation should be effected by two canals, the northern and southern, taking off from each end of the weir, with a combined capacity of 1,000 cubic feet per second. The Bikaner State was to share the canal supplies and meet a proportionate part of the cost. The canals were constructed with famine labour in 1896-97. and began to irrigate in the Monsoon of 1897.[42]

Area Irrigated

The areas commanded in British and Bikaner territory were 130 and 117 square miles, and the irrigable areas were 53 and 35 square miles, respectively. There were 95 miles of main canals and 24 of distributories; and the total capital outlay to the end of March, 1904, .was 6.3 lakhs, of which 2.8 lakhs was debited to Bikaner. These canals were never likely to show any return on their capital cost, as only part of the irrigated area was assessed to land revenue only.[43]

The Hajiwah Canal

The Hajiwah canal was included in the Lower Satluj system. It was a private canal constructed in the time of Maharaja Ranjit Singh, and its administration was taken over by the British Government in 1888 in consequence of the mismanagement of the owners. This action was authorised by the terms of a deed executed in 1886, which the British Government had given the owners a grant of 60,000 acres of land served by the canal, and it was upheld by the Privy Council 1901. The canal had a bed-width of 30 feet, an average supply during the flood season of 500 cubic feet per second, and a length of 39 miles. The average area irrigated was only 53 square miles, as the alignment was defective.[44]

Sidhnai Canal

Sidhnai Canal is an irrigation work, taking off from the left

---

42. Panjab Administration Report, 1896-1897, pp. 196-199.
43. Hissar District Gazetteer, pp. 144-145.
44. Panjab Administration Report 1897-98, pp. 233.
    Lahore District Gazetteer, pp. 120-131.

bank of the Ravi and watering part of Multan District. It derived its name, meaning 'straight', from a remarkable reach of the Ravi, which extended in a perfectly straight cutting for 10 or 12 miles from Tulamba to Sarai Sidhu. It was opened for irrigation in 1886. The headworks consisted of a weir 737 feet long, built across this reach. The main line had a bed-width of 90 feet and a maximum discharge of 1,820 cubic feet per second. After 30 miles it divided into two large distributories, which between them took nearly one-third of the whole supply. The very short length of the canal compared with the area irrigated was one cause of its financial success. There were in all thirteen main distributory channels taking off from the main line, and three subsidiary canals which took off from the river above the dam.[45]

Area Irrigated

The gross area commanded in 595 square miles, of which the greatest part was Government waste, and was settled by Colonists brought from various parts of the Panjab the land being given out for the most parts in 90-acre plots. Although the whole of the water in the Sidhnai reach could be turned into the canal, the Ravi in the winter was often absolutely dry, owing to the supply taken by the Bari Doab Canal, so that the spring crop had to be matured by the aid of wells. The average area irrigated, was approximately 190 square miles, and the capital outlay was about 13 lakhs, giving the average annual profit more than 11 per cent.[46]

Chenab Inundation Canals

This was a system of inundation canals, taking off from the left bank of the Chenab below its confluence with the Ravi, and irrigating part of the Multan and Shujabad tahsils of Multan District. They were for the most part constructed by the Pathan rulers of Multan and Shujabad, and were once thirteen in number; but by amalgamation the heads in the river were reduced to four, the Mattihal, Wali Muhammad Sikandarabad, and Sikandrawah. As the canal-irrigated land was much lower than the

45. Panjab Administration Report 1896-97, pp 207-208.
46. Panjab Administration Report 1897-98, pp. 231-232. Multan District Gazetteer, pp. 149-150.

river-level in July and August, the outer banks of the canals were made specially high and strong to keep the flood waters from pouring over the cultivated land, and in certain lengths of the river embankments were constructed. In this way there was a chain of protection about 80 miles long on the east bank of the river.[47]

Discharge of Canals

The maximum discharge of the canals was 5,200 cubic feet per second; there were 252 miles of main canals and 46 miles of Government distributories. The system by which the cultivators, in lieu of paying for the water, provided labour for silt clearance were abolished, and occupiers' rates imposed. No capital account was kept for these canals. The gross revenue approximately averaged 3.3 lakhs yearly, and the net revenue Rs. 47,000. The average area irrigated was more than 214 square miles.[48]

Muzaffargarh Canals

Muzaffargarh Canals groups was an Imperial system of inundation canals, taking off from the left bank of the Indus and the right bank of the Chenab, and irrigating portions of Muzaffargarh District. They were for the most part constructed the native rulers of the District, and improved by Sawan Mal, Governor under Maharaja Ranjit Singh. After annexation these canals remained for many years under the management of the Deputy Commissioner and were transferred to the Canal Department as a 'minor' work in 1880. The system of canal clearance by the labour of the cultivators was finally abolished in 1903, when occupiers' rates were introduced. The Indus series, which was by far the more important of the two, consisted of eight canals with an aggregate length of 1.38 miles of main, branch, and distributory channels, and a total average discharge of 2,570 cubic feet per second. There were five canals in the Chenab series, with a total length of 232 miles and a discharge of 740 cubic feet per second.

Area Irrigated

The gross area commanded by the canals was 1,205 square

47. Panjab Administration Report 1896-97, pp. 203-206.
48. Multan District Gazetteer, pp. 147-148.

miles, of which 1,055 were cultivable and 547 irrigable, the area irrigated approximately averaged 457 square miles, of which 366 square miles were watered from the Indus. To protect the irrigated country, embankments were constructed, stretching for 119 miles along the Indus and for 40 miles along the Chenab. No capital account was kept for the system. The gross revenue was estimated at 6 lakhs and the net revenue 3.3 lakhs.

Indus Inundation Canals

The Indus inundation canals was the group of an imperial system of inundation, taking off from the west bank of the Indus and irrigating part of Dera Ghazi Khan District. They were fourteen in number and covered a river frontage of 175 miles, protecting a low-lying narrow strip of country from 6 to 16 miles wide, known as the Sind. These were mostly constructed by the Mirani chiefs and other native rulers, and were greatly improved by Sawan Mal Governor under Maharaja Ranjit Singh. Five, however, were constructed by Baloch Chiefs in 1862-63 for the use of their tribal lands, but proving a financial failure were bought up by the British Government.

Area Irrigated

The gross area commanded was 1,374 square miles, of which 661 were cultivable. The greatest area of crops matured was 348 square miles, and the average about 300 square miles. The normal period of flow was from the beginning of May to the end of September; consequently, while the autumn crop was matured entirely by canal water, the supply in the spring harvest was sufficient only for ploughing and sowing, after which wells were used.

The average discharge of the whole series was, 2,400 cubic feet per second. There were 680 miles of main canals and branches, of which 108 were constructed under British rule, 75 miles of distributories, and 7 of drainage cuts and escapes. As the irrigated tract was below the flood-level of the Indus, a system of embankment 75 miles long was built, and also works for training the river and protecting the irrigation works. The capital sum expended from 1854 to the end of March, 1904, was 8.6 lakhs. Until 1897 there was practically no net revenue; in that year, by the revised settlement of Dera Ghazi Khan District, the indirect revenue was substantially increased and a low occupiers rate imposed. The gross revenue was about 4.1 lakhs and the net revenue 1 lakh, or 11.88 per cent, on the capital expenditure. A considerable income was derived from Government lands on the Dhundi canal.[49]

TRIPLE PROJECT

(1) Upper Jhelum; (2) Upper Chenab; (3) Lower Bari Doab Canal.

The Lower Chenab Canal took the whole available supply of the Chanab river. But it did not command a large area in the Rechna Doab lying in the west of Gujranwala, in which ran cultivation was very risky and well cultivation was costly. No help could be got from the Ravi, as the Upper Bari Doab Canal exhausted its supply. It was, thus, desirable to extend irrigation in the area mentioned above. The bold scheme known as the Triple Project which embraced the construction of the Upper Jhelum, Upper Chenab and Lower Bari Doab Canals, had based on the belief that the Jhelum river had even in the cold weather water to spare after feeding the Lower Jhelum Canal.

The true 'Raison D'etre' of the Upper Jhelum Canal whose head-works were at Mangla in Kashmir a little north of the Gujarat district, was to throw a large volume of water into the Chenab at Khanki, where the Lower Chenab Canal took off, and so set free an equal supply to be taken out of the Chenab higher up at Murala in Sialkot, where were the head-works of the Upper Chenab Canal. But the Upper Jhelum Canal had also water annually some 345,000 acres in Gujarat and Shahpur. The Upper Chenab Canal thus irrigated 648,000 acres in Gujaranwala, and carried across the Ravi by an aqueduct at Balloke in the south of Lahore. Henceforth the canal was known as the Lower Bari Doab, which watered 882,000 acres, mostly owned by the State, in the Montgomery and Multan Districts. On the other two canals the area of Government land was not large.

1. Upper Jhelum Canal

In the first year of irrigation from this canal supply reached

49. Panjab Administration Report 1896-1897, pp. 209-210.

five-eighths of its maximum discharge. A large new canal with high embankments required a continuous increase in supply. The area irrigated was only 117,605 acres as against 245,000 acres anticipated in the Project forecast. The shortage was due to the fact that irrigation commenced a year later than was anticipated.

2. Upper Chenab Canal: Area Irrigated

The monsoon was above the normal and the 'kharif' crops were very fair in the year of 1916-1917, but the winter season was again abnormally dry and the river supplied again usually low; great difficulty was consequently experienced in maturing the 'rabi' crops. 9 per cent. of which failed. The increase in the 'kharif' area (from 159,152 in 1915-16 to 285,917 acre during the year 1916-1917) was remarkable, but the 'rabi' area, on the other hand, dropped from 165,910 to 151,560 acres. The total direct receipts forecast, but the indirect receipts (Rs. 2,54,872) were short by Rs. 4,98,744; this was because the system of indirect credit on this canal was complicated and had not been fully settled. The Deg diversion embank was maintained intact although the flood water reached as high a level as in 1914; the diversion channel had scoured satisfactorily and the possibility of damage by floods had been reduced.

3. Lower Bari Doab: Area Irrigated

The total area irrigated by the Lower Bari Doab Canal (514,936) acres was short by 135,064 acres in 1916-17 as compared with tthe Project forecast. The working of this canal had not been fully established as yet owing to the supply in the Upper Jhelum Canal (which was opened in December 1915—a year later than anticipated in the Project) having been still short of full design. Cautious increase of the Upper Jhelum Canal supply was necessary for safety. The Lower Pari Doab Canal supply was however more than enough for the area allotted and the canal was in advance of colonization. Proprietory lands were broken up and were being irrigated. The total area of Crown waste land allotted at the end of the year 1916-17, was 656,391 acres out of the 791,994 acres of culturable area commanded.[50]

---

50. Panjab Administration Report 1916-17, p. 43.

Assessment Of The Canalisation : Divided Into Three Classes

System of the canalisation of the Panjab may thus be divided into three broad classes. (a) In the first canal water was applied to land, already largely cultivated by old settled inhabitants who relied for the ripening of their crops on the rainfall, eked out occasionally by wells. The loss due to vicissitudes of season were heavy in 1922 the Director of Land Records found that in the province as a whole the normal rate of crop failure mainly due to deficient or unseasonal rainfall, was 21 per cent. Since then irrigation was widely extended and the average failure was 15 per cent, it was sometimes as high as 65 per cent. The summer (kharif) crop was the heavier sufferer, and the percentage of failure then was 21 per cent, as compared with 14 for the 'rabi' or winter crop.

Seasonal Vicissitudes

On an acreage of 30 million, the total loss from this cause was enormous, representing to the cultivator a waste of immense labour, time and expenditure. Were this loss concentrated into one area, it would receive far more attention than it did. A cautious estimate would put it at round about eight to ten crorés, a heavy toll to be paid by the Panjab cultivators as the price of seasonal vicissitudes. In those settled areas, the canals had reduced these loss and increased the profit of cultivation; they had made agriculture more safe and given to the worker greater command over this operations, including a greater choice over the crops he may grow. They had further encouraged him to put under the plough much land formerly left waste or cultivated only in seasons of good rainfall.

Two Outstanding Results

Two outstanding results may be mentioned; formerly the cotton grown was limited to the requirements of the home and little left the village, now a great trade had grown up and the area shown had increased to meet the demand from a wider market. Secondly, the cultivator had been enabled to grow more wheat with the result that it had largely displaced the millets in the daily diet, even of the poorer classes.

2. The second class of State canals were either cuts designed

to inundate large areas on the banks of the rivers during the flood season or were reconstructions or replacements of those by channels with head regulators gave a controlled supply. To a considerable extent the areas served by these had previously been partially cultivated, with the aid of wells, but the new works brought water to large tracts which previously had possessed little settled cultivation. Multan and Muzaffargarh contain examples, and the extension to new areas is illustrated by the Sidhnai Canal colony. As these canals were originally designed to function during the flood seasons only, their main object was to moisten the land for 'rabi' (winter) crops and to ripen such summer (kharif) crops as could be sown. For the ripening of the winter crops, wells were required and their construction was made a compulsory condition of grants in the areas colonised under these non-perennial canals.

3. The third class of canal is the great group of colony works designed to bring water to vast areas of desert waste in the great Panjab Doabs in the centre and south-west of the province. In these areas the annual rainfall was usually below 15 inches; in a large part it was below 12 inches and in the south-west it was below 7, in all cases too little to ensure the ripening of crops unaided by wells or other artificial means. Here, irrigation was not designed to assist agriculture and diminish the losses from seasonal vagaries, but to create it where before it did not exist. Scattered about were old wells, and in odd depressions where rain collected a little precarious cultivation had been possible; but there is little exaggeration in describing this great Central and South-western area as mainly desert prior to the inauguration of the great Chenab, Jhelum, Bari Doab and Triple Canal projects.

Gave Great Prosperity to the Panjab

The Upper Jhelum differed from the rest in as much as it had no weir across the river, this triumph of engineering being skillfully designed to make use of a natural shingle bar; the rest were provided with weirs and the water in the rivers was under strict control. The great colonies made possible by these huge works were the creation of a great co-operation between the most skilled body of water engineers in the world, constructive administrators of the Panjab. They enjoyed a prosperity such as the older settled districts could match and they bore witness to the high standard of perfection both of the irrigation system and of the schemes of colonization. As Lord Curzon remarked they had converted the province from a battlefield of frontier warfare into a home of contented and peaceful peasantry. Upon the human element their effect was no less remarkable; the opportunities for hard work under more responsive conditions then prevailed in their home districts had moulded the character of the colonists and developed a sense of pride in their economic well-being that should strengthen the opposition to any tendency towards a lowering of the standard of living.

New Experiments

For the student of rural economics, these great experiments, will afford much material for the scientific examination of many theories. It is unfortunate that the standard areas for grants were fixed not with any relation to economic needs of a family but to fit in with a survey but, as it happened the square or rectangle adopted (25 or 27.8 acres) represents about double the area considered by the people as that which can be managed with a single yoke of oxen, and the ordinary holding of a tenant is half a square or rectangle.

Land Belonged to the State

Again, the land belonged to the State, and such rights as then existed were derived directly from the State although opportunities for purchase were provided in the conditions of the grants. The political theorist who advocated the nationalisation of the land would find here in existence the conditions he demanded, although much of his dreams would be dissipated by the reality. The continuous agitation from the State tenants for more and ever more concessions could serve as a warning to those who urged that the abolition of the private landlord would remove all the troubles of agriculture; moreover the dangers of political pressure from a powerful body of the State tenants, seeeking their own selfish advantage at whatever cost to their less fortunate brethren, could illustrate the need for caution in bringing the Government into too close touch with the people.

In the realms of education, public health, medical aid, roads etc., the demand for more amenities from the State could be countered by the State's demand for more taxes to meet the ever increasing expenditure; but only a part of the Panjab was then irrigated, and concessions granted to those who enjoyed the benefits were apt to bring less not only to those but to the less fortunate holders of land dependent on rain who might be called upon to make up part of the deficit entailed by granting valuable privileges to others.

Statistics

It is unfortunate that the statistics for the areas colonized was not kept distinct from those of the administrative districts in which they lay, with the result that they were confused with those of sometimes distinctly backward tracts.[51]

The above five districts included the greater part but not the whole of the Canal Colonies; the irrigated area sown in a single year was over six million acres, while of the area dependent on rainfall less than one million acres was cultivated before 1930, and of that over half was in Shahpur where the rainfall was 15 inches a year. Montgomery had slightly over 10 inches, Lyallpur 13, Multan 6.8 and Jhang 10 inches. The colonies extend into Gujranwala and Sheikhupura with nearly one and a half million acres irrigated, but they also include old settled areas.

51. Some idea of development within fifty years (1881-1931) may be derived from the following figures for population at different census enumerations :—

District	1881	1891	1901	1911	1921	1931
Montgomery	384,312	416,599	429,674	481,865	685,690	999,772
Lyallpur	53,832	46,829	576,926	824,470	957,881	1,151,351
Multan	555,516	634,538	709,297	813,357	889,328	1,174,900
Jhang	390,630	402,341	426,225	524,803	570,559	664,863
Shahpur	382,652	478,289	488,149	645,001	719,918	821,490
Total:—	1,731,942	1,978,693	2,630,294	3,289,496	3,823,376	4,912,346

Trade and Commerce Flourished

It would be difficult to give anything approaching an accurate estimate of the new wealth annually accruing from those great schemes; they had revolutionised the economic position of the Panjab and its people, not only of the colonists but of the great trading classes, and they had brought undreamed of wealth to the professional classes in the large towns. Elsewhere it will be shown how small was the commerce in Panjab products, how little the imports before the great schemes achieved fruition; and the enormous addition to the wealth of the province was reflected in its cultural as well as in its material progress.

In old settled districts a large proportion and in the colonies the whole of the annual yield must be credited to irrigation. In Amritsar, for instance, the Director of Land Records had estimated that the outturn of wheat was five maunds more on irrigated than on unirrigated land, although the annual rainfall was on the average over 24 inches. In Lyallpur the same authority estimated the difference at nine maunds. But some addition to that could be made for the greater area that failed to mature in unirrigated land. The Irrigation Department gave annually a modest estimate of the value of crops ripened under canal water; in 1928-29 Rs. 46 per acre; in 1929-30 Rs. 41 per acre; in 1930-31 owing to the great depression the figure fell to Rs. 25 per acre. It might be estimated that in a normal year crops worth from Rs. 40 to 50 crores were raised on irrigated lands, of which from Rs 25 to 33 crores are entirely due to the canals.

A Precaution

Of the canals in the province the greater works were productive; others were primarily protective, that is to say, designed to protect the tract against famine or severe scarcity. On the continuous efficient working of the system millions of people were dependent for the means of subsistence; the greater part of the area in the colonies had few wells and insufficient rainfall in a normal year to ripen a crop, so that the breakdown which interrupted the flow of water for a lengthy period would bring widespread disaster in its train. To ensure that the canals were kept in good working order and to save millions from the threat of loss of their livelihood if not of actual starvation, there was engaged a highly skilled body of engineers and subordinates, and large sums were yearly to be placed at their disposal to avoid risk.

The irrigation system then involved the province in 3 items of heavy responsibility, the interest charges on the capital sum borrowed, the cost of administration and the cost of maintenance and repair. To cover these there was levied a charge per acre irrigated and matured which was locally known as 'abiana' or water-rate. As this charge was repeatedly coming under criticism, not always well-informed, it seemed desirable to explain the economic aspect. The sums collected as water-rate were so large in the gross that they appeared excessives, and critics were apt to assume that there was room for reduction.

THE BHAKRA DAM AND OTHER PROJECTS

The above projects were merely provided for diverting the ordinary flow of the rivers into channels whence it could be used for irrigation. They made no provision for the utilization of the enormous surplus available when the rivers were swollen by the melting Himalyan snows in summer. The Satluj Valley Project was based on a minimum expectation of 6,500 cusecs, and the river flow had fallen below that in dry winters, yet 400,000 cusecs went down in flood just as the Sulaimanki weir was reaching completion.

There was plenty of arid land. It was for the impounding of some of it that the Bhakhra Dam on the Satluj was designed. The dam first proposed was to be 395 feet high to hold up a lake with a capacity of two and a half million foot-acres which was sufficient to give 6,000 cusecs for 200 days in the year. A bigger scheme contemplated making the dam a hundred feet higher (495 feet in all) and storing river below Phillour, from which point a new canal be four and three quarters million foot-acres.

The lesser scheme would add one and three million acres to the acres irrigated by the Sirhind Canal and by taking some of the work then done by the Western Jumna Canal it could enable the latter to irrigate another half million acres. This involved the enlargement of the existing Sirhind Canal and the construction of a weir on the Satluj constructed to take a portion of the irrigation of the existing Sirhind Canal. A new channel was to be constructed from the tail of the Main Line of the existing Sirhind Canal, across to the Sirsa Branch of the Western Jumna Canal which would in future be fully supplied from thence. The supply in the Western Jumna Canal thus set free, the Sirsa Branch was to be utilized for the irrigation of all the unirrigated land south-west of the Western Jumna Canal. The Project was estimated to cost about fourteen and a half crores to give an increased irrigated area of over two million acres, and to yield a return of 7 per cent, on the capital outlay.[52]

The Wular Project

Under this scheme irrigation was to be extended, irrespective of territorial boundaries, wherever physically possible in the tract between the Satluj and Jumna rivers, excluding the submontane tract, which, however, could subsequently be irrigated by means of tube-wells if sufficient water power was developed by the project. A much smaller project of the same nature was the Wular Lake Barrage Project which provided for the construction of a barrage on the river Jhelum at Sopor, just below its exit from the Wular Lake in Kashmir, the project was to impound water in that lake during the summer, for use in the winter by the Panjab Canals, offtaking from the Jhelum and the Chenab rivers. This project still formed the subjects of negotiations with the Kashmir State Government.[53]

Thain Project

The Ravi could also apparently be headed up at Thain, in a reservoir for the use of the Lower and Upper Bari Doab Canals, thereby increasing their cold weather supply by 20 per cent, with presumably the power to take double the amount in the summer. Much could also be done with the tributaries of the great rivers. The Degh was an absurd channel which ran through Gujranwala. A narrow miserable stream in the winter, it came down in great spates, Road, and causing water-logging in various areas watered by the Upper Canal. A good proportion of its run-off could be held up within the hills and let down quietly as required, thereby substituting an irriga-

52. Panjab Administration Report p. 381.
53. Panjab Administration Report p. 382.

tional canal for a periodically destructive torrent.

The Chakki torrent was familiar to travellers to Dalhousie and Dharamsala. Its bed was merely sand and boulders for much of the year. But at intervals it became a raging stream which did much damage in Gurdaspur and at the headworks of the upper Bari Canal. If, as believed, it could be dammed with success, the holding up of the waters could also had a double value in utilizing an element which was then purely destructive.

2

THE PANJAB STATE (1849-1947)

The Native States with which the Government of the Panjab had political relations were of two classes, viz., Dependent and Feudatory States and Independent States. There were 34 Dependent and Feudatory States. A brief account of these states is given for the general interest of students of history. The political position of these states in the north of India for about two centuries had been so important such as to deserve individual treatment at our hands.

Panjab Gun Saluted States

Out of 34 Panjab States, 14 were entitled for gun salutes.

Name of the State	Area in sq. miles	Population of State (1921)	Annual Revenue	Salute in guns
1. Patiala	5,932	15.0 lacs	163 lacs	19
2. Bahawalpur	15,000	7.81 "	49 "	17
3. Kapurthala	630	2.84 "	491 "	15*
4. Jind	1,259	3.08 "	28 "	15
5. Nabha	928	2.63 "	25 "	13
6. Faridkot	643	1.51 "	19 "	11
7. Malerkotla	168	80,000	14 "	11
8. Mandi	1,200	1.85 lacs	13 "	11**
9. Chamba	3,216	1.42 "	9 "	11**
10. Nahan	1,200	1.40 "	6 "	11**
11. Bilaspur	448	98,000	3 "	11**
12. Suket	420	54,000	2.34 "	11**
13. Loharu	222	21,000	1.31 "	9
14. Bashahr	3,820	86,000	3.34 "	9
Toal		40.93 lacs	384.99 lacs	

* Includes the income of about 20 lacs from Oudh Estate.

** In Simla Hill

The salute of guns was in recognition of the princes by which they were enjoying their respective positions and prestige.

THE PHULKIAN STATES

Geography

The three Phulkian States[1] of Patiala, Jind and Nabha formed a political agency under the Panjab Government. They occupied, with Bahawalpur and Hissar, the bulk of that great wedge of light loam and sand which Rajasthan, physically considered, pushed northwards almost of the Satluj. In the Phulkian States this consisted of two tracts the Powadh and Jangal Des. The former, which occupied the north and north-east of their territory, possessed a light fertile loam soil and a very moderate natural water level, so that well irrigation was easy. The Jangal Des was a great tract of sandy loam and sand in the south-west. Water lay too deep for the profitable working of wells, but the harvests were far less insecure than one could look to the scantiness of the rainfall. The soil was wonderfully cool and drought-resisting.

Cultivation

The dry cultivation consisted of millets in the Autumn, and of gram and mixed crops of wheat or barley in the spring harvest. These three erstwhile states had rather more than a one-third share in the Sirhind Canal, and the portions of the Powadh and Jangal Des were irrigated. In the case of Powadh there had been in some places over irrigation considering how near the surface the water table was. The Narwana tahsil in Patiala and the part of Jind which lay between Karnal and Rohtak was a bit of the Bangar tract of the south-eastern Panjab, with a strong loam soil and a naturally deep water level. The former received irrigation from the Sirsa, and the latter from Hansi branch of the Western Jamna Canal. The outlying tracts of the south of Rohtak and Gurgaon, acquired after the Mutiny of 1857, were part of the dry sandy Rajasthan desert, in which the 'kharif' was the chief harvest, and the millets and gram the principal crops.

---

1. Area 7919 sq. miles.

In addition, Patiala State had an area of 294 square miles of territory immediately below and the Simla Hills. The territory of the Phulkian States was scattered and intermixed, and they had pockets in British districts and vice versa, a natural result of their historic origin and development.

History

Phul was the sixth in descent from Baryam, a Sidhu Jat, to whom Babar gave the 'Chaudhriyat' of the wild territory of the south-west of Delhi, making him in effect a Lord of the Marches. The country and more which elapsed between the grant of the 'Chaudhriyat' and Phul's death in 1652 were filled with continual fighting with the Bhattis. Phul's second son Rama obtained from the Governor of Sirhind the 'Chaudhriyat' of the Jangal Des. When Ahmed Shah defeated the Sikhs near Barnala in 1762, Rama's son, Ala Singh, was one of his prisoners. He was a Chief of such importance that his conqueror gave him the title of Raja and the right to coin money. But Ala Singh found it prudent to join next year in the capture of Sirhind. From the division of territory which followed the separate existence of the Phulkian States began and they came under British protection in 1809. The Raja of Patiala was the British ally in the Anglo-Gurkha War in 1814, and received the Pinjaur tahsil. The active loyalty displayed in the Mutiny of 1857 was suitably rewarded by accessions of territory. The right of adoption was conferred, and special arrangements made to prevent lapse, if nevertheless the line in any state failed.

1. PATIALA

Geography

Patiala occupied five-seventh of the Phulkian inheritance. The predominant agricultural tribe was the Jats, over three-fourths of whom were Sikhs. The cultivated area was 4/5th of the total area. Over one-fourth of the former was irrigated, 27 p.c. from wells, and the rest by the two canals. In an area[2] extending with breaks from Simla to the Rajasthan desert the variations of agriculture were of course extreme. The state was

2. Area, 5,412 square miles.

excellently served by railways.

Nizamats

There were five 'nizamats' or districts, Pinjaur, Amargarh, Karmgarh, Anahadgarh and Mahindargarh. Their united area was equivalent to that of two ordinary British districts. The Pinjaur nizamat with headquarters at Rajpura covered 825 square miles. Of its four tahsils Pinjaur contained the submontane and hill tract, part of the latter being quite close to Simla. The other three tahsils Rajpura, Banur and Ghanaur were in the Powadh. The Amargarh nizamat with an area of 855 square miles comprised the three tahsils of Fatehgarh, Sahibgarh and Amargarh.

The first two were rich and fertile well tracts. Amargarh was in the Jangal Des to the south-west of Sahibgarh. It received irrigation from the Kotla branch of the Sirhind Canal. The Karmgarh nizamat with an area of 1835 square miles contained the four tahsils of Patiala, Bhowanigarh, Sunam and Nirwana. The headquarters were at Bhawanigarh. The first three were partly in the Powadh and partly in the Jangal Des. Nirwana was in the Bangar. There was much irrigation from the Sirhind and Western Jamna Canals. The Anahadgarh nizamat lay wholly in the Jangal Des. It had an area of 1836 square miles, and was divided into three tehsils, Anahadgarh, Bhikhi, and Govindgarh. The headquarters were at Barnala or Anahadgarh. The Mahindargarh nizamat lay far away to the south on the borders of Jaipur and Alwar. Its area was only 576 miles and it had two tahsils, Mahindargarh or Kanaud and Narnaul. Kanaud was the headquarters.

History

Raja Ala Singh, the founder of the erstwhile Patiala State died in 1765 and was succeeded by his grandson Amar Singh (1765-1781), who was occupied in continual warfare with his brother and his neighbours. His son, Sahib Singh (1781-1818), came under British Protection in 1809. Karam Singh (1813-1845). his successor, was the British ally in Anglo-Gurkha War. Maharaja Narinder Singh, K.C.S.I. (1845-1862), was a wise and brave man, who gave manful and most important help in the Mutiny of 1857, to the British Government. His son, Maharaja Mahinder

Singh (1862-1876), succeeded at the age of ten and died 14 years later. His eldest son, Maharaja Rajindar Singh (1876-1900), was only four when he succeeded and died at the age of 28. In the Anglo-Gurkha Campaign, in the Anglo-Sikh Wars, and in the Mutiny, the forces of Patiala lent their valuable aid to the British Government.

In the critical days of 1857 Maharaja Narinder Singh was instrumental in saving Panjab; and Lord Canning himself at a later date officially acknowledged his services as being of incalculable value. Maharaja Narinder Singh died in the prime of life in 1862 after having governed his territories with wisdom, firmness and benevolence, while performing the most eminent service to the British crown. Maharaja Rajinder Singh improved the resources of the State by large extensions of irrigations, and interested himself much in the extension of education, sanitation and medical relief. He offered his forces to the Government of India for the Manipur expedition of 1891 and the Malakand Campaign of 1895. In 1897 his troops joined the Mohmad Field Force and later took part in the Tirah Expedition, the Maharaja himself serving on the staff in the field. In 1900 His Highness died suddenly when only twenty-eight years old, having left a reputation for generosity, hospitality and sportsmanship.

Maharaja Bhupindar Singh

The services of Patiala State for the British Government were notable. In addition to the Imperial Service Corps while in the crisis of 1918 during the First World War Maharaja Bhupindar Singh offered to raise three Battallions of infantry in addition to maintaining the flow of recruits to the units already in the field. The total expenditure on the State War service during the war, including contribution to the various loans, amounted to one and one-third crores of rupees. The personal efforts of His Highness and his State which were recognized by inviting him to participate in the War Conference in 1918, where he did much good work winning for him fresh laurels as a statesman.[3] At this juncture, over sixty thousand men from this State, which had a total higher than the best of any British District

3. Ruling Princes & Chief of India, pp. 261-62.

and four times as much as that of any other Indian Princely state, went to the front.[4] He developed into a first class sportsman, an astute politician and an able administrator. It was he who was mostly responsible for giving Patiala a prominent place on the political map. Well above the average in Princely order, he was practically a life Chancellor of the Chamber of Princes. He attended the Imperial War Conference in 1918 as a representative of the Indian States, and in 1928, he presented the Princes' case before the Indian States Committee. He was also selected as one of the representatives of the Princes at the Round Table Conference in London in 1930. Maharaja Bhupindar Singh died in 1938.

Maharaja Yadvindra Singh

Maharaja Bhupindar Singh was succeeded by Maharaja Yadvindra Singh. His Highness Maharaja Yadvindra Singh was born on January 7, 1913. On the completion of his education at the Aitcheson College, Lahore in 1930. He succeeded his father to the gaddi on March 23, 1938. Like a progressive ruler, as he is, he immediately ordered the repeal of all oppressive laws like the Shikar and Nazul laws and abolished as many as eleven Shikar or Game Preserves to provide more land for agriculture and to save it from its enemies. On the out-break of World War II in 1939 he founded the Khalsa Defence of India League which sent thousand of stalwart Panjabis to the colours. He also personally went to the Italian theatre of war, the Middle East and Malaya.

His Highness has been a guiding light in the politics of the Princely Order ever since he became the Pro-Chancellor of the Chamber of Princes in 1943. He took leading part in the negotiations with the Cabinet Mission in 1946.

Patiala State under Maharaja Yadvindra Singh gave 65,000 recruits to the Indian Army. This was in addition to the recruitment going on for the Patiala State Forces. The Recruiting Officers, Jullundur, Hissar, Ferozepore, Ajmer and Delhi were paying visits to various places in the State and were provided with every facility to carry on the work of recruitment for the various branches of the Indian Army.

---

4. A History of the Sikhs, Vol. II-Khushwant Singh, p. 160.

Military Contributions

The Patiala Rajindra Lancers, the Ist Rajindra Sikhs and the 2nd Yadvindra Infantry remained on active service. All the expenses of these units were borne by the State. Four infantry battalions were expanded to full active regiments and an Infantry Training Battalion was raised. The Army Training School, the Mechanical Transport Section and the Patiala Wireless Section were re-organised as separate units. A full Mechanical Transport Company was raised and remained on active service. The new recruits were given fullest possible training in all branches of modern warfare. On account of reorganisation of the Patiala State Forces, the military budget which used to be Rs. 15 lakhs had risen to about Rs. 45 lakhs.

His Highness on the War Front

No sooner the Second world war (1939-45) was declared than His Highness in keeping with the hallowed martial traditions of his House cherished a keen desire to be amidst fighting forces on any one of the war fronts. But in the Second World War maintaining of the home front as well as the morale of the people was no less important than fighting on the war front. As later events showed His Highness' presence at home front proved of immense value in building up the huge war effort in sending up a continuous stream of men at the various theatres of war. His Highness as the accredited leader of the Sikhs, not only arrayed the great potential strength of the Sikh community against the enemies of freedom but was also responsible for keeping up the state war efforts to its colossal dimensions. His Highness had returned from a tour of Italy and the Middle East. During the course of his last tour extending over a month he visited troops in Egypt, Syria, Palestine, Paiforce and Italy. This was His Highness' third tour of a battle-front.[5] Despite his heavy pre-occupations, His Highness paid a visit to Malaya Peninsula just before the attack by the Japanese took place on Singapore. His Highness was the first Indian prince to pay a visit to this theatre of war. Subsequently His Highness visited the Assam front when the Japs were indulging in an attempt to

5. The Patiala Post, April-May 1945, pp. 33-34.

invade India.

He was one of the first prince who acceded to the Union of India and helped in the integration of the country with the formation of State Unions on the lines of British Indian provinces. The covenant of Patiala and East Panjab States Union was signed on May 5, 1948, and it was inaugurated on July 15, 1948, by the Hon'ble Sardar Vallabhbhai Patel with His Highness as its life-Rajpramukh. His Highness took over the administration of the Patiala and the East Panjab States Union on August 20, 1948.

2. JIND

Geography

One third of the population of Jind[6] consisted of Hindu and Sikh Jats. There were two nizamats, Sangrur and Jind: the latter consisted of the tahsils of Jind and Dadri. The Sangrur villages were interspersed among those of the other Phulkian States, and formed a part of the Jangal Des. Jind was in the Bangar, and Dadri, was separated from Jind by the Rohtak district, and partly in the sandy Rajasthan desert. The rainfall varied from 17 inches at Sangrur to ten inches at Dadri. Sangrur was irrigated by the Sirhind Canal and Jind by Western Jamana Canal. Dadri was a dry sandy tract, in which the Autumn millets were the chief crops. The revenue in 1911-12 was 19 lakhs (£126,700).[7]

HISTORY

Raja Bhag Singh

The real founder of the State was Gajpat Singh, who was a chief of great vigour. But the ruling family of Jind also belongs to the dynasty of Phul, descending from Chandhari Tiloka. His son Sukhchain Singh was the father of Raja Gajpat Singh, with whom the history of the State is especially connected with Gajpat Singh was born in the year 1938 and grew up to a fine handsome youth, well skilled in all military exercises. He con-

6. Area 1,259 square miles.
7. Panjab and the N.W.F.P. & Kashmir, Douie, p. 276.

quered Jind in 1774, deprived of his relative, the chief of Nabha and Sangrur. He died in 1789. His successor, Raja Bhag Singh, was a good ally of the British Government. His daughter Bibi Raj Kaur was the mother of Maharaja Ranjit Singh. Raja Bhag Singh assisted Lord Lake in his operations against the Marathas. Raja Bhag Singh was the first of all the great Cis-Satluj chiefs to seek an alliance with the British Government. Lord Lake wrote of him "a friend and an ally." He died after a long and successful career in 1819. His son, Fateh Singh, survived him by three years. Sangat Singh succeeded to troublous times and died childless in 1834. His second cousin, Raja Sarup Singh, was allowed by British Government to inherit only the territory acquired by Gajpat Singh, from whom he derived his claim.

Raja Sarup Singh

In 1822, Sangat Singh ascended the throne and on his death in 1839 Government recognised Sarup Singh, a third cousin of his, as the nearest male heir. During the Mutiny of 1857, Raja Sarup Singh's services were of a most valuable nature. The Jind forces marched in advance of the British Column. Raja Sarup Singh joined the British Camp at Alipore and in the battle of Badli Serai the Jind troops behaved most gallantly and were complimented on the field by the Commander-in-Chief, who sent one of the captured guns to the Raja as a present. The Jind force took a prominent part in the assault of Delhi, scaling the walls side by side with English troops. He was the only chief who was present with his Armyat Delhi, and in recognition of his services Dadri Ilaqa and 13 villages close to Sangrur were granted to him. Certain other privileges, such as the power of adoption in case of failure of a male issue[8] was also granted. He died in 1864.

Raja Raghubir Singh

His son Raghubir Singh (1864-1887) was a vigorous and successful ruler. He gave loyal help to British Government in the Kuka outbreak (1872) and in the Second Anglo-Afghan War. He was one of the most able and enlightened rulers, indefatigable in his efforts to promote the prosperity of his people.

8. Ruling Princes & Chiefs of India, p. 288.

He was awarded the title of Raja-i-Rajgan for furnishing a contingent of troops during the Second Afghan War, in perpetuity.

Maharaja Ranbir Singh

Maharaja Ranbir Singh, the grandson of Raja Raghubir Singh, was only eight when he succeeded, and Jind was managed by a Council of Regency for a number of years. Full powers were given to the chief in 1899. The Dhuri-Jakhal and Jind-Panipat railway lines were constructed during the reign of Maharaja Ranbir Singh. He received the title of Maharaja in 1911. His services during the First Great World War (1914-1918) were highly appreciated by the Government of India. He died in April, 1948, when the state acceeded to India & joined the Patiala and the East Panjab States Union.

3. NABHA

Geography

Nabha consisted of twelve patches of territory in the north scattered among the possessions of Patiala, Jind, and Faridkot, and two other patches in the extreme south on the border of Gurgaon. The northern section of the state was divided into the eastern nizamat of Amloh in the Powadh and the western nizamat of Phul in the Jangal Des. Both received irrigation from the Sirhind Canal. The Bawal Nizamat was part of the arid Rajasthan desert. Jats, who are mostly Sikhs, constituted 30 p.c. of the population.[9]

The Nabha State territory was scattered throughout the area occupied by the Phulkian States and consisted of three main divisions Phul, Amloh and Bawal. The total area was 968 square miles, the population, according to the census of 1921, was 263,394.

History

The real founder of the Nabha State was Hamir Singh a grandson of Phul's grandson, Gurditta. He joined with his Sikh bretheren in the capture of Sirhind and received as his reward

9. Panjab and the N.W.F.P. & Kashmir—Douie, p. 277.

the pargana of Amloh. He added many villages to the possessions inherited from his grandfather. Gurditta founded the present town of Nabha, struck coins in his own name, and exercised all powers of an independent Ruler for some years before his death in 1783. Nabha, with the other Cis-Satluj States, was taken under British protection in 1809.

Raja Jaswant Singh who was then on the 'Gaddi' was succeeded in 1840 by his son Devindar Singh. After the First Anglo-Sikh War, Devindar Singh was deposed and one-fourth of the Nabha State was confiscated.

Raja Bharpur Singh

During the Mutiny, however, Bharpur Singh, the successor of Devindar Singh, acted with exemplary loyalty and his troops rendered valuable services both at the siege of Delhi and elsewhere; in recognition of these services, the 'parganas' of Bawal and Kanti yielding a lakh of rupees of revenue were made over to the Nabha State and certain privileges conferred upon its Chief.

Raja Hira Singh

Raja Bharpur Singh was offered a seat in the Legislative Council on the Government of India in 1863. In 1871 Bhagwan Singh, the then ruler, died issueless and Raja Hira Singh, the Chief of Badrukhan, and a cousin of the Raja of Jind, was selected as his successor. During his long reign he gave repeated proofs of his desire to contribute to the power and prestige of the Empire and proved himself an energetic and able Ruler of the old school. The State furnished a contingent which did excellent service on the frontier during the Anglo-Afghan War of 1879-80 and its Imperial Service troops were also employed on the Tirah and Buner expeditions of 1897. The State also offered aid in the operations on the Frontier in 1908 against the Mohmand and Zaka Khel tribes.

Salute Raised

Raja Hira Singh's salute was raised to 13 guns as a personal distinction in 1877 and to 15 guns in 1893. The dignity of a Grand Commander of the Stars of India was conferred upon him in 1879, and the title of Raja-i-Rajgan in 1893 in recognition of the excellent administration of his State. He was invested with the insignia of a Grand Commander of the Order of the Indian Empire at Delhi, in January, 1903, and was also at the same time appointed Honorary Colonel of the 14th (King George's Own) Ferozepur Sikhs. He was invited to the Imperial Coronation Durbar at Delhi in December 1911 and proceeded to Delhi, but owing to the illness which ended in his death on the 15th December 1911 was unable to do more than attend the private reception by His Imperial Majesty the King-Emperor. The title of Maharaja was conferred upon him as an hereditary distinction on the day of the Durbar. He was succeeded by his son Maharaja Ripudaman Singh, born in 1883.

Maharaja Ripudaman Singh

The State was transferred from the Political charge of the Political Agent, Phulkian States, to the Agent to the Governor-General, Panjab States, on 1st November 1921. Nabha ranked fourth among the States in the Panjab. The Ruler of Jind was given precedence over Nabha on public occasions, but a return visit by His Excellency the Viceroy was paid to Nabha before the return visit to Jind. The permanent salute of the State was raised to 13 guns on the 1st January 1921. The Ruler was a Member of the Chamber of Princes.

On the outbreak of the War in 1914 Maharaja Ripudaman Singh offered his Imperial Service Troops, and duly rewarded his good services. In 1917-18 His Highness made contributions to various war funds and also gave a donation of three lakhs of rupees towards the expenses of the Expeditionary Forces and two and half lakhs for the additional aeroplanes for the defence of London.

Under Indian State Forces scheme Nabha maintained a force of infantry 450 strong. In July, 1923, the Government of India assumed control of the State in accordance with an agreement entered into by the Maharaja whereby he voluntarily separated himself from the administration, retaining his salute and titles. Owing, however, to his failing to abide by the terms of his agreement, he was deprived in February 1928 of the title of Maharaja and all rights and privileges pertaining thereto and ordered to reside until further notice at Kodaikanal, in the

Madras Presidency.[10]

His Highness Maharaja Partap Singh was born on 21st September, 1919, and succeeded his father Maharaja Ripudaman Singh in July 1923. The administration of the State during his minority was entrusted to an Administrator appointed by the British Government. Maharaja Partap Singh assumed full powers in 1938.

After an active service of 5 years overseas, the Nabha Akal Infantry returned to India in December, 1945 and arrived at Nabha on the 11th December, 1945. It was received at the Nabha Railway Station by His Highness the Maharaja Sahib Malvendra Bahadur, the gentry, Military Adviser, Panjab States Forces and Assistant Military Adviser, Panjab States Forces. As the train steamed into the station, scenes of great excitement were witnessed as fathers, mothers, sisters and brothers of the soldiers thronged the station platform and entrance hoping to meet their near ones returning to their homes after a long absence of glorious service.[11] He ruled the Nabha State up to August, 1948, when Patiala and the East Panjab States Union was formed.

4. KAPURTHALA

Geography

The main part consisted of a strip of territory mostly in the valley of the Beas, and interposed between that river and Jullundur. The State consisted of four tahsils; Bholath, Dhilwan, Kapurthala and Sultanpur. There was a small pocket of territory of Bhunga in Hoshiärpur, and a much larger one, the Phagwara tahsil, projecting southwards from the border of that district into Jullundur. Two-thirds of the area was cultivated and the proportion of high-class crop was large. The chief agricultural tribes were the Muslim Arains and the Sikh Jats.

HISTORY

Sardar Jassa Singh Ahluwalia

The real founder of the Kapurthala State was Sardar Jassa

10. Ruling Princes & Chief of India, p. 270.
11. Administration Report of Nabha State, 1945-46, p. 12.

Singh Ahluwalia, who in 1763, when Sirhind fell, was the leading Sikh chief in the Panjab. He captured Kapurthala in 1771 and made it his headquarters. He died in 1783. A distant relative, Bagh Singh, succeeded him, whose successor, Fateh Singh, was a sworn brother of Maharaja Ranjit Singh, with whom he exchanged turbans. But an alliance between the weak and the strong was not free from fears, and in 1826 Fateh Singh, who had large possessions south of the Satluj, fled and sought the protection of the British Government.

Sardar Fateh Singh

However, Sardar Fateh Singh returned to Kapurthala in 1827, and the Maharaja Ranjit Singh never pushed matters with Fateh Singh to extremities. The latter died in 1836. His successor Raja Nihal Singh (1836-1852) was a timid man, and his failure to support the British in 1845 led to the loss of his Cis-Satluj estates. When the Jullundur Doab came under the Dominion of the British Government in 1846, the erstwhile Kapurthala State, was maintained under the independent possession of the Kapurthala Ruler, conditional on his paying a commutation in cash amounting to Rs. 1,31,000 annually for the service engagements by which he had been previously bound to the Sikh confederacy. At the same time the Bari Doab estate was leased to the head of the House in perpetuity. This annual tribute of Rs. 1,31,000 a year was remitted by the Government of India in perpetuity later in 1924 in recognition of the splendid war record and uniformly efficient administration of the State.

Maharaja Jagatjit Singh 1877-1948

Raja Nihal Singh was succeeded by Raja Randhir Singh (1853-1870). His valuable services to the British Government during 1857-58, were rewarded with the title of Raja-i-Rajgan, the right of adoption and other concessions, in addition to the territories in the United Province of Agra and Awadh. He was succeeded by Raja Kharak Singh, (1870-1877). Raja Kharak Singh reigned for seven years only, when he died. He was succeeded by his five years old son, Maharaja Jagatjit Singh.

On the 24th November, 1890, Maharaja Jagatjit Singh G.C.S.I. attained his majority and assumed the Government of his State, the formal ceremony was performed by Sir James

Lyall, the then Lieutenant-Governor of the Panjab. At the Darbar the Governor spoke of the Prince and his illustrious family in terms of the highest regard and affection, and expressed every confidence as to the future welfare of the State under His Highness' benign and enlightened rule. His Highness was widely travelled Prince.[12]

In October, 1928, at the invitation of His Majesty the King, His Highness paid a State visit to the Court of Spain. His Highness the Maharaja, the Tikka Raja (Heir apparent) and his staff, were all put up in the Royal Palace. A shooting party was arranged for His Highness in which the King in person accompanied the Maharaja. The most brilliant function was the magnificent and most sumptuous banquet given by the King and Queen in honour of His Highness the Maharaja, at which, besides all the Members of the Royal family, the whole Spanish Court was present, the ladies in their beautiful jewels and coronets and the gentlemen in their full dress uniform with decorations. His Highness went again to Geneva on the 1st of September 1930 for the third time to represent India and the Ruling Princes of India on the 10th Assembly of the League of Nations, a unique distinction which had not been enjoyed by any other Ruling Prince in India so far.

Major-General C .O. Harvey, C.B., C.V.O., C.B.E.M.C., Military Adviser-in-Chief, Indian States Forces accompanied by Lieut. Colonel F. C. Codard the Military Adviser, Panjab States Forces visited Kapurthala on 17-18 March 1946 and was much pleased with the general efficiency of the State Forces and improvements made and gave an excellent report on the annual inspection of the Kapurthala State Forces.

The Military Adviser, Panjab States Forces and his assistants paid their usual visits and were fully satisfied with the high standard of efficiency in all branches of training and administration and made various complimentary remarks in their tour notes.

His Highness the Maharaja Jagatjit Singh announced in his birthday Durbar Speech in 1946 that for the Post War Development Schemes in the State a sum of Rs. 30 lacs may be set apart which would be spent in a period of five years beginning from

12. Ruling Princes & Chiefs of India, p. 279.

1st April 1946. The interim report of the Committee appointed under his order on Post War Development was perused by His Highness and he was very highly pleased to see a useful note prepared by the committee which contained details of what was required to be done for the benefit of his people. His Highness was further pleased to order that Post War Development work may be entrusted to Maharajkumar Karamjit Singh as adviser and to the Chief Minister for the execution of proposals embodied in the report.[13]

5. FARIDKOT

Geography

Faridkot was a small wedge of territory encircled which almost divided the Ferozepore district in two. The population was composed of Sikhs forty-two and a half, Hindus and Jains 29, and Muslims 28-1/2 p.c. Sikh Jats were the strongest tribe. The country was flat. In the west it was very sandy, but in the east the soil was firmer and was irrigated in part by the Sirhind Canal. The Chief like the Phulkians, was a Sidhu Barar Jat, and, though not a descendant of Phul, united his line with the Phulkians further back.

The ruling house of Faridkot has also a common ancestor with the Phulkian Chiefs and the Bhais of Kaithal in Barar, some twelve generations before Phul. Sidhu Barar lent his name to the tribe of the Barar Jat Sikhs to which the Faridkot family belongs. He was a contemporary of the Lodhis and Sanghar, a descendant of his, and the Mughal Emperors Babar and Humayun. His son, Bhallan, was a contemporary of Akbar the Great, and was always in armed conflict with the Bhattis, whose leader Mansur Khan was his chief rival. He had no male issue, and was, therfore, succeeded by his nephew Kapura, son of Lala. He was born in about year 1628 and lived up to 1708. He founded the town, of Kot Kapura at the suggestion of Bhai Bhagtu, the well-known disciple of Guru Arjan and the ancestor of the Bhais of Kaithal. Kapura received the 'Phul', or the Sikh baptism of Guru Govind Singh, and is known to history by the name of Kapur Singh. Kapur Singh was succeeded by

13. Report on the Administration of the Kapurthala State (1945-46), pp. 17, 64.

his son, Sardar Sukhia Singh, who was followed, in about 1732, by Sardar Jodh Singh. He always had his relations strained not only with the chiefs of Patiala but also with his own real brothers, Hamir Singh and Bir Singh, who complained about it to the leaders of the Khalsa Dal. Sardars Jassa Singh Ahluwalia and Jhanda Singh Bhangi brought about a compromise between the brothers. Sardar Hamir Singh succeeded his brother Jodh Singh's son, Tek Singh. He built the fort of Faridkot and made it his capital. His son, Mohar Singh, was deposed by Charhat Singh who in turn, was attacked and slain by his uncle, Dal Singh, And Dal Singh was assassinated by a cousin, Fauja Singh, who acted as the guardian of the minor chief Gulab Singh, son of Sardar Charhat Singh. The territory of Faridkot was invaded and occupied by Maharaja Ranjit Singh in 1807. It was, however, restored to Sardar Gulab Singh in 1809 in consequence of the Maharaja's treaty with the British. Sardar Gulab Singh was murdered in 1826 and was succeeded by his young son, Atar Singh, who died soon afterwards in August, 1827. Sardar Pahar Singh was then considered the rightful successor to the 'gaddi' of Faridkot.

Sardar Pahar Singh was an able ruler, and he devoted himself to the prosperity of his people. He dug canals and extended the cultivation, and thus doubled the income of his State within twenty years of his peaceful reign. He helped the British in the Anglo-Sikh War 1845-46, and his timely information to the British Commander about the position of the Sikhs Army in the battle of Pherushahr saved not only the British Army but also the British Government in India from a disaster that stared them in the face. The services of Sardar Pahar Singh were rewarded with the title of Raja and a grant of territory and some other favours.

Raja Wazir Singh

Raja Wazir Singh succeeded his father Raja Pahar Singh in 1849. He sided with the British in the Second Anglo-Sikh War. During the Mutiny of 1857 he rendered active assistance to the British in guarding the Satluj Ferries against the passage of rebel troops. With a squadron of his cavalry and two guns, he personally attacked a strong rebel Sham Das and destroyed his stronghold. The title of Brar Bans Raja Sahib Bahadur was bestowed upon him and he was accorded a salute of 11 guns. He died at Thanesar in 1874 after a reign of 25 years.[14]

Raja Bikram Singh

Raja Bikram Singh succeeded his father in 1875. Well skilled in languages and an able Ruler, he administered the State with conspicuous ability and enacted various reforms. During the Second Anglo-Afghan War he furnished a contingent of 250 horse and foot soldiers, and as a reward for his loyalty and the progressive nature of his Rulership he was honoured by the British Government with the hereditary title of Farzand-i-Sadat-i-Nishan, Hazrat-i-Kaisar-i-Hind Brar Bans.

Raja Balbir Singh

Raja Bikram Singh died in 1898, and was succeeded by his elder son, Raja Balbir Singh, who expired in 1906, after a short reign. He erected several buildings, such as Cantonment lines for his company of sappers, a clock tower as a memorial to Her Majesty the late Queen-Empress Victoria, and the Raja Mahal Palace. He had no direct issue, but adopted his nephew. His Highness Major Maharaja Brijender Singh Sahib Bahadur, as his heir.

Maharaja Brijender Singh

Maharaja Brijender Singh was born in 1896 and accended the 'gaddi' on the 15th March, 1906, at the age of ten. During his minority, the administration was placed in hands of a Council of Regency. His Highness was sent for his education to the Aitchison Chiefs' College, Lahore. His Highness assumed full Ruling Powers in 1916, but, unfortunately, died after too short a reign, on the 22nd December 1918.

First World War

On the outbreak of the First Great World War, His late Highness, following the traditional loyalty and unflinching devotion of his House to the 'gaddi' and person of His Imperial Majesty the King-Emperor, offered the services of his Imperial Service sappers and placed all the resources of his State at the

---

14. Ruling Princes & Chiefs of India, p. 285.

disposal of the British Government. A Company of Sappers and Miners was sent to East Africa in October 1914, and served there with distinction for more than three years. In 1916, at few days' notice, the Faridkot Darbar supplied as many as 405 camel men and muleteers, and a Second Company of Sappers of the recruiting services of the State during the War were eminently noteworthy.

On the lamented and untimely death of the late Maharaja Brijinder Singh, his elder son, Raja Harinder Singh, who was born on 28th January 1915 succeeded his father on 23rd December, 1918. As he was a minor, the administration of the State was conducted by a Council of Administration consisting of five members.

In December 1913, the State was transferred from the Political charge of the Commissioner, Jullundur Division, to that of the Political Agent, Bahawalpore Agency, under the control of the Panjab Government. Since the 1st November, 1921, it had been in the political charge of the Hon'ble the Agent to the Governor-General, Panjab States.[15]

Raja Brijinder Singh, came to the 'gaddi' in 1906 and died in 1918. He was succeeded by Raja Harinder Singh in 1928 till 1948, when the State was acceeded to India and joined the Patiala and East Panjab States Union, in 1948.

6. KALSIA

Geography

Kalsia consisted of a number of patches of territory in Ambala and an enclave in Ferozepore known as Chirak.[16] The Kalsia State originally formed a part of the territories of the Karor-Singhia Misal, founded by Sardar Shyam Singh, a Jat of Narli. It was, later on, consolidated by Sardar Karora Singh of Barrki, who lent his name to the Misal. After Sardar Karora Singh's death in the battle of Taraori in 1761, he was succeeded by the celebrated S. Baghel Singh of Jhabal who greatly extended his exploits and territories, both to the north and the south of the Satluj, with his headquarters at Hariana in the district of Hoshiarpur and Chhillaudi in the district of Karnal.

15. Ruling Princes & Chief of India, p. 236
16. Area, 168 square miles.

Sardar Jodh Singh was a devoted friend of Maharaja Ranjit Singh. In 1807 he joined him in the attack of Naraingarh in Ambala and received the estates of Badala Kheri and Shamchapal. He also fought for him in many a battle in the Panjab and his services were rewarded with the grant of the 'ilaqa' of Garhdiwala in the district of Hoshiarpur. He played a conspicuous part in the last battle and victory of Multan in 1818 and was left there in command of troops along with Sardar Dal Singh and Khalsa Dewa Singh to look to the repairs of the Multan fort and the city-wall and its ramparts. It was there that he died in 1818 of the wounds received in the battle. His son and successor, Sardar Sobha Singh, was for some time under the guardianship of Maharaja Karam Singh of Patiala. Sardar Sobha Singh ruled the Kalsia State for forty years and died in 1858, just at the close of the Mutiny, during which he remained devotedly loyal to the British Government.

Sardar Lehna Singh

He was succeeded by Sardar Lehna Singh (died 1869) who was followed in quick succession by his son Sardar Bishan Singh (died 1883) and grandson Sardar Jagjit Singh (died 1886). As the last named Sardar died at the age of seven, he was succeeded by his younger brother, Sardar Ranjit Singh, during whose minority the administration of the State was entrusted to a Council. Full powers were conferred on the Chief in 1906, and he died two years later in July 1908, leaving an infant son, Sardar Ravi-Sher Singh. The hereditary title of Raja was conferred on him in 1916 in recognition of the services rendered by him during the Great War. Raja Ravi-Sher Singh died on January 4, 1947, and was succeeded by second son Raja Karan Sher Singh. The Kalsia State acceded to the Indian Union on the lapse of British paramountcy in August 1947 and joined the Patiala and East Panjab States Union in 1948. The town of Kalsia and a number of small enclaves were transferred to the Panjab and the Himachal Pradesh in 1950 in exchange of territories taken over by the Patiala Union from these States.

7. BAHAWALPUR

Geography

Bahawalpur was by far the largest of the Panjab States.

But the greater part of it was desert, and the population, except in the river tract, was very sparse.[17] Bahawalpur stretched from Ferozepore on the north to the Sindh border. It had a river frontage exceeding 300 miles on the Satluj, Panjnad, and Indus. The cultivated area was about 1451 square miles, and of this 83 per cent was irrigated and 10 per cent flooded.

The rainfall is only five inches and the climate is very hot. South and east of the rivers was a tract of low land known as the "Sindh", which widened out to the south. It was partly flooded and partly irrigated by innundation canals with the help of wells. Palm groves were a conspicuous feature in the Sindh. Behind it was a great stretch of strong loam or "pat", narrow in the south, but widening out in the north.

It was bounded on the south-east by a wide depression known as the Hakra, probably at one time the bed of the Satluj. At present little cultivation was possible in the 'pat'. South of the Hakra was a huge tract of sand and sand dunes, known as the Rohi or Cholistan, which was part of the Rajasthan desert.

Nizamats

There were three nizamats, Minchinabad in the north, Bahawalpur in the middle, and Khanpur in the south. The capital, Bahawalpur, was close to the bridge at Adamwahan by which the North-Western Railway crossed the Satluj.

HISTORY

Sadiq Muhammad Khan

The ruling family belonged to the Abbasi Daudpotra clan, and came originally from Sindh. Sadiq Muhammad Khan, who received the title of Nawab from Nadir Shah, when he invaded the Derajat, in 1739, may be considered the real founder of the State.

Nawab Bahawalkhan

The Nawab of Bahawalpur rendered great assistance to British troops marching through his territory on their way for the Kabul campaign and his zealous services were rewarded by the British Government by the grant of Bhung and Kotsubzal in

17. Area, 15,917 square miles.

1842. In 1848 the Nawab offered all the resources of his State for assistance of the British Government in the Multan War, which resulted in the surrender of Multan and the defeat of Dewan Mul Raj, making Multan British possession. These important services were duly acknowledged by the Government by the grant to the Nawab of a life pension of one lakh of rupees anually.

Nawab Fateh Khan

Nawab Bahawal Khan died in 1852 and was succeeded by Nawab Fateh Khan. At the outbreak of the Indian Mutiny in 1857 this Nawab rendered every assistance to the British Government. Nawab Fateh Khan died in 1858 and was succeeded by his son Nawab Bahawal Khan IV, who after an eventless rule of about eight years died in 1866 and was succeeded by his son Nawab Sadiq Muhammad Khan IV. It was from this year that the modern history of the Bahawalpur State began. Nawab Sadiq Muhammad Khan was only four years old in the year 1866 when he succeeded his father, and in consequence of his minority a British Agency was established for the administration of the State, which lasted up to 1879. During this minority a marvellous improvement in the organisation of each department under British supervision was soon manifested and within a few years the State was brought into a flourishing condition.

Nawab Sadiq Muhammad Khan IV

In 1879 Nawab Sadiq Mohammad Khan IV was invested with full powers of a Ruling Chief. He rendered important service in the Kabul War of 1879 in recognition of which he was created G.C.S.I. in 1882. He received the personal thanks of the Government of India on the occasion of the visit of His Excellency Lord Ripon, Viceroy and Governor-General of India to Bahawalpur in 1880.

His father having died as early as 1907, the present Ruler came of age in 1924 and was invested with full powers in the same year by Lord Reading, the then Viceroy, His Highness had taken very keen interest in reorganising State troops and, for being of soldierly habits, his personal example had gone a long way to improving the Army.[18] At the time of partition of India, Bahawalpur State acceeded to Pakistan.

8. MALERKOTLA

Geography

Malerkotla consisted of a strip of territory to the south of the Ludhiana District.[19] The capital was connected with Ludhiana by railway. The Nawab kept up a company of Sappers and Miners for imperial service. Nawab Ataullah Khan also joined Lord Lake against the Marathas in 1803 and was taken under British protection by the treaty of 1809. He died in 1810 and was succeeded by Nawab Wazir Ali Khan, who, in turn, was followed by Nawab Amir Ali Khan (1821-46), Mahbub Ali Khan (1846-57) and Sikandar Ali Khan (1857-71). During this period the Malerkotla State helped the British in the Anglo-Gorkha Wars and the Mutiny. Nawab Sikandar Ali Khan received a salute of nine guns in 1861. He died in 1871. He had no male heir. His adoption of Ibrahim Ali Khan (and nomination as Nawab), the eldest son of his cousin, Dilawar Ali Khan (in Ataullah Khan's branch), under a Sanad granted to him in 1861 conferring the right of adoption, was upheld by the British Government.

The Kukas

In January 1872, a number of Kuka Sikhs, also called the Namdharis, attacked the kine-killing butchers of Malerkotla. Mr. Gowan, the Deputy Commissioner of Ludhiana, and Mr. Douglas Forsyth, the Commissioner of Ambala, unduly magnified this little affair into a mutiny of grave political importance, and blew by the guns as many as sixty-five of the Kukas. Baba Ram Singh, the leader of the sect, was deported to Rangoon where he died on November 29, 1884. Full account of Kuka-Movement has been dealt separately.

For reasons of health, Nawab Ibrahim Ali Khan withdrew from worldly affairs, and the State was managed by Nawab Amir-ud-Din Khan of Loharu as Superintendent appointed by

---

18. Ruling Princes & Chiefs of India, p. 267
19. Area, 167 square miles.

the Government of India. Nawab Ibrahim Ali Khan's son, Sahibzada Muhammad Ahmed Ali Khan, became Regent of the State on February 1, 1908. He was invested with ruling powers on January 5, 1909. He helped the Government of India during the Great Wars of 1914-18 and 1939-45 and was duly rewarded for his services. He was succeeded on his death on October 16, 1947, by his eldest son, His Highness Nawab Muhammad Iftikhar Ali Khan. Malerkotla acceded to the Indian Union on the lapse of British paramountcy and joined the Patiala and East Panjab States Union in 1948.

9. NALAGARH

Nalagarh was by far the oldest State in the Union. The Chief of Nalagarh, in common with that of Bilaspur, traces his origin to a Chandel Rajput who came from Garh Chanderi. Originally both these States were one unit, but a difference between two brothers led to the separate formation of Nalagarh under its own independent rulers, the first of whom Ajai Chand assumed power in 1100 A.D.

Raja Ram Saran Singh

The most important prince of the line was Raja Ram Saran Singh who reigned for about sixty years and died in 1849. It was during his time that, at the invitation of the Raja of Bilaspur, the Gorkhas came from Nepal in 1803 and subdued the various Hill Chiefs, including the Raja of Nalagarh. During the Anglo-Gorkha War of 1814, Raja Ram Saran Singh joined the British Commander, General Sir David Ochterloney, and helped him in the expulsion of the Gorkhas. At the conclusion of the war, he was re-instated in his ancestral territory. He improved and strengthened the fort of Palasi in the plains, on the bank of the Satluj, with the sum of one lakh of rupees received from the British Government as indemnity for the Satgarha forts returned to the Raja of Bilaspur after the Gorkha War.

Raja Bije Singh

He was succeeded by his son, Raja Bije Singh, who, on his death in 1857, was followed by his brother, Raja Agar Singh, an intelligent ruler. Raja Agar Singh's succession was held in abeyance for a period of three years during which the State was directly ruled by the British. It was due to the help of his neighbour, Maharaja Narendar Singh of Patiala, who took it on his shoulders to bring justice to a brother ruler in distress, that the 'gaddi' was again restored to the Ruling House of Nalagarh.

Raja Joginder Singh

Raja Isari Singh succeeded his father, Raja Agar Singh, in 1876. But he did not prove to be a capable ruler. The administration of the State was, therefore, entrusted to a Council. On the death of Isari Singh in 1911, his brother, Raja Joginder Singh, came to the 'gaddi' and administered the State with zeal and ability. He improved the State finances, revised the settlement of forests, opened a large number of primary schools, making education free, and established co-operative societies, with a Central Co-operative Bank at Nalagarh, the capital of the State.

Raja Surinder Singh

On his death he was succeeded by his son, Colonel Raja Surinder Singh. On succeeding to the 'gaddi' he, with the approval of the Crown, entered into a treaty with the Patiala Government, as a result of which his State was jointly administered with Patiala State. This action, in view of the changing times, stood out as unique and far-sighted, as proved by later developments, in the history of Indian States. During the short period of his rule he managed the affairs of the State creditably and was always popular. Like the other Panjab States, Nalagarh acceded to the Indian Union on the lapse of British paramountcy and joined the Patiala and East Panjab States Union in 1948.

PATAUDI, DUJANA AND LOHARU

The three little Muslim States of Loharu, Dujana, and Pataudi are relics of the policy which in the opening years of the nineteenth century sought rigorously to limit the British Government responsibilities to the west of the Jamna. Together they had an area of 275 square miles, a population of 59,937 persons, and a revenue of Rs. 269,500 (£18,000). Loharu State, 222 square miles in area and with a population of 20,621 according to 1921 census, was situated in the south-east corner of the Panjab on the border of Rajasthan.

Nawab Sir Amir-ud-Din Ahmed

Nawab Sir Amir-ud-din Ahmed Khan Bahadur, K.C.I.E., succeeded his father in 1884. He had been a Member of the Panjab Legislative Council (1889-1900), additional Member of the Viceroy's Legislative Council (1895), and was created a K.C.I.E., in 1897. From 1893 to 1902 he had been the Superintendent of the erstwhile Malerkotla State and was in 1903 granted a salute of nine guns as personal distinction. During the First Great World War, in addition to the services of the State, he offered his personal services and was sent to Basra on special duty under the Political Resident. In recognition of the meritorious services of the State in the First Great World War the personal salute was made permanent to the Ruler of the State in 1918.

Nawab Ali-ud-Din Ahmed Khan

In 1920 Nawab Sir Amiruddin Ahmed Khan voluntarily abdicated in favour of his son, Nawab Ali-ud-din Ahmed Khan, but was permitted to retain his title and salute as personal distinction.

Nawab Aiz-ud-Din Ahmed Khan

Captain Nawab Aiz-ud-din Ahmed Khan reigned from April 1920 to October 1926. He was granted the Military rank of Captain on account of his personal services in the Anglo-Afghan War of 1919, and passed his short period in strenuous efforts to overhaul the finances of the State. He was a zealous Member of the Chamber of Princes.

Nawab Aiz-ud-din Ahmed Khan was succeeded by his eldest son Fakharuddaulah Nawab Minuddin Ahmed Khan II, who was born on March 23rd, 1911. He was duly installed by the Hon'ble the Agent to the Governor-General, Panjab States, in a Darbar held in 1926. He was educated at the Aitchison Chief's College, Lahore, and was under Judicial and Revenue training at Jullundur under the supervision of the Commissioner of the Division for some time. During his minority the State was being administered by a Council of Regency, with Nawab Sir Amiruddin Ahmed Khan as its head.

The State ranked 18th in order of precedence among Indian States in the Panjab, was a member of the Chamber of Princes in its own right, and the Ruler was titled to be received by His Excellency the Viceroy, and was granted a Sanad in 1923 conferring upon him the power of capital sentence. Under the Indian States Forces scheme, the State also maintained a small force, the chief part of which consisted of a Camel Transport Company.

10. MANDI

Geography

Mandi[20] is a tract of mountains and valleys drained by the Beas. With Suket, with which for many generations it formed one kingdom it was a wedge thrust up from the Satluj between Kangra and Kulu. Three-fifths of the area was made up of forests and grazing lands.[21] The 'deodar' blue pine forests on the Kulu border were valuable. At Guma and Drang an impure salt, fit for cattle, was extracted from shallow cuttings. A considerable part of the revenue was derived from the price and duty.

HISTORY

Raja Joginder Sen

The rulers of the Mandi State were Chandarbansi Rajputs. The direct line came to an end in 1912 with the death of Bhawani Sen, but to prevent lapse the British Government had chosen as successor, a distant relative, Joginder Sen.

His Highness Joginder Sen Bahadur, ascended the throne when he was only eight years of age. The administration during his minority was carried on by officers deputed by the British Government. These deputed officers not only completed the Land Revenue and Forest Settlements, but also organised the various

20. The capital town Mandi had been the principal trade market on the Hoshiarpur-Yarkand trade route. It was an ancient city which abound in old temples, which are very interesting from the archaeologist's point of view. Out of the many places of interests in the State most important is the holy lake of Riwalsar which attracted large number of Hindus and Buddhist pilgrims.

21. Mandi was lying on the upper reaches of the river Beas which drains nearly the whole of its area some 1,200 square miles. The country is mountainous. A considerable portion is covered with beautiful forests containing a variety to useful timber.

departments of the State on the lines of administration in British India. The State forces were also reorganised.

His Highness after his education at the Aitchison Chiefs' College, Lahore, went through a course of Judicial and Revenue training in the Panjab. In 1923 His Highness married Princess Amrit Kaur, the only daughter of His Highness the Maharaja of Kapurthala and was blessed with a son and Heir, Sir Josodhan Singh.

His Highness assumed the reins of Government in February 1925 and appointed Rai Bahadur Dewan Dina Nath, Bar-at-Law, who had been the Superintendent of Mandi for some time, as his Chief Executive Officer, and with this able and experienced officer entered upon his onerous duties. Ever since his accession to 'gaddi', His Highness devoted himself to the improvement of the administration in every possible way.

11. SUKET

Geography

Suket lay between Mandi and the Satluj.[22] Its Raja Ugar Sen, like his distant relative, the Raja of Mandi came under British protection in 1846. His great-grandson Raja Bhim Sen. His Highness Raja Lakshman Sen Bahadur was the 51st descendant of the Sen Rajput family that founded the State in the 8th century. His Highness comes down of the ancient Chander Bansi Rajputs of India. The Raja Sahib was educated at Aitchison Chiefs' College, Lahore. After that he received his administrative, judicial and political training under the most distinguished officers of the Panjab Government and the Hon'ble Judges of the Panjab Chief Court.

His Highness succeeded, in 1919, his brother, His Highness Raja Sir Bhim Sen, C.I.E., who died in 1919. Immediately after taking the reins of Government in his hands, he devoted all his time and energy for establishing a system of Government after the model of British Indian administration. Many commercial and traffic facilities were granted to the public, which had placed the State in closer touch with other parts of the country. His Highness commanded the full confidence of his subjects and en-

---

22. Area 420 square miles.

joyed the esteem of the British Government.[23]

12 SIRMUR (NAHAN)

Geography

Sirmur (Nahan) lay to the north of the Ambala district, and occupied the greater part of the catchment area of the Giri, a tributary of the Jamna.[24] It was for the most part a mountain tract, the Chor to the north of the Giri rising to a height of 11,982 feet. The capital Nahan (3207 feet), near the southern border was in the Shivalik range.

In the south-east of the State was the rich valley known as the Kiarda Dun, reclaimed and colonized by Raja Shamsher Parkash. There were valuable 'deodar' and 'sal' forests. In 1815 the British Government having driven out the Gorkhas put Fateh Parkash on the throne of his ancestors. His troops fought on the English side in the First Anglo-Sikh War. His successors, Raja Sir Shamsher Parkash, G.C.S.I. (1856-98), and Raja Sir Surinder Bikram Parkash, K.C.S.I. (1898-1911), managed their State with conspicuous success.

In the Second Anglo-Afghan War in 1880, Sirmur sent a contingent to the frontier, and the Sappers and Miners, which it kept up for Imperial Service, accompanied the Tirah Expedition of 1897 also.

Lieut. Colonel His Highness Maharaja Sir Amar Parkash Bahadur, K.C.S.I., K.C.I.E., succeeded his father Raja Sir Surendra Bikram Parkash Bahadur in 1911 A.D. having been installed on the 'gaddi' on the 26th October 1911 by Sir Louis Dane, the Lieutenant-Governor of the Panjab.[25]

13 CHAMBA

Geography

Chamba lay to the north of Kangra from which it was divided by the Dhauladhar.[26] The southern and northern parts of the State were occupied respectively by the basins of the Ravi and Chenab. Chamba is a region of lofty mountains with some

24. Area 1198 square miles.
25. Ruling Princes & Chiefs of India p. 281.
26. Area 3216 square miles.
23. Ruling Princes & Chiefs of India, p 321.

fertile valleys in the south and west. Only about one-nineteenth of the area was cultivated. The snowy range of mid-Himalaya separated the Ravi valley from that of the Chenab, and the great Zanskar chain with its outliers occupied the territory beyond the Chenab, where the rainfall was extremely small and Tibetan conditions prevailed. The State contained fine forests and excellent sport was to be got in its mountains. There were five 'wazarats' or districts, Brahmaur or Barmaur, Chambat, Bhattoyat, Chaura, and Pangi.

History

Chamba was one of the oldest Indian States, having been founded in the middle of the sixth century A.D. In 1847 after the First Anglo-Sikh War, the State came under British control. It contained 50 small sub-divisions, called 'parganas' or ilaqas, each under its own staff of officials.

Raja Sri Singh

Raja Sri Singh ruled from 1843 to 1870, and was followed by his brother Raja Gopal Singh who abdicated in 1873 in favour of his elder son Raja Sham Singh. The last named was a great builder and did much to embellish the capital as well as open up the State by the construction of good roads.

Raja Bhuri Singh

Raja Sir Bhuri Singh (1904-19) continued the work and among other improvements, provided an electric installation and a good pipe water supply to the town. His great distinguished service during the First Great War (1914-1918) won for him the distinctions of K.C.S.I. and K.C.I.E. from Government, and for the State an honoured name among the principalities of the Panjab. The formal installation of His Highness was performed by His Honour the Lieutenant-Governor of the Panjab, at Chamba on April 24, 1920.

SIMLA HILL STATES

The Deputy Commissioner of Simla was political officer with the title of Superintendent of nineteen, or, including the tributaries of Bashahr, Keonthal, and Jubbal, of 28 states with a total area of 8355 square miles, a population of 410,453, and revenue amounting to a little over ten lakhs (£66,000). The States varied in size from the patch of four square miles ruled by the Thakur of Buja to the 3881 square miles included in Bashahr.[27] The chiefs were all Rajputs, who came under the protection of the British Government at the close of the Gorkha War.

The watershed of the Satluj and Jamna ran through the tract. The range which formed the watershed of the Satluj and the Jamna started from the Shinka Pass on the south border of Bashahr and passed over Hattu and Simla. In Bashahr it divided the catchment areas of the Rupin and Pabar rivers, tributaries of the Tons and therefore of the Jamna, from those of the Baspa and the Nogli, which were affluents of the Satluj, West of Bashahr the chief tributary of the Jamna was the Giri and of the Satluj the Gambhar, which rose near Kassauli. In the east Bashahr had a large area north of the Satluj drained by its tributary the Spiti and smaller streams. In the centre the Satluj was the northern boundary of the Simla Hill States. In the west Bilaspur extended across the river. The east of Bashahr was entirely in the Satluj basin.

BILASPUR

This was true also of Bilaspur or Kahlur, which had territory on both banks of the river.[28] The capital, Bilaspur, was on the left bank only 1455 feet above sea level.

BASHAHR

The chain which formed the watershed of the Satluj and Jamna rose from about 12,000 feet Hattu in the west to nearly 20,000 feet on the Tibet border.[29] Two peaks in the chain exceeded 20,000 feet. Further north Raldand to the east of Chini was 21,250 feet high, and in the north east on the Tibet border there were two giants about 1000 feet higher.

Bashahr was divided into two parts, Bashahr proper and

27. Only four other States had areas exceeding 125 square miles, namely, Bilaspur (448), Keonthal (359), Jubbal (320), and Hindur or Nalagarh (256). Excluding feudatories the revenues varied from Rs. 900 (or a little over £1 a week) in Mangal to Rs. 190,000 (£12,666) in Bilaspur.
28. Area 448 square miles.
29. Area 3881 square miles.

Kunawar. The latter occupied the Satluj valley in the north-east of the State. It covered an area of about 1730 square miles and was very sparsely peopled. In the north of Kunawar the predominant racial type was Mongoloid and the religion was Buddhism. The capital of Bashahr, Rampur, on the left bank of the Satluj was at an elevation of 3300 feet. The Gorkhas never succeeded in conquering Kunawar. They occupied Bashahr, but in 1815 the British Government restored the authority of the Raja.

CONCLUSION

The Panjab States numbering 34, with which the Government of the Panjab had political relations till 1921 were of two classes, viz., Dependent and Feudatory States, and Independent States (including frontier tribes).[30]

The relations of the Dependent and Feudatory States—viz., Kashmir and Bahawalpur—with the British Government were regulated by treaties: those of Patiala, Jind, and Nabha by Sannads, or rescripts of the Governor-General Kashmir payed an annual tribute of shawls and shawl-goats; Patiala, Jind and Nabha furnished a quota of horsemen for general duty in British territory. A 'nazaranah' or relief was payable to the British Government by the last three Chiefs, on succession of collaterals to the Chiefship: and the Chiefs were bound to execute justice, and promote the welfare of subjects to prevent 'Satti', Slavery; and female infanticide, to cooperate with the British Government against an enemy; to furnish supplies to troops, and to grant, free of expense, aid required for railroads and imperial lines of road. On the other hand, the British Government guaranteed them in full and unreserved possession of their territories. They differed from the remaining feudatories in the fact that these were granted full powers of life and death over their subjects, and that the Government undertook not to receive any complaints from their subjects, whether 'muafidars' 'jagirdars',

30. The Dependent and Feudatory States 34 in number, viz., Kashmir, Patiala, Bahawalpur, Jind, Nabha, Kapurthala, Mandi, Sirmur (Nahan), Kahlur (Bilaspur), Bashahr, Hindur (Nalagarh), Keonthal, Malerkotla, Faridkot, Chamba, Kalsia, Pataudi, Loharu, Dujana, Bhagal, Jubbal, Kumaharasain, Suket, Bhajji, Mailog, Balsan, Dhami, Kuthar, Kunihial, Mangal, Bija, Bhagat, Darkuti, Taroch.

relatives, dependants servants or other classes.[31]

Sir Walter Lawrence preferred to live in the Indian States than in British India, on account of perhaps the better administration and other facilities available to a British representative.

"Then in Lahore I knew well the representatives of the Panjab States, dignified men, who always thought first of the dignity of their Chiefs, last and least of their financial interests. I met too the grand old men, who had been friends and advisers of Ranjit Singh, and had spoken their minds in the den of the famous Lion of the Panjab. They too talked of the dignity of power, and taught me that power comes from knowing men (Adm-Shinasi). They were wits, masters of words, and conversation, but seemed asphyxiated by the cut and dried system of our administration. Then for many years along the frontier of the Panjab and the State of Jammu and Kashmir, every day comparing the advantages and noticing the differences of the two systems of Government. And my conclusion is that, if I were a humble peasant, or an ambitious young Indian of fair education, I would rather live in an Indian State than in a British Province."[32]

Slavery Worse Than Self-Murder

Loss of independence results in slavery; slavery brings self-humiliation, and self-humiliation is worse than self-murder. So to live in the British India or to live in one of the Princely states in India cannot make much difference with respect to the fundamental values that all human beings in all nations cherish dearest to their heart one of the greatest of such values being to put it in the words of Lokmanya Balgangadhar Tilak: "Swaraj is my birth-right".

Choice Between Two Evils

It is a choice between two evils: Foreign evil and native evil. And if we look upon these two evils from a closer perspective we will find that the slavery under a native Rajah or Nawab should not be so humiliating as the one under the British Government. Slavery under a foreign government certain to

31. Punjab Administrative Report—1869-1870 p. 9.
32. Ruling Princes & Chiefs of India (Introduction)

be condemned more vociferously than the slavery under the native rulers however degenerate their rule might be. The histories of democracies everywhere have not shown a brighter picture of moral standards and social values than the ones obtaining in the various Indian States. Democracies have been witnessed in recent times degenerating into worst type of criminality, corruption and bestiality. The only satisfaction to democratic people is that the debauchery to which they have reduced themselves it is of their own choosing, their own doing, a result of their own most avaricious desires and ambitions. Indian States, for that matter, cannot be condemned more severely, though democracy has made it a fashion to cry down everything that did not grow under a democracy. By arguing thus I hold no brief for the Indian Princes or the British Raj, but I have sought to make this comparative, differentiation to place my finger, as an objective of history, on the wrong here, there and whenever it be. While I uphold the spirit of democracy, I decry its functioning when democracy degenerates into bureaucracy, oligarchy or into some form of fascist regime.

Double Slavery in States

A point that may be made out on the side of the British Government is that while people living on the territory directly governed by the British lived under British slavery, the people living in the Indian States were living under a double slavery—first that of the Rajahs and secondly, that of the British Government whose interference and functioning in the Indian States was more than visible. But this argument amounts to a theorem meant only to exercise the mind of the students in a certain direction having no political or historical validity.

Another point is that all the States could not be treated at par. There were several States in India, like Mysore, Gwalior, Baroda, Kashmir, to quote some of them, where the Rajahs ruled with wisdom and far-sight, showed uncommon statesmanship and concerned for their subjects and carried their respective states forward to the goals which were so loudly set by a democratic nation. Just to quote one example, Mysore was the state where there was 97% literacy when India became free in 1947. Moreover, several Rajahs, especially those in Rajasthan, Madhya Pradesh and Maharashtra lived wisely with restraint and moderation and some of them strictly according to their religious traditions and the customs of their own 'gharanas'. The sins of Maharaja Bhupindar Singh could not be spread and scattered over.

3

MAHARAJA OF PATIALA AS CHANCELLOR OF CHAMBER OF PRINCES

The question of the position of the Rulers of the Panj States in the policy of India and the British Empire has great interest in view of the Constitutional Reforms. Mr. Panikar's narrative of His Highness the Maharaja of Patiala as Chancellorship of the Chamber of Princes, had appeared at an opportune moment.

To some extent the form in which the question of the position of the Rulers was raised and the federal proposals were the outcome of the activities of the Chamber of Princes, which at least since 1922, when Maharaja of Patiala was its Chancellor, had pressed for a careful examination and inquiry into the future position of the Indian States.

Chamber of Princes Inaugurated—1921

The Chamber of Princes was instituted, as a result of the desire of the rulers of Indian States for an organization which would enable the Viceroy and the Princes to come together and to deliberate on matters relating to the British Empire and the States as a whole. Lord Hardinge who found informal consultation with Princes valuable, during the critical days of the first Great World War, was sympathetic towards this idea. The Princes' Conference came into existence in 1916 and continued to meet every year till the Chamber of Princes was formally inaugurated in 1921.

As Honorary General Secretary to the Princes' Conference from 1916 to 1921 and as the first Chancellor of the Chamber of Princes from 1921 to 1926, it fell to the lot of the Maharaja of Patiala to shoulder the responsibility of organizing and conducting the work of the Conference and the Chamber.

Great Responsibilities

Throughout this period of ten years His Highness the

Maharaja of Patiala was closely associated with much important duty including that of working out a preliminary scheme while on a small Committee of Princes assisted by some Ministers, at a later stage, the formulation in collaboration with the officers of the Government of India, of the final proposals relating to the establishment of the Chamber its constitution, rules and regulations, its functions and composition, and other allied matters; and on various important Conferences and Committees, and especially the Princes' Standing Committee.

In the Chancellorship of the Maharaja of Bikaner in 1926 it was his privilege to propose at an informal meeting of the Princes the name of His Highness the Maharaja of Patiala as his successor who subsequently bore the burden and responsibilities of that difficult task and at times unenviable office, for a total period of some eight and a half years:—

"I am thus in a position to speak from considerable first-hand knowledge of His Highness the Maharaja of Patiala's great work—both inside and outside the Chamber of Princes and of his personal contribution to the problems which faced the Princes during one of the most important junctures in the modern history of the Indian States".[1]

THE GENESIS OF THE BUTLER REPORT

Princes and the First World War

The Indian Princes adopted the Imperial cause as their own during the First Great World War in 1914-1918 for which they were compensated by a change of policy and attitude on the part of the British Government. It was felt that the old policy of isolation had long since been out-worn. One result of that policy was the institution of the Chamber of Princes in which the rulers of some prominent States took the opportunity of Joint Consultation to clear their position as regards the incidence of paramountcy. They felt that their treaty rights had been solemnly eroded by the development of political practice and they desired to set up a barrier against further encroachments. They were now brought into direct contact with the Government of India.

1. The Indian Princes in Council—Panikkar, Foreword

New code

In response to their wishes, an effort was made to modify political practice so far as that was feasible. It was, however, found impossible to bring the major problems of the Crown to intervene to redress misrule within the framework of the new code. Moreover, a fresh instance of Paramountcy soon forces itself on the susceptibilities of the Princes in the historic correspondence between the Nizam of the Hyderabad State and the Government of India. The Nizam claimed that in regard to internal matters his Government was independent and on a position of equality with the British Government. He denied the right of the British to make binding decisions on matters relating to his controversies with the Government of India.

Lord Readings' reply

Lord Reading replied (March 1926) "It is the right and privilege of paramount power to decide all disputes that may arise between States or between one of the States or itself. The sovereignty of the Crown is Supreme in India. Its supremacy is not based only upon treaties and engagements but exists independently of them."[2] A problem of equal importance forced itself on the attention of the Princes. British India was agitating strongly for self Government in the event of its grant in whose hands would paramountcy vest in the Indian Government or the Crown.

Representation of the Princes—1927

Accordingly in the spring of 1927 the standing committee of the Chamber of Princes put forward proposals before Lord Irwin at a Round Table Conference between the Viceroy and some high officials of the Government on one side and certain members of the standing committee on the other hand. The Princes wanted an imperial and judicial examination of the question of relationship between the States and the Paramount Power in the light of their respective treaties 'Sanads' and other documents. The standing committee followed this up by sending its Ministers to England in the ensuing summer to seek authori-

2. Indian States and the Government of India—Panikkar p. 138.

tative legal advice from eminent lawyers upon certain aspects of their legal position.

Indian State Committee

The request of the Princes was conceded to and on December 16, 1927 Earl Birkenhead, the Secretary of State for India appointed the Indian States Committee with the following terms of reference:—

1. To report upon the relationship between the Paramount power and the Indian States with particular reference to the rights and obligations arising from Treaties, Engagements and Sanads and usage and sufference and other causes.
2. To enquire into the financial and economic relations between British India and the States and to make any recommendations that the Committee may consider desirable or necessary for their more satisfactory adjustment.

The Committee Consisted of Three Members

The committee was to consist of three members including the President Sir Harcourt Butler, an old and distinguished member of the Political Department, having been for several years political Secretary in the Government of India and well acquainted with the policy as had been in actual operations in relation to the states. The other members of the committee were Prof. Holdsworth—a legal writer of eminence and Mr. Peel.

Soon after the announcement of the Committee the Standing Committee of the Chamber of Princes appointed a Committee of Princes to prepare the case for the States to be presented to the Committee. At the same time they engaged an eminent lawyer.

All Princes Were Not Unanimous

Sir Leslie Scott was to help them in the preparation of their case and to present it to the Committee when it was ready. This action of the Standing Committee met with unqualified approval of an informal Conference of the Princes. More than this the Chancellor and several Members of the Standing Committee proceeded to England along with their Counsel so as to be able to more effectively press for and obtain proper relief for the Princes' grievances. It must here be mentioned that the representation though not quite unanimous[3] was supported by an overwhelming majority of the Princes and even those few Princes who preferred to approach the Committee directly with their individual grievances were not opposed to the presentation of their case of the whole order to which they belonged.

Inquiry in Camera

The inquiry was held in camera and the Committee denied itself by a too narrow interpretation of the terms of reference the opportunity of hearing the views of the people of the Indian States on the important question raised before the Committee. The Committee, however, allowed States Subjects Association to put their views in written statements. The Committee visited fifteen States among them Hyderabad, Kashmir, Patiala, Baroda, Mysore, Gwalior, Bikaner and examined 48 witnesses. The most important evidence on behalf of the States was however put before the Committee in London by Sir Leslie Wilson in October and November, 1928. Sir Leslie and his colleagues had scrutinized very closely the existing treaties and their alleged infringement.

Paramount Power had the Right to Intervene in the Internal Affairs of the States

The Princes Counsel said that the relationship of the States to the Paramount Power was a relationship to the Crown and that the treaties made with them were treaties with the Crown. Sir Leslie confined paramountcy to the conduct of the foreign relations of the States, including inter-State relations. It was admitted as a corollary of these principles that the Crown had a right to intervene in the internal affairs of a State. Such intervention was necessary for the purpose of exercising the rights of fulfilling the obligations of the Crown in connection with foreign relations and external and internal security and not otherwise.

---

3. For several important States like Hyderabad, Baroda, Mysore, Travancore-Cochin and other States declined to be represented by Sir Leslie Scott and preferred to state their own cases in written replies to the questionnaire.

Butler Report Unanimous

The views of the Princes did not meet with the favour of Sir Harcourt Butler and his colleagues proved from the nature of their Report. The Report of the Indian States Committee was signed on the 14th February, 1929, was presented to the British Parliament on the 15th April and simultaneously published both in England and India. The Report was a short one and unanimous.

1. It was recommended that the Viceroy and not the Governor-General in Council should in future be the agent of the Crown in its relations with the Princes and that important matters of dispute between States themselves, the States and the Paramount Power and between the States and British India should be referred to an Independent Committee for advice.

2. The Committee held that treaties, engagements and 'Sanads' had been made with the Crown and that the relationship between the Paramount Power and the Princes should not be transferred without the agreement of the latter to a new Government in British India responsible to an Indian Legislature.

3. The Committee accepted the plea of the States that they should be consulted on all external affairs regarding defence. The final voice was to remain with the Paramount Power as being responsible for the defence both of British India and the Indian States. Paramountcy was however to remain paramount fulfilling its obligations and adopting itself according to the shifting necessities of time.

4. The Butler committee laid great stress on the recruitment and training of political officers who should be recruited separately from the British Universities for service in the States alone. The Committee recommended the advice of Lord Irwin for a fixed privy purse, security of tenure in the public services including the establishment of an Indian Judiciary.

Financial and Economic Relations

Touching the question of the financial and economic relations between British India and the States the committee recommended the appointment of an expert body to enquire into

1. Reasonable claims of States or groups of States to a share in the customs revenue.

2. The adequacy of their contributions to Imperial burdens. They also recommended the experts to consider the question of a zellverein which they considered to be ideal solution of the problem.

3. The committee recognized that there would be matters of common concern to British India and the States in which the interests of the two might clash. For adjustment in these matters they recommended that the Viceroy should appoint committees to advise him and in cases, where such committees failed to agree, the Viceroy might appoint more formal committees with impartial chairman of not lower standard than that of high court judges. In the event of their advice not being taken, the matter was to be referred to the Secretary of State for India.

Butler Report opposed by all States

The Butler Report was met with a mixed reception both in India and England. Long before its publication some of the Princes gave expression to their sense of disappointment at the probable result of the inquiry and a perusal of the Report made it quite clear that their anticipations were fully justified. The main request of the princes was that the present powers of intervention should be more clearly defined and limited. This request the Butler Committee definitely refused, they rather reaffirmed the existing positions with an ever greater emphasis than that contained in previous pronouncements. The Report was duly considered at the ninth session of the Chamber of Princes. The Maharaja of Patiala called the report "as a mixture of good and evil" but spoke strongly against the Butler statement of the implications of Paramountcy. His Highness the Nawab of Bhopal declared that the Butler Report was a sad illusion, while the general trend of the speeches expressed disappointment at the Report.

Report denounced by the Public Organs

The Indian Press and the Indian public men never expected any fruitful results from this enquiry. The Report was denounced by eminent public men and the leading organs of public opinion in India as a deliberate attempt to drive a wedge between British India and Indian States and made the question of evolving a new constitution for India even more difficult than it was. This was because the Report had accepted the princes' stand that they were not to be 'controlled' by Government of India but by the Crown.

Tej Bahadur Sapru

Commenting on the Butler recommendations Sir Tej Bahadur Sapru said: "Constitutionally this doctrine overlooks the difference between the paramountcy of the paramount power and the form of Government which that power may establish in India. Politically it is a negation of Indian claim to the Status of a Dominion".

Ram Chandra Rao

Indian public opinion was well represented in the remarks of Dewan Bahadur Ram Chandra Rao, who said: "The British Imperialists have been thinking for some time of a plan by which the demand for Dominion Status can be defeated and no better plan could be devised for that purpose than the present proposals of the Butler Committee which constitute a negation of Dominion Status for all times."

Recommendation of the Nehru Committee

Far different and much more logical were the recommendations of the Nehru Committee appointed to consider the problem of Indian Constitutional advance. The Princes had made a fetish of their direct relationship with the Crown. The Committee brought it home by inexorable force of logic that even admitting its existence the change in the nature or composition of the Governmental machinery in India could not alter the situation. The Crown did not mean the British Government in constitutional theory and practice. The new Government envisaged was to be the King's Government in India whether it was responsible to the British Parliament or the India. If they had no objection to the political secretary of the Government of India exercising vast powers over them, there was no logic in their refusal to deal with a similar official appointed by the Dominion Government of India.

ADEQUATE SAFEGUARDS

The Committee provided adequate safeguards to the interests of the Princes when they clashed with British India. In justifiable matters they suggested that in case of differences between the Commonwealth and the Commonwealth Government on any matter arising out of the treaties, the Governor-General in Council might, with the consent of the State concerned, refer the matter to the Supreme Court for decision; its constitution being so devised as to inspire the confidence of all parties. In regard to non-justifiable matters involving financial and administrative relations they suggested settlement by means of mutual conference. These recommendations were a definite improvement of the 'Status Quo' but the princes rejected them.

Suggestion by Sir John Simon

There is no doubt that the Butler rebuff to the Princely point of view had much to do with the emergence of the Princes as a political factor and their fear of political progress in British India. The announcement of a Round Table Conference for the discussion of Indian constitutional reforms was welcomed by the Indian Princes who looked forward to it for a satisfactory settlement of the various questions which they had raised before the Butler Committee. Indeed the main reason given by Sir John Simon for suggesting such a conference was the interconnection between the Indian States and British India and the necessity of an adjustment of the relations between them which was involved in the determination of the future status of British India, was necessary.

Maharaja of Bikaner

In the course of an interview which His Highness the Maharaja of Bikaner gave to a press representative he said, he welcomed cordially the Viceregal statement about the Round Table Conference and declared. "It is now for Indian States as well as British India to demonstrate to the world at large that they are jointly and unitedly capable of dealing successfully with solving the problem involved. The Princes have no desire to hamper the attainment of Dominion Status by British India or to be a drag on its constitutional advancement".

The Maharaja further said that a federation was the best solution of the problem and that the States could not be expected to agree to any proposals involving a violation of their "Sovereign" rights.

Unanimous Resolution of the Chamber of Princes, 1930

The Maharaja of Patiala, the Nawab of Bhopal and other Princes expressed similar sentiments. These statements were confirmed by a unanimous resolution passed in February 1930 by the Chamber of Princes welcoming the Viceregal announcement. It is interesting to note in this connection that a delegation of Indian States subjects waited on the Viceroy at Bangalore and urged upon him the necessity of including representatives of States peoples to the Round Table Conference. Natural as was the feeling of disappointment when the Viceroy declined to do, it was not possible for him to give any other reply than the one he gave, pledged as the British Government was to a policy of non-interference in the internal affairs of the Indian States".

Princes in Favour of Federation

The attitude of the Indian Princes at the first Round Table Conference, inaugurated on November 12, 1930 by the King, cleared them in the eyes of those British Indians who suspected them of reactionary tendencies. In answer to the speeches of British Indian spokesmen especially Sir Tej Bahadur Sapru that their vision of the future of India was that of a federation including the Indian States the princely delegates cordially responded and thus removed from the path of the Conference a most delicate problem. In the words of the Prime Minister, "The Declaration of the Princes has revolutionized the situation. It has at once not only opened our vision, not only cheered our hearts, not only let us lift our eyes to see a glowing horizon, but has simplified our duties. The Princes have given a most substantial contribution in opening up the way to a really united federated India".

Principle of Federation of Three Stipulations

The delegation however felt it necessary to qualify their assent to the principle of federation by three stipulations:

1. That entry into the federation should be at the discretion of each individual state.

2. That the 'rights' of the States should be safeguarded and maintained intact subject only to delegation of such powers to a federal Government as the rulers might decide to make voluntarily by treaty with the Crown.

3. That all matters affecting the Rulers personally or their dynasties should be reserved for decisions by the Viceroy as agent of the British Crown.

The Chamber of Princes at their meeting in March 1931 endorsed the action by its delegates and empowered them further to carry on negotiations with due regard to the interests of the States and subject to the final ratification by the Chamber and each individual State.

Maharaja of Patiala's Manifesto

Some of the Princes however were weakening in their allegiance to the federal idea. This became certainty with the publication by the Maharaja of Patiala, the then Chancellor of the Chamber of Princes, of a manifesto which had the support of many other rulers and in which he formally announced his preference for a scheme intermediate between the system in vogue and an All India Federation. He wanted to see the Princes themselves organised for corporate action into a sort of a confederation particularly in their relation with British India before he was prepared to enter into the sort of federation outlined at the first Session of the Round Table Conference.

The Second Round Table Conference

It became clear at the Second Session of the Round Table Conference which opened on September 7, 1931, that the Patiala scheme had found support. The rulers of the important States of Dholpur and Indore agreed with him. They proposed that all the States should enter a Confederation through the Chamber of Princes which "enlarged and constitutionalised" would then be an electoral college for electing the States representatives to the Federation Legislature. The representatives of the other States were cautious to the verge of despair. The British India's representatives went so far as to openly allege that certain members of the Political Department were working against the movement towards federation. Some princes were heard to echo these complaints. As Mr. Wilson further says, "I am inclined to believe that the Princes have been encouraged in certain high quarters. The weaker members of the Princely order whose states are not in too healthy a condition or whose private extravagance have made them somewhat amenable to Government of India discipline have been used to check the impulses and desires of the larger and stronger states for federation".[4]

Political Officers Lost Much of Their Powers

This was but natural for the political officers of the Government of India who wielded such powers had to lose much of their power. The result of these moves was that practically every question which came up before the Committee of the Round Table Conference bristled with difficulties and its discussion marked with titancies. Bigger States like Hyderabad refused to be put on the same level as the smaller ones. In fact there was just about as much unity among the Indian Princes as there was among their countrymen in British India. Even the hints in the Premiers' speech winding up the second Session of the Round Table Conference that some form of diplomatic pressure would be brought upon the princes to induce them to hasten more speedily and to produce solutions of the deadlocks created gave no assurance to British Indian patriots who only knew too well that the declaration of Statesmen in England did not necessarily carry weight with the 'Politicals'.

PRINCES IN FAVOUR OF FEDERATION

Many of the Princes were, however, far sighted, and knew that if the idea of federation was to fail the political department would gather the reins in its hand more firmly than ever. The wiser heads then knew that the only way to escape from tightening effects of an unending intelage was for the States to pursue a path of constitutional Reforms wherein a power could be brought into existence within the state itself to check the natural faults of autocracy. They also knew the benefits likely to accrue to them from a federation duly evolved. They were however afraid of taking the first plunge.[5]

4. The Indian Chaos—Wilson, p. 94.
5. The Indian Princes in Council—Pannikar, pp. 43-44.

Third Round Table Conference

The complex problem of the States vis-a-vis British India assumed a more hopeful aspect at the third Session of the Round Table Conference which was held from November 17 to December 24, 1932 intended to be 'business' conference. Problem dealt with at the previous Sessions received fuller examination. The mode by which the States were to federate was settled. The new federal Government in so far as the States were concerned was to get its power not by Act of Parliament because legislation by Parliament could not apply to the States.

Two Stages

And in as much as the treaties of the States were with the Crown the procedure would consist of two stages:

1. Each State by an instrument was to transfer these powers to the Crown for the specific purpose of vesting them in the new Government.
2. The Crown would then transfer these powers to the Federal Government.

Next emerged a practical question of Cardinal importance. Were all States bound to federate in respect of every subject scheduled as federal or had each State the freedom to limit its adherence to selected subjects? On the one hand certain States had as the result of treaties special rights in such federal matters as posts, currency etc. but it would not be reasonable to expect them to surrender at the inception of the new arrangements. On the other hand the New Government would be seriously weakened if the range of exceptions was going to be at all wide.

The Solution Reached

The solution reached was in the nature of a practical compromise that while States could reserve their special rights by their respective instruments of instruction the Crown could refuse the entry of states which did not offer to become partners with a substantial interest by the new concern. The list of federal subjects like dealings customs etc. was next examined by a Sub-Committee. Certain general conclusions were reached but it was felt that the 'content of each subject' should receive expert scrutiny so that there might be no doubt about the precise powers transferred to the federation.

TWO HOUSES: UPPER CHAMBER, LOWER CHAMBER

Two Views on Legislature

1. As was to be expected, much time was devoted to the Legislatures. On the strength of the two houses of the federal legislature there were differences of opinion amongst both British India and the States delegates. One school of thought favoured small houses, the other voted for larger ones. On the States side the cleavage was broadly speaking between the larger states and the smaller ones. The former were anxious that they should wield in the federation an influence proportionate to their importance while the latter starting from the position that all the States represented in the Chamber of Princes were sovereign contended that there should be absolute equality of representation in the Upper Chamber among such States.

Difference on the Weightage

2. Another point of difference arose about the weightage to be given to the States in the Upper Chamber. The general opinion was that the States should get 40% while a section of the State representatives asked for 50%. On these three important questions the sizes of the legislatures, the members of the States representatives and the allocation of seats among the States could not reach any agreement.

Four important points on which the States expressed anxiety were conceded to:

Firstly in spheres outside those covered by the federation, the relation of the States with the Crown should remain unaltered and in charge of the Viceroy as representing the Emperor.

Secondly, when the federation had a complaint for default against a state it would involve the aid of the Governor-General.

Thirdly that the protection of the rights of the States should be a special responsibility of the Governor-General.

Fourthly, as the Crown had treaty obligations in regard to the defence of the Indian States the Viceroy should have special powers to implement this obligation effectively.

The setting up of a federal government was unanimously agreed to. On the complicated questions connected with federal finance there was much more agreement at the conference than on any previous occasion.

Conclusion

Pressed for a timetable the Secretary of State put forward the formula. The organs of the Federal Government used to be set up by proclamation as soon as a sufficient number of States with more than half the population and possessing more than half the voting strength in the Houses signified their willingness to enter the Federation.

Sir Samuel Hoare also promised to do his best to bring about federation and use his good offices with the princes to this end. Throughout the proceedings of the 3rd Session of the Round Table Conference the British Indian delegates evinced a keen appreciation of the special points of view of Indian States and it was believed that the third Conference brought the realisation of an All India Federation nearer than ever before.

Bi-Cameral Legislature

These proposals were duly incorporated into "White Paper issued by His Majesty's Government in March 1938". Under this document the Federal Legislature would be bi-cameral. The Upper Chamber of Council of States was to consist 260 seats of whom 100 would be filled by the nominees of the States members of the Federation. The Lower Chamber would consist of 375 members of whom 125 would be appointed by the rulers of the States. This sort of representation may not be conducive to the consummation desired for the harmonious beneficial and progress of a federal system was necessary that the administrative and other methods adopted in the different parts should be substantially similar. Different parts should not pull in different directions.

The proposed Federal Legislature was to consist of elected representatives of British India and of representatives of Indian States appointed by their rulers. They were vassals of the British Crown and generally under the thumb of the Political Officers who it was apprehended might use all their influence to urge the princes to order their nominees to support official policies.

Apart from this, however, the conditions set before the Federation could come into existence made many people doubt as to whether it would ever come into being in the near future. British Indians had not grudged over representatives of the states in the proposed federation, but they expected at the same time that the Princes would throw no obstacles in its way.

4

THE PANJAB RIYASTI PARJA MANDAL—1928-1946

The Panjab States Subjects Movement came into existence in 1928, under the name of the Panjab Riyasti Parja Mandal, but since then the representatives of the various Panjab States including Kashmir had been meeting more regularly and pressing their viewpoint more systematically than before. It was time that all such organisations in India co-ordinated their efforts and made a common cause to achieve their object by forcing the Panjab States Rulers to establish their Governments on democratic lines.

Divided Into Four Groups

The Panjab States were divided into four groups for the administrative purposes by the Political Department of British Indian Government:—

1. Kashmir State had a resident.
2. Fourteen saluted States of the Panjab had an Agent to the Governor General whose headquarters were at Lahore.
3. Simla Hill States were under the Deputy Commissioner of Simla who also acted as Superintendent of Simla Hill States. He was under the Panjab Government.
4. Dujana, Pataudi, Kalsia and a couple of other States were under the Panjab Government which were non-saluted.

It will thus be seen that the Political Department was directly concerned with Nos. 1 and 2. In these big states there was glaring mis-management and maladministration.

First Meeting—1929.

The Riasti Parja Mandal through the efforts of the leading

Zamindars of the Panjab States, convened their first meeting at Lahore on December 30, 1929. Sardar Inder Singh of Talwandi, Patiala State and Sardar Ranjit Singh of Malerkotla State were provisionally elected President and Secretary of the Mandal. A Committee of the following members, from the Panjab States was formed:—

1. Sardar Thakar Singh Domeli, Kapurthala State
2. Chaudhari Abdul Aziz Begowal, Kapurthala State
3. Sardar Kartar Singh, Patiala State
4. Sardar Kehar Singh Kabuli, Faridkot State
5. Sardar Kahan Singh Mandar, Kalsia State

This Committee was formed to unite the State subjects to find out the means and ways to redress their miseries and to explore the means and ways for liberation from the suppression of the Princes. So far there was no political body in the States, on the pattern of the Indian National Congress, Muslim League or the other Indian political parties. They were the pioneer workers who took the initiative to raise voice against the tyrannical and self-willed rule of the Panjab States Rulers.

Spadework in the States

All the members were required to tour in their respective States and to establish branches of the Riasti Parja Mandal at various places to enlist the support of the people. It also fell to their lot to draft the rules and regulations of the Mandal. A few observations of the first conference of the Riasti Parja Mandal are given here. Various activities of the Panjab States Rulers were discussed in the open assembly of this conference which was held on December 30, 1929, at Lahore.

Patiala State

The Maharaja of Patiala had acquired a great unpopularity for detaining unlawfully, without trial, many public-spirited, peaceful and influential men of his State for a long period. The long detention of Sardar Sewa Singh Thikariwala, Chairman of the first Reception Committee of the Riasti Parja Mandal, was taken up by the people very seriously. He was released only when he could no longer be detained. Sardar Harchand Singh

Jaiji was also detained without a trial for more than a year. A full account of the unprecedented sacrifice of Sardar Sewa Singh Thikariwala is given in the coming pages.

Kashmir State

His Highness of Kashmir was another prodigy. He was shuffling and reshuffling the portfolios of his top heavy administration and instead of introducing reforms in the State he took pleasure in the bringing about a renaissance of ante-diluvian usages and customs in the 20th century. His insistence on all gazetted officers presenting themselves every Tuesday in a certain gaudy dress to tender "Jaideva" was much felt by the officers and the public. If a few of his subjects betrayed the temerity to approach the Paramount Power they were treated with severe punishments forthwith. Education and sanitation were at a sad discount and the taxes were greedily assessed and relentlessly collected. There was a tax on every head of a goat, a sheep, a kid, a lamb, milch buffalo, bullock, every fire place, every shop, every tree of pear, apple or walnut etc. The poor Kashmiris had to migrate to the British India to seek sustenance.

Malerkotla State

His Highness the Nawab of Malerkotla was the ruler of a comparatively small territory and his chief concern was to outdo his brother Princes in pomp and grandeur. His State had long been in extremes. He legalised "Satta" gambling in his State the ramifications of which could be traced in the neighbouring districts of the Panjab.

Princes Protection Act

The Princes Protection Act was passed principally at the instance of His Highness the Maharaja of Patiala who was the first ruler to avail himself of it. It was enacted in the Patiala-Nabha dispute and the Political Department was prevailed upon by the Maharaja of Patiala to pass some such measures as a protection to him from the onslaughts of the sympathisers of the ex-Maharaja Ripudaman Singh of Nabha.

The immediate necessity having ceased to exist either the Act should have been repealed or its preparation restricted by more adequate safeguards. The subjects of the Indian State could not ventilate their grievances before their rulers without running the almost sure and serious risk of imprisonment on one pretext or the other. Until the passing of the Princes Protection Act they could depend on calling Paramount Power's attention to their sufferings. Obviously enough therefore this, only source of help of the Panjab States had been stopped by this enactment. Fortunately the Act was seldom resorted to.

Good Work Done By The Mandal

The good work done by the first Riasti Parja Mandal Committee went a long way to unite the people of the States against their self-willed rulers. Their propaganda created public opinion. It spread like a wild fire among the down trodden people. There was great response from every branch of the Mandal recently established by the enthusiastic members of the Mandal. Hardly four months had passed when the people of the States wanted to strengthen the body and to bring further the government on the democratic lines.

Conference At Ludhiana April, 1929

It was considered advisable to convene meetings in the British area instead of within the States. The next conference of the Parja Mandal was held in the Town Hall, Ludhiana, on April 7, 1929, under the presidentship of Sardar Jaswant Singh Danewalia, Gurdaspur District. Delegates from the Kashmir, Kapurthala, Nabha, Patiala, Jind, Malerkotla and Faridkot States attended the conference.

It was discussed that there were 669 States in India. Out of these 109 were entitled to gun salutes. According to the agreements of 1857 the British Government could not interfere in the internal managements of the States. Thus the Indian rulers had acquired almost the divine rights over their subjects. Under this privilege, like Henry VIII of England, the Princes had become despots. The subjects were ground under the suppressive measures of the rulers. Anybody, whoever wished to seek some sort of reform in any branch of the State administration, the ruler could throw him into the Jail, without telling him any cause of his offence. Condign punishments were awarded to agitators. False cases were often made against the people even to curb their lawful and constructive activities.

00.50 per cent of his income for the purpose. Sikh States exer-

The Political Agents

Administration of the States based on wrong principles was the target of a great criticism. It was customary in the past that if the ruler committed wrong, his brothers or subjects used to acquire possession of the throne themselves. Since the time of the British Government this tradition has changed into Divine Right Theory with regard to the Princes. The rulers cared more for the British Political Agents than their subjects.

Mandal Consisted Men Of All Religions

The Panjab State Riasti Parja Mandal consisted men of all castes and religions. Efforts were made to get the men from all religions to join in large numbers. The Mandal had opened its branches at Faridkot, Nahan, Nabha, Patiala and Simla and in other States. Pamphlets were published against the Rulers in the States. The Princes reacted promptly to spread their propaganda in foreign countries and every ruler of the State paid cised excessive tyrannies. As the Sikhs were oppressed more, they joined in larger number than the men of other religions, Being inspired by the political advancement in the British India the people of the States also came forward to check the despotic rules of the Panjab Princes. They held rallies, conferences and meetings to enlist the public voice against the suppressive rules of the State rulers. Under this spirit the following resolutions were passed in this conference.

Resolutions

It was resolved that a conference should be held at Lahore on a large scale. Mr. P. N. Kaul proposed the following resolutions:—

1. That this meeting of the Riyasti Parja Mandal requests the Government of India to intervene and take up the administration in their hands of the States whose finances were not controlled.

2. It was requested to invite the special attention of the Maharaja of Patiala and the Government of India to do justice with the people of Patiala State who were arrested without fault and were oppressed even up to the danger of life. The

Maharaja of Patiala's attention should also be drawn towards the rumoured forthcoming arrests of Akalis in the so called conspiracy cases. The Maharaja of Patiala should also fully explain the serious allegations which were circulated against him in the Press.

3. The rulers of the States were requested to pay special attention to the due demands and feelings of their subjects, to appoint responsible Governments and to form regular courts for justice.

4. The arrests and oppressions caused to the innocent respectable people by the Maharaja of Patiala were condemned. The Indian States People Conference was requested to help the State subjects by enquiring into the matter.

This Conference had a desired affect on the people of the Panjab State and there was great response to workers. There was a stir against the Princes in the people and began to unite themselves for the Common cause. The leaders felt a need to call another political conference to unite the people and to achieve the object.

Pseudo Panjab Riasti Parja Mandal

The Panjab States Rulers were more expert in Machiavellian tactics than Niccolo Machiavelli himself. They at once created a counter Riasti Parja Mandal. A typical letter addressed to His Highness of Patiala is produced hereunder to form an idea of the nefarious tactics planned by the Maharaja of Patiala to undo the activities of the real Riasti Parja Mandal.

"I hope you (The Maharaja of Patiala) will be glad to know that to represent the real sentiments of the people of the Panjab States and to counteract the mischievous propaganda of the Panjab Riyasti Parja Mandal whose activities are very injurious for the interest of the State subjects. Some real and earnest well wishers of the Panjab States, have organised a body entitled Panjab Riyasti Parja Pratinidhi Mandal. Its aims and objects are to create a feeling of love and co-operation amongst the rulers and the ruled and to try for the betterment of the Panjab States subjects".

"I am approaching you with the request to kindly let me know if your state administration has got any objection in the creation of this useful body and whether you are prepared to co-operate with it in your own interest and that of your State peoples. I may assure you that like Panjab Riasti Parja Mandal it will have no mischief behind it and it shall always have its motto 'Love & Co-operation'.

"A large number of Panjab States subjects have been enrolled as its members and efforts are being made to make it a fully representative body".

"If it be desirable I can meet you and discuss the details".

"An early reply will extremely oblige".

Huge amounts from the State Treasuries were spent to establish a counter Panjab State Parja Pratinidhi Mandal. Records of the erstwhile Panjab States reveal, how the opportunists were approaching the rulers to undo the work of the Panjab Riasti Parja Mandal workers. High officers of the States were in fact at the back of such activities, but this body of the opportunists could not survive long.

Conference at Ludhiana—October, 1930.

Annual Conference of the Panjab Riasti Parja Mandal was held again at Ludhiana under the Chairmanship of Sardar Sewa Singh Thikriwala, on October 11, 1930. A branch of the Panjab Riasti Parja Mandal was started at Ludhiana and all necessary precautions were taken in avoiding or overcoming the adverse forces and the mischievous propaganda that were threatened to be used and as a matter of fact were actually employed by some of the States and other interested persons. Later hirelings stooped to most unscrupulous means and were up to anything unfavourable and hostile atmosphere for the conference.

Head Office

The activities of the Riasti Parja Mandal could be carried out, outside the State. The Head Office of the Association was situated in Lahore. Some important places in the States were not made the centres of activities, because the conditions and existence of plots, interplots and intrigues were common in the

1. Confidential letter dated 2nd October, 1930 from the General Secretary, Panjab Riyasti Parja Pratinidhi Mandal Railway Road, Lahore. (File No. 156/90 of 1930 regarding Panjab Riasti Parja Pratinidhi Mandal, Lahore p. I).

States. The rulers awarded inhuman punishments to the workers and they could go to any extent to crush the political activities. Examples are numerous where the rulers crossed the limits of humanity to do away with the public workers. It was well-nigh impossible for a man to avoid them. Speaking of a reform in the States in those days meant inviting troubles and courting arrests of the worst type.

Session Began

The proceedings in the open session began at about 11 forenoon on October 12, 1930 on the arrival of the President. The spacious Pandal was packed to its utmost capacity with the delegates. The raised dais was thronged with distinguished visitors, State officers, reporters, etc. The admission to the conference was by tickets and it may be mentioned that some interested persons insisted on being given delegate tickets so that they could have an opportunity of speaking to create a fuss but were not allowed.

Sardar Sewa Singh, Chairman of the Reception Committee, read out his address that the Conference was held for the purpose of having some effectual voice for safeguarding the interests of 34 States of the Panjab. He gave a brief account of the maladministration of the States, before the audience.

Jammu and Kashmir

The State of Jammu and Kashmir was the biggest in the Panjab. It was being governed by His Highness Maharaja Hari Singh in a most despotic manner. Tens of thousands of his State subjects had not the least voice in matters of administration. Forced labour and other pinching laws made the people miserable and Kashmir which had so often been compared by poets to "Heaven on the surface of this earth", was turned into "Hell".

Sad Plight Of The People Of Patiala

The people of Patiala were sick of the tyrannies of Maharaja Bhupinder Singh since long. Tyrannies included murders, rapes and other heinous offences went on increasing day by day. Being tired of these oppressions people of Patiala submitted a strong memorial to His Excellency the Viceroy of India wherein the despotic rule of Maharaja were detailed and it was earnestly prayed that the oppressed people of the Patiala State be helped and taken care of. Though no special notice was taken of the said memorial by the British Government yet the All India States Peoples Conference appointed an Enquiry Committee to enquire into the oppression as alleged in the said memorial. The Enquiry Committee collected sufficient material by touring round the State and by staying in Panjab for many days and as a result of its findings published a Report in the form of a voluminous book known as "Indictment of Patiala". The Report contained twelve serious charges made against the Maharaja of Patiala and evidence was led in proof of these charges.

Resolutions

Keeping in view such many cases of maladministration and other sad affairs in administration in the Panjab States and the tyrannous rule of the Princes the Riasti Parja Mandal unanimously passed the following resolutions:—

1. The Princes of the Panjab States nominated to the Round Table Conference were not their real nominees.

2. The nomination of Maharaja of Patiala to the Round Table Conference was a serious blunder on the part of the Indian Government.

3. The demand of the Indian Princes that they should be directly responsible to the British Crown and not to the Government of India was highly unjustifiable and detrimental to the people of the States.

4. On Government's refusal to hold an open enquiry, as suggested, the Ryasti Parja Mandal lost all confidence in Mr. Fitzpatrick's enquiry.

5. The despotic, monarchial and one-man rule established in the States was daily becoming more and more intolerable to the people. Until and unless responsible Government on Parliamentary lines is not substituted and the administration of the States made satisfactory, the State subjects will not remain idle.

6. In declaring the proprietary zamindars of about seven hundred villages as non-proprietors by the Maharaja of Patiala was condemned. It was held that the proprietors of these village zamindars should make a bold stand for their rights.

Nabha State

This session of the Panjab States Peoples' Conference strongly condemned the attitude of the Nabha Admnistration in its repealing the established laws such as those relating to Loan Alienation of Land, Banks, Diminution in the number of persons attending the marriage parties etc.

Jind State

The laws were enacted by the Jind State to the detriment and the distress of the people. The attitude of the Administration of Jind was improper that it was putting into trouble by imprisoning fifty respectable residents of the State for their raising voice against the above-mentioned enactments.

Kalsia State

The ruler of the Kalsia State did not care for his subjects. The escheated land were openly auctioned to other persons and their rights were totally ignored.

Federal Scheme

The question which was monopolising public attention all over India was that of the Federal Scheme evolved in London at the Round Table Conferences. So far the scheme needed little elaboration. Position of the State subjects stood outside the picture altogether. British Indians, on the other hand, could get a large constitutional advantage, full provincial autonomy and responsibility at the centre over the whole field, excepting defence and foreign affairs and subject to certain reservations. Whether these exceptions and qualifications made too large a deduction from Swarajya, was a question which was then agitating public opinion in British India. No such disturbing question arose for the State subjects. The scheme did not propose to give even a jot of power to the people in the States. Whatever power fell to the share of the States was to go to the rulers and no part of it to the people.

Scheme Harmful To The State Subjects

The rulers, however, were making a notable improvement in their position in every way. Federation usually entailed some sacrifices on the federating units. They had to part with their independence and sovereign powers over certain matters in favour of a common government which they helped to bring into existence by means of federation. They underwent this sacrifice cheerfully, because only in that way could a uniform regulation of certain general concerns which required to be centrally administered be secured.

Democracy At The People's Cost

It would be an act of neighbourliness on the part of British Indian leadership, at the Round Table Conference that they stood firm like rock on the demand of the States' people that the States' representatives in the Federal Parliament should be elected instead of nominated. It was a modest demand. Only those subjects were being made federal which were, under the exclusive control of the Government of India. The Princes had no voice in their management.

Essential Conditions Of Federation

The people of the Indian States did not desire the Federal idea to be frustrated. It was desired that the federation should be of the genuine type:

1. That it should comprehend not merely subjects which the Princes no longer control, but all subjects of real all-India concern;

2. That elected representatives of the people should sit in the federal legislature;

3. That fundamental rights of citizenship should be guaranteed by the federal constitution and should be enforced by the federal judiciary;

4. That residual powers should vest in the Federal government and not in the governments of the provinces and the States;

5. That the federal government should exercise rights of paramountcy over the States' Governments so long as these were not brought under popular control.

If federation of this character was possible, the people would welcome it; but federation of the character proposed was not only of no advantage to States subject but was positively injurious to their interest.

No Public Check On The Finances.

The great desideratum in the States was a check of the finances. The rulers considered the State treasury as their private purse, and the State as their estate, being responsible to none to count for the expenses they incurred. Many of the rulers were openly accused by their people of wasting the State money not only on luxuries, 'shikar parties', lavishly entertaining European guests—official and un-official, and on their expensive tours to Europe and America. In several cases 50% and over of the State revenue was spent for the person of the rulers and his family leaving very little for such nation-building departments as education, medical relief and sanitation. Money taken from the people as taxes was not returned to them in one form or the other, but went mostly into the pockets of psycophants.[2]

Forced Labour Universal In States

'Begar' or forced labour was widely prevalent in all States. It was as if some communities, specially the depressed classes, were ordained from time immemorial for this very purpose. Not only that the whole rural population, including agriculturists, who formed 80 to 90% of the payment was always inadequate in theory, and often refused in practice too.[3]

Congress And The States

The question was often asked why the Congress agitation in the States had suddenly flared up since 1930. It will be re-

2. In connection with the very luxurious equipment in the palaces of Princes the late Mr. E. S. Montagu while sitting in a Maharaja's palace writes in his "Indian Diary" as follows:—"Everywhere are cigarette boxes in the form of motor cars or aeroplanes, or a stroke to lift the cigarette out. On the dining table is an electric pump working a fountain. One has often been inclined to wonder what becomes of this sort of ingenuity when one sees them at jewellers or bazars of Naples, or Dresden and so forth, and the answer seems to be that they all go to the Indian Dominion."
3. Instances are quoted in the "Indictment case of Patiala" of compulsory labour being exacted for Shikar parties, construction and clearance of canals, and for cultivating State gardens & Bullocks and camels were also impressed for transport, and provisions specially milk and ghee were exacted with inadequate, probably no payment.

membered that the Congress had passed a resolution to the effect that the Congressmen in British India should not interfere in the affairs of the States till the people themselves were able to stand on their legs and agitate for their rights and privileges on their own account.

During the few years, which lapsed since the formation of Congress Ministry in British India, two powerful forces were at work, which were silently levelling up the hitherto almost inert mass of States People. These two forces were in the first place the frequent communications, which were passing between the Government of India and the State authorities on the question of federation. The whole position of the States vis-a-vis British India and their place in the federation as time and again came prominent before their eyes. The Viceroy and his representatives had not only spoken on the subject of the princes joining the federation at an early date but they had also paid personal visits to the States. The Princes had met in conferences and so had also their ministers. To discuss the various naughty questions arising out of their new relationship with the Paramount Power and the protection which they would legitimately be able to receive from the British Government in India.

The second force equally powerful to excite attention was the coming of the Ministries and the independence spirit in which they had been working, the spirit of independence which they had been evincing in their relationship with the Govt. of India. They realised that these were the people with whom the States were to deal. The smooth working of a federation composed of two unequal partners was considered to be not practicable. Both the Princes and their subjects began to review the situation in the light of what was taking place in the Congress managed Ministries. It was because of these two forces that there had been a sudden awakening among the State subjects.

The States People's Conference—1933.

The proposals contained in the White Paper were utterly unacceptable to the State subjects as they embodied the decision of the three Round Table Conferences[4] which had no represent-

4. a. The first Round Table Conference was inaugurated on November

atives of Panjab States subjects was the verdict of the All India States People's Conference given by Mr. Patwardhan the Chairman of the States People's Conference held in New Delhi, on April 7, 1933.

The White Paper

In March, 1933 the British Government came out with the White Paper containing the proposals of the British Government, indicating the line on which the new constitution of India was to take shape. It was drafted in the light of the conclusions arrived at during the three Round Table Conferences. The White Paper, however, contained some points of departure from what was decided at the Conferences. But all these innovations were retrogressive and were introduced to make it more palatable to the Conservative majorities which were now present in both the Houses of the British Parliament. In April, 1933, a joint Parliamentary Select Committee was appointed to discuss in detail the proposals of the Government contained in White Paper. It considered of 16 members from both the Houses of the British Parliament with a clear majority of the Conservative members, with Lord Linlithgow as its Chairman. The representatives from British India and the Indian States were invited to appear before it as expert witnesses. Sir Samuel Hoare acted as the chief spokesman of the Government in his capacity as the Secretary of State for India.

The Report of the Committee was published on November 11, 1934. As was expected, the Committee made the White Paper still worse, from the Indian point of view, and introduced some more reactionary provisions. The White Paper had recommended direct election to the popular House of the Central Legislature. The Joint Select Committee discarded all democratic prin-

---

12, 1930 by the King and was presided over by Mr. Ramsay Macdonald.

b. The Second Round Table Conference was opened on September 7, 1931. Between the Gandhi-Irwin Pact and the Second Round Table Conference significant changes had taken place. Lord Willington had succeeded Lord Irwin. In England, the Labour Government was replaced by the National Government.

c. The third Round Table Conference was held from November 17 to December 24, 1932.

ciples and usages and recommmended indirect election for the House. The scope of the separate electorates was extended. The representatives of the States were to be nominated by the Princes. The power to abolish the Second Chambers in the Provinces had been given to the Central Legislature of India by the White Paper: the Committee kept this power back in the hands of British Parliament. Restriction on the powers of the Federal Court were increased, so as not to make it the final court of appeal in India on any point and to leave the supremacy of the Privy Council intact, in all cases. A bill was drafted on the basis of the Report of the Committee and became the Government of India Act, 1935, after receiving the Royal assent in August, 1935.

A Protest

The Conference had expressed its empathatic protest against the exclusion of representatives of States' people from all the three Round Table Conferences and registered its opinion that the White Paper which embodied the conclusions of those conferences could never be acceptable to them since they had been ignored throughout and all the rights and privileges that were opposed for the States were to be conferred upon Princes and their nominees.

The Problems

This conference further discussed difficult problems of the people of the Panjab States. The political activities were being curbed through the unlawful means by the Princes. The fundamental laws were being denied to the people. The conference by passing the resolutions, speeches and writing memorandums to the Princes and the British Government apprised them of the will of the people. The Press was freely used to express the hardships of the States Subjects, which indirectly helped the State Subjects to publicize their grievances throughout India and abroad. Indian States Peoples Committee raised the prestige of the Panjab Riasti Parja Mandal by which the Panjab States subjects were highly emboldened to lay their grievances before the Princes and in representing their cases to the Paramount Government of the country. On the other hand, the Princes were alerted and had checked their tyrannious methods to deal with the subjects, though outwardly they did not show any sign of demoralisation. In this conference the following measures were taken to safeguard the interests of the people of the States.

Fundamental Rights

1. The new Constitution should guarantee the right elementary citizenship to people of the States, being opened to them to seek redress for infringement of these rights from the Federal Court.

2. The States entering into federation should not be permitted to reserve the management of any subject mentioned in the list of Federal Subjects.

3. Residuary powers should be vested in the Federal Government.

4. AMENDING THE CONSTITUTIONS

A special stress was laid on procedure for amending the constitution but when the amendments were passed by the requisite majority it will automatically come into force without separate ratification by British Indian provinces. The enlargement of the Federal list of subjects and the method of selection of representatives of the federal subjects should be particularly specified as fit subjects for amendment.

5. Federal laws should not require being adopted by the States for taking effect in Federating States in British India. The Federal Government should deal individually with each.

6. The conference made special appeal to British Indian leaders of all parties to reject the constitution it did not satisfy the above demands of the States people and a declaration of rights for them.

The administrative flaws of almost all the Panjab States were discussed in the special meeting of the Committees. A special stress was laid upon the rulers of the following States.

Malerkotla And Patiala States

By another resolution, the conference recommended the appointment of a non-official inquiry committee composed of leaders from other provinces, to go into the alleged maladministration in Malerkotla.

A third resolution referred to the alarm felt by the conference about the condition of the hunger-strikes in Narnaul

Jail in Patiala State. They requested the A.G.G. to the Panjab States to look into the matter.

Bahawalpur State

The last resolution requested His Highness the Nawab of Bahawalpur for taking immediate steps to remove the grievances submitted by a deputation of Hindu subjects that waited upon him on December 21, 1932. These demands related to the ban on the entry of newspapers in the State. The repeal of conversion law, restraint over Hindu festivals, sale of beef in thoroughfares, ban on lawyers in the State.

Sardar Sewa Singh Thikriwala

Sardar Sewa Singh Thikriwala, popularly known as "Kirpan Bahadur" was the real hero to found the Panjab Riasti Parja Mandal to raise the voice of the people against the despotic rule of the rulers of the Panjab States. It was due to his pioneer work and patriotic spirit that some more political parties had come into being in the Panjab States, e.g.

1. The Muzara Movement,
2. The Kirti Kisan Sabha,
3. The Akali Agitation, and
4. The Biswedari Movement.

It was a time when the State rulers were terror to their subjects. The people had no right even to have the access to lay down their genuine grievances before their rulers. Rural areas were neglected terribly where the officers had their own Raj. The honour of their females was always in danger.

Under such old times and the despotic rulers, "the lion of the Panjab States Subjects", Sardar Sewa Singh Thikriwala had come into the rescue of millions of the down-trodden people when he united them to stand against injustice. Whatever has been narrated here, with regard to the political awakening in the States was due to the untiring and devoted efforts of Sardar Sewa Singh. Like the great patriots or reformers of the world, Sardar Sewa Singh had to face the dire consequences from the hands of the rulers. A brief account of his ultimate sad but most worthy end is given hereunder:—

Sardar Sewa Singh Kirpan Bahadur was the son of Sardar Dewa Singh of village Thikriwala, Tehsil Barnala. Ever since the abdication of the ex-Maharaja Ripudaman Singh of Nabha he was actively backing the agitation of Akalis in favour of the exiled Maharaja against the British Government.

Charges Framed Against Sardar Sewa Singh

The first annual meeting of Riasti Parja Mandal was held in December, 1929, a few days before the annual session of the Indian National Congress at Lahore, under the presidentship of Mr. Chudgar. Sardar Sewa Singh was the Chairman of the Reception Committee. He was appointed President of the Panjab Riasti Parja Mandal for the next year in the same meeting.

In the month of September, 1929, Sardar Sewa Singh along with the Akalis of his party toured in the Patiala State and the villages of the British territory adjoining the Panjab States territory, held Diwans. Before huge gatherings, he delivered speeches against the maladministration of Government of Patiala.

In October, 1930 during the second annual session of the Panjab Riasti Parja Mandal which was held under the presidentship of Mr. Raghuvinder Rao Sharma, Sardar Sewa Singh again became the Chairman of the Reception Committee; and before its session he on his own behalf invited the people by means of printed posters especially the subjects of the State to attend the meeting. On that occasion on October 12, 1930, in the capacity of the Chairman of the Reception Committee, Sardar Sewa Singh read an address in Urdu which had been printed beforehand to a public gathering numbering about one thousand persons including about 200 to 250 inhabitants of the Patiala State also.

The portions of the said address brought into hatred or contempt or excited feelings of disaffection towards the person and Government of His Highness the Maharaja of Patiala. It was found from the various reports received at different times from the officers of the Barnala District that the address read by him had really excited the feelings of disaffection among the State subjects and brought the State Government into hatred and contempt. "In these circumstances, I respectfully request that necessary sanction may kindly be obtained to launch a case under Section 124 A of the I.P. Code against Sewa Singh who, by reading over the address and distributing copies, therefore, to the public has brought into hatred or contempt or excited feelings of disaffection towards the person and Government of His Highness Shri 108 Maharaja Dhiraj Mohinder Bahadur of Patiala."[5]

Shriman Panth Rattan Sardar Sewa Singh of Thikhriwala, President, Panjab Riasti Parja Mandal, President, Akhil Jatha, Patiala State, Akal College Guru Sagar Mastuana, Malwa Pratinidhi Khalsa Dewan and President of many other societies, incharge of the Shiromani Gurdwara Parbandhak Committee, who had come out of the Patiala Jail after 4 years' rigorous internment was again arrested by the Patiala police at 12 in the night of 3rd November, 1930 in his village Thikriwala.

Hearing At Barnala

The first hearing of the case in the Court of the Special Magistrate, Barnala, came off on November 7, 1930. Santa Singh of Thikhriwala, Harnam Singh Sufedposh of Barnala and other traitors appeared as Crown witnesses. Statements of 18 subjects of the Patiala State witnesses were recorded. The Crown witnesses stated that Sewa Singh Thikhriwala distributed to them copies of his address with his own hands in the village. On reading the copies they came to know of the campaign of calumny and lies which had been started against the Maharaja of Patiala. They went to the Police Station and reported that the copies had been delivered to them by Sewa Singh himself.[6]

Defence

After taking down the statements of Crown witnesses the Court declared that proceedings on behalf of the Crown being over, Sewa Singh should present his defence, if any. He wanted to produce unlike the Crown not only 5 or 10 witnesses but one or two thousand witnesses and asked for writing materials being supplied to him to prepare a list of his witnesses. He gave a list of some 5 to 7 hundred witnesses including prominent leaders in the country such as S. Kharak Singh, Mahatma Gandhi, Mr.

5. Proceedings against Sewa Singh Akali of Thikhriwala under Section 134 A, I.P.C.; Case No. 92/C of 1930, p. 11.
6. Notice No. 1, issued by the Panjab Riasti Parja Mandal, Patiala, dated 24-4-1930.

Patel, Chudgar, Amritlal Sethi and others, besides these he gave the names of the distinguished men from the British territory.

Warning

Leaders of all the political parties, in sympathy with the down-trodden people of the Panjab States, with particular reference to the subjects of the Patiala State, had warned them to be united against the tyranical rule of the Maharaja. Since the popular worker of Sardar Sewa Singh was unlawfully arrested to throw him into the jail, never to come out of it alive. They invited the Patiala State Subjects, who suffered at the hands of high officers of the State to represent their genuine grievances. All such persons were publicly invited to come to Barnala to appear before the Magistrate who was trying Sardar Sewa Singh.[7]

Proceedings Continued

The proceedings in this case continued from day to day. Leading Akalis were engaged on behalf of Shiromani Akali Dal, Shiromani Gurdwara Parbandhak Committee and the Panjab Riasti Parja Mandal. The people were told to endorse the address delivered by Sardar Sewa Singh at the Ludhiana conference word by word. In favour of Sardar Sewa Singh a thousand people thronged the Barnala court. The Patiala police had to take special measures to check the huge gatherings of the people because the people were fully aware of the direct consequences of the popular leader. They knew it well that the Maharaja of Patiala would not spare him at any cost.

Sardar Sewa Singh was a well-known Akali leader. He belonged to Thikhriwala, a village in Patiala State, where he was a Biswedar. He was a silent worker, very sweet and humble in his ways but strong and determined in his will.

He entered public life as a member of the Akali organisations, the S.G.P.C. and the Shiromani Akali Dal. In 1923, when these bodies were declared illegal, he was arrested along with

7. Proceedings against Sewa Singh Akali of Thikhriwala under Section 124 A, I.P.C.: Case No. 92 of 1930, p. 61.

other Akali leaders. In 1926 he was released along with them, but he was taken direct from the Central Jail, Lahore to the Central Jail, Patiala, where he was detained for more than three years until he was released on 24th August, 1929, as a result of a representation made by Sir Sunder Singh Majithia, Sir Joginder Singh, Sir Saljit Singh, Gyani Sher Singh, etc. Pressure had also been put for his release by the agitation carried on by the Shiromani Akali Dal, of which he was the Vice-President.

Another body had by the time become prominent in voicing the grievances of the people of the Panjab State. It was the Riasti Parja Mandal, Panjab, Sardar Sewa Singh became its President of the Malwa Pratinidhi Khalsa Diwan in October 1930, the Riasti Parja Mandal held a big conference at Ludhiana. Sardar Sewa Singh acted as the President of the Reception Committee. When he returned to his village after the conference, he was arrested by the Patiala police on the charge of having distributed in his village some copies of his address as Chairman of the Reception Committee. He was sentenced to six years' imprisonment, but was let off only four months after. As president of the Riasti Parja Mandal he took part in agitation carried on against official interference in the matter of holding Diwans in the States of Sangrur and Malerkotla. The agitation ended in a compromise.

After some time the Panjab Riasti Parja Mandal organised agitation and public demonstrations against the Maharaja of Patiala in Amritsar. But Sardar Sewa Singh did not take part in them, as he was busy in his village in maknig preparation for his daughter's marriage. He was, however, arrested by the Patiala police. He did not put any defence in imprisonment, with a fine of Rs. 1,500/- or in default a further incarceration in Jail. He never came out of it.

According to press reports, it was on account of his solitary confinement, coupled with other unnecessary restrictions, that he went on hunger-strike. This hunger-strike he maintained for about nine months, i.e. from May last up to the end of his life. When the rumours of his hunger-strike were published, there was great agitation in the press, and the Shiromani Akali Dal inquired from the Prime Minister, Patiala, about the truth of the rumour. After this, on the 8th June, 1934, a graver rumour appeared about the death of the Sardar.

On this, the son-in-law of Sardar Sewa Singh, the Shiromani Akali Dal and the Riasti Parja Mandal sent telegrams to Patiala State Government, the Viceroy and the Political Agent enquiring if there was any truth in the rumour. The reply was that the rumour was unfounded. To put an end to the anxiety, the son-in-law and the wife of the Sardar applied for interview which was eventually granted, and on July 4, his wife and a relative saw him in jail. He had been reduced to a mere skeleton, and his weight decreased from 145 lbs. to 80 lbs. It was with great difficulty that he had been able to recognise his wife. It was learnt at the interview that on June 2 and 3, he swooned for about three hours. That caused the rumour of his death. No interview was allowed after this.

His condition seemed to have deteriorated. His relatives were sending telegrams for permission to be allowed to live near him, or if that were not possible to be informed daily of his condition. In despair they sent a telegram to the Political Agent. On August 19, a letter was received from the Secretary to the Agent intimating that no useful purpose would be served by an interview with the Sardar; and after two days a telegram was received from the Agent that the Sardar was comfortable and his condition was ameliorated. Another letter was sent to the Agent on September 7, 1934, but receiving no reply to it, the relatives gave up all hope. The Shiromani Akali Dal then tried to get permission for an interview, but failed to arouse a response. The Sikh Societies and the Indian States People's Conference passed resolutions urging the Patiala Darbar to order the release of Sardar Sewa Singh on the ground of humanity. The appeals proved abortive. The Maharaja of Patiala determined to dispense with him. It is said that under his orders, Sardar Sewa Singh was administered poison. Though the account of his last days is official, yet the truth can be gleaned by a careful perusal of it.

"Convict prisoner Sewa Singh of Thikhriwala started vomiting blood on the afternoon of 18th January, 1935. Dr. Jagdish Singh, M.B.B.S., Medical Officer, Jail and subsequently Dr. Biel, Offg. Director of Medical Services, in the absence of Dr. Seelig, examined the patient soon after, took him into their hands and rendered all possible assistance they could. I was informed of it late in the evening on 18th and went to the jail on the morning of 19th January and saw the patient for himself. Both the doctors were present and I was told that his condition was serious. I, therefore, sent for Dr. Seelig, Director of Medical Services who had returned to Patiala in the morning. I stayed there for about 2 hours. Dr. Seelig examined him and advised that he should be removed to the Rajindra Hospital with a view to facilitate the treatment".

Removed To The Hospital

"Sardar Sewa Singh was accordingly removed in a motor lorry to the Rajindra Hospital on the afternoon of 19th in charge of Dr. Jagdish Singh, Medical Officer, Jail and under the direct supervision of Dr. Seelig. All possible comfort and treatment were provided for him in the Rajindra Hospital. The patient however died at about 1-30 A.M. on 20th January, 1935. I informed you of his death on the telephone personally at about 10 A.M."

"A telegram was sent to the Nazim, Barnala, to communicate the news of his death to his relations at Thikhriwala. Hari Singh, a cousin of the deceased, who happened to be at Patiala, was also informed and he came to the Rajindra Hospital on the morning of 20th and was the chief mourner. The cremation was delayed till 5 P.M. to afford a reasonable time to the relations of the deceased to come to Patiala, but none came. Hari Singh provided a 'Doshala' for the dead body. The dead body was treated with due respect and all religious ceremonies were duly performed. It was not possible to wait any longer for the relations of the deceased because it was contrary to religious usage to cremate the dead body after sunset, so the dead body was cremated at 5 P.M." Jathedar of Thikhriwala came to the jail this morning at about 9 A.M. and demanded the ashes of the deceased to be taken to Thikhriwala, as desired by the wife of the deceased. The dead body of the deceased was cremated at the public cremation ground near the Rajindra Hospital and the jail authorities rightly think that they have no longer any concern in this matter,[8]" according to the statement of the Law Minister.

---

8. The cremation ground where Sardar Sewa Singh was cremated was guarded by the armed police for several years. Even the ashes of the Sardar were not allowed to be moved.

"It is neither desirable nor possible under the law to refuse their request. I am however apprehensive that these and other Akalis are likely to make a fuss over the ashes and that there is a probability of hostile demonstrations being held during the transit of the ashes to end at Thikhriwala and possibly at other places. I am therefore asking the Inspector General of Police to make adequate arrangements to avoid all kinds of hostile demonstrations. I believe the Inspector General of Police will get into touch with you on the phone today for instructions in this matter. Herewith enclosed please find a copy of the report of the Superintendent, Central Jail, in this connection.[9]"

The death of Sardar Sewa Singh Thikhriwala not only caused an irreparable loss to Shiromani Akali Dal, but also shocked subjects of Patiala State, for whom he sacrificed his life. People all over the country were bereaved to learn the death of a great fighter against tyranny. The apprehensions of Patiala State Government are well understood by the perusal of a confidential demi-official letter of a special C.I.D. officer, who was deputed to report about the reaction of the people:—

"I am desired to inform you that it has been reported from a reliable source that at a private meeting of prominent Akali and other political workers which was held in the office of the Shiromani Akali Dal at Amritsar on the 27th January, 1935, under the presidency of Master Tara Singh, the workers of the Riasti Parja Mandal consulted Dr. Kitchlew and other Congress and Akali agitators regarding the agitation in connection with the death of Sardar Sewa Singh of Thikhriwala. Dr Kitchlew advised the Parja Mandal workers that the Congress could not take part in any agitation which they might organise against the Patiala Government and suggested that the Panjab Riasti Parja Mandal should carry on a constitutional agitation independently which would receive his assistance and also that of Master Tara Singh. The Riasti Parja Mandal workers then held a separate meeting of their own in which they adopted a resolution expressing sympathy with the relations of Sardar Sewa Singh, warning His Highness the Maharaja of Patiala that he could not escape responsibility for Sardar Sewa Singh's death and de-

9. No. 247/C, Case No. 411 of 1934, Patiala, dated 21-1-35, p. 169.

manded that the Government of India should make an open enquiry into his death."[10]

Though the death of Sardar Sewa Singh caused a serious setback to Riasti Parja Mandal, yet the movement received a great impetus by the death of Maharaja Bhupinder Singh in 1938.

It was reported that the people intended to hold open elections at the headquarters of various Tehsils in order to form a Central Riasti Parja Mandal Body for the whole State of representatives who were elected by delegates from Tehsils. The toppling down of Congress like a house of cards after the arrest and prosecution of Siri Ram Kaushak, left no other alternative for its members than to join Parja Mandal organisation.

This was followed by the prompt publication of posters from a Ludhiana Press announcing a programme of election of the Patiala Parja Mandal. These posters were circulated in the State through their own agency.[11]

It was announced that the Programme pertaining to Narnaul would be published later. It was also announced in a note that the elections of Parja Mandal of Patiala State would be subsequently held at Sunam on March 29, 1939 and that the delegates of all Tehsils should attend there at 2 P.M. It was also laid down therein that only registered members could be able to take part and vote and the members and Tehsil Committee were urged upon to pay the due subscription in order to exercise the right of vote. One member of Central Body of Patiala State Parja Mandal would be elected by twenty elected representatives of a Tehsil. The posters in Urdu and Gurmukhi bore the superscription "Inqlab Zindabad" and were issued on

---

10. D.O. No. 227-R/Misc.-4/35. Case No. 411/C of 1935, p. 267.

11. The following programme appeared to give the widest publicity:—

Name of Tehsil	Date of election	Place of election
Sunam	24th Phagan	Sunam
Bhatinda	26th Phagan	Bhatinda
Barnala	28th Phagan	Barnala
Dhuri	29th Phagan	V. Kanjhla
Dhawanigarh	2nd Chet	Bhawanigarh
Patiala	4th Chet	V. Kaurwala
Rajpura	5th Chet	Bhoghlan
Sirhind	6th Chet	Mandi Sirhind
Pael	7th Chet	Mandi Doraha

behalf of Jangir Singh Joga, a well-known Socialist Parja Mandalist.

First election

According to the programme the first elections took place at Sunam for the Sunam Tehsil. The problem of Parja Mandal Movement which was gradually gaining momentum in Patiala State and the necessity of retarding its growth so that it might not become a serious menace to absolute authority, attracted the attention of Patiala State Government.

According to the Hidayat of 1988, Parja Mandal as political organisation was to be registered. District Magistrate Sunam served a notice on Jangir Singh Joga that by not registering Parja Mandal, sections 2 and 3 of the aforesaid Hidayat had been violated and thus the activities of Parja Mandal were ultra-vires and he was liable to be prosecuted. The District Officers were generally of the opinion that an effective check should be provided to this growing menace to the stability of the State[12].

The Quit-India Movement

After the meeting of the Working Committee of the all-India National Congress at Bombay in August 1942, which resulted in the wholesale arrests of the members of Congress High Command and Congress unrest in India, the residents of the Patiala State especially those imbued with Congress ideas did not organize a meeting or procession or any demonstration in the State territory. They did not resort to any demonstration whatsoever as an expression of their sympathies with such arrests in British India nor did they give vent to any particular feeling of disapprobation over the arrest of Mahatma Gandhi.

Brish Bhan, a pleader of Sunam, acting President of the so called Panjab Riasti Parja Mandal, who alone from Patiala State had gone to attend the meeting of the All India Congress Working Committee at Bombay, on his return, contemplated holding a meeting in the State to take the decision of starting Civil Disobedience Movement in compliance with Mahatma Gandhi's orders, but he could not do so and the Parja Manda-

12. Activities of the Workers of the Panjab Kisan Committee, in Panjab State. Case No. 830/C of 1938, dated 27-2-39, p. 225.

lists did not show any noticeable activity. Necessary precautionary measures were adopted to check the agitation or any other trouble in the State that might have resulted from mass movement arising out of the Congress resolution.

Objectionable posters relating to Congress unrest were, however, found from the letter boxes of Patiala City. Such posters were also thrown in Idgah on the last Id day and in Mahendra College, Patiala. Similar posters were distributed also at Bhatinda and Narnaul.

Disturbance at Narnaul

Congress unrest, which followed the arrest of Congress leaders had affected some politically minded persons of Narnaul proper. The result was that 18 persons planned to create a disturbance at Narnaul by performing acts of sabotage but before they could realise their object, the explosion of a country-made bomb pricked the bubble and as a result of careful enquiries the accused were arrested and challaned after investigation.[13]

Bhatinda

Ten Urdu posters entitled "Zummewari Kis Par Hai" absolving the Congress of its responsibility from the Congress unrest were found from the house search of Kundan Lal Aggarwal of Bhatinda, where his sons, Harbans Lal Vakil, Kalwant Rai, Parkash Sarup and Jagan Nath lived. As a result thereof, the person and his four sons were arrested and a case u/s 39 Patiala Defence Rule 1996 vide F.I.R. No. 260 dated 26-2-43 was registered and culprits were duly challaned.

Sunam

Brish Bhan, Pt. Narain Datt and Autar Singh, Pleaders, Nauhar Chand, petition writer, and Dr. Harbhajan Singh of Sunam were reported to have held a small meeting in camera only to express feelings of sympathy over the fast of Mahatma Gandhi. Brish Bhan Pleader was arrested by Ambala Police on March 19, 1943 at the Railway Station Sunam in connection with the distribution of objectionable Congress posters.

---

13. Case No. 830/C of 1939, dated 24-8-43/8-5-20, p. 363.

Meetings of the Panjab Riasti Parja Mandal were held at Kanti, Bawal & Nabha. Shah Nawaz Khan, the well-known I.N.A. Officer, did not turn up at the meeting at Kanti as previously announced. The meeting was presided over by Seth Damodar Das, M.L.A. who, accompanied by Bhagat Singh of Delhi and Manohar Sham of Kanti reached the Railway Station Ateli (about 6 miles from Kanti) by goods train at 11 A.M. Thence they were taken on an elephant in procession to Kanti. Resolutions demanding responsible Government in Nabha State and the abolition of the Hidayat of 1988, and urging the release of Col. Bhonsle, Col. Manohar and other I.N.A. personnel were passed at the meeting. One Kamla Bai a lady from Sirohi Nangla made a speech in which she exhorted the ladies present to follow the example of Rani of Jhansi, Chand Bibi etc.

Among the prominent visitors from outside in the meeting at Bawal were the aforesaid Kamla Bai of Sirohi, Gopi Shankar of Jaipur and Ajudhya Parshad of Narnaul. Captains Shiv Narain and Kirpa Ram, Ex-officers of the I.N.A., both residents of the Bawal Ilaqa also made speeches at this meeting urging upon the people to fight for freedom. At the end of the meeting, office-bearers of the local Panjab Riasti Parja Mandal were elected.

The meeting at Nabha was preceded by a procession through the City which terminated in the Anaj Mandi. This meeting was presided over by Hardial Singh Vakil where the following resolutions were passed:

(a) That the land revenue be reduced;

(b) That immediate responsible Government be established in Nabha State;

(c) That the Acts promulgated in place of the Hidayat of 1988 also be repealed, and

(d) That the salaries of the State employees be increased.

At the end of the meeting, a Congress Flag was hoisted at the office of Panjab Riasti Parja Mandal in the centre of the town by two local Vakils namely Babu Ram and Sant Ram.[14]

---

14. Office of the Chief Minister, Nabha State, File No. 509/E-46 Part A, Basta No. 12, Subject: Formation of Parja Mandal in Nabha State and Muslim League.

Kapurthala State

The Panjab Riasti Parja Mandal came into being in Kapurthala State at a meeting convened by the Kapurthala National League to express indignation at the death of Shankar Singh in the Kotwali while under police custody on July 30, 1938. The National League speakers were considered too moderate in their views by a party led by the Central Zamindara League workers such as Chanan Singh of Dhoot and Roor Singh of Dhaliwal Bet, who interrupted the meeting and took its control. The meeting was then styled as "Meeting of the Parja Mandal" and since then the members of Parja Mandal elected the following office-bearers and carried on agitation.

1. Bahadur Singh—President
2. Roop Lal, Kapurthala—Vice-President
   Kirpal Singh Chilwan -do-
3. Chanan Singh Dhoot—General Secretary
4. Labhu Ram Chopra—Secretary
5. Swami Saran—Cashier

The society held its meetings in secret, and its object was to raise discontent with the heavy land revenue demand and to re-summon the State Assembly. Thakar Singh Domeli who was also put in jail in Fisher's time was a moving spirit in the agitation. He was an adherent of a party supported by Sir Sunder Singh Majithia who took keen interest in him.

Later, the Riasti Parja Mandal became more enthusiastic and started the work actively. In 1939, the following office-bearers were elected:—

President—Bahadur Singh
Vice-President—Roop Lal
General Secretary—Chanan Singh Dhoot
Secretary—Labhu Ram Chopra
Joint Secretary—Hari Dutt
Cashier—Swami Saran

This Committee founded branches at Tehsil headquarters. Labhu Ram, the Secretary, was in touch with Achint Ram who was the Life Member of the Servants of the Peoples Society, Lahore, and who was a terror to the British Government in India. Achint Ram was a very active organiser who gave an impetus to the working of this body. In the Kapurthala State the Kisan Movement played a very dominant role, account of which is separately dealt with. However, after the 'Quit India Movement' of 1942, the Riasti Parja Mandal came in the fore-front. Almost all the members were Congressmen.

The Parja Mandalists supported the Zamindara Movement and fought for the remission of the revenue payment. For this purpose Subhas Chander Bose was invited to address the Parja Mandal Conference held at Phagwara on May 20, 1939.

The following resolutions were passed at the meeting of the Parja Mandal Tahsil Phagwara under the presidentship of Thakur Singh of Naroor:—

At ths meeting it was demanded from the State Government adequate remission of the revenue payment due to the destruction of the two continuous crops and having consideration of the economic conditions of the peasants.

5

KISAN AND MUZARA MOVEMENT IN STATES

Early History

The Muzara popularly known as Kisan Movement had in Patiala State long before the preventive measures could be taken by the Committee was not registered and had no office in the state. In the year 1930/1931, the Akali Movement assumed different political shapes, i.e. Panjab Riyasti Parja Mandal, Kisan Movement, Muzara Movement and Socialists etc. In the first instance, a Gurmukhi weekly newspaper under the caption "Muzdur Kisan", came to the notice of the C.I.D. It contained articles of revolutionary nature against the Patiala Darbar. This paper was banned in the State.[1]

Conference at Congowal

Up to the year 1935, this movement remained dormant. After it had appeared in the press than a Kisan Conference would be held at Longowal, near Sunam, Gurmukhi posters under the caption "Shandar Kisan Conference" published by Mansa Ram of Dhohar, near Dirbha, Propaganda Secretary, in which it was announced that the conference would be held at Longowal on the 7th and 8th of November, 1936.

The contents of the posters revealed that a spirit of agitation would be spread among Agriculturists and non-agriculturists against the Mahajan class and Shahukars as a community sucking the blood of Zamindars and in order to blame the Government, the State administration was to be criticised. The attention of the district authorities was invited towards this by the then I.G.P. directing to take legal steps to prevent the holding of the Conference which was against law and

1. Under Ijlas-i-Khas orders No. 1 dated 14-7-31.

Hidayat 1988.[2]

Bhagwan Singh Longowalia, a great public spirited young man of Patiala State had done a great work for the down-trodden peasants. He remained in Budhlada where he stayed in those days in a local Gurdwara. Prem Singh son of Jaswant Singh Dharamgarh, who was then in the employment of S. Sewa Singh[3] was at Amritsar was reported to have distributed the posters in question.[4]

The well-to-do villagers of Longowal did not support Conference which was proposed to be convened at their village. They opposed the activities of the workers at the instance of the Patiala Government.

On July 11, 1936, when Hira Singh Bhathal, along with his wife, Hardit Singh Bhathal, Bakhshish Singh Kattu, Hazura Singh Dhansula belonging to the Nabha State and two other Akalis reached Longowal to join the Conference, the villagers forced them to leave the village.

Karam Singh Mann President

On July 24, 1936, Karam Singh Mann, Bar-at-Law, Lahore, was elected to preside over this conference, Mohan Lal Gupta Gujranwala and his wife, Feroze-ud-din Kansur, Inder Singh Sansapur, Jullundur District, Khalil Ahmed "Sabri", Amritsar and Comrade Gurmukh Singh Ambalvi, workers of Kirti Kisan Party, reached village Longowal. The people of Longowal, numbering about two hundred met them and told them that no Conference was to be held there and that someone had issued a false poster, which, they said, had already been contradicted by the Panchayat of Longowal. They further told them that as the villagers were against the holding of Kirti Kisan Conference so it was proper for them to go back. Accordingly all Kisan workers had returned disappointed.

---

2. "Whereas in agreement with the Jind and Nabha States, it had been deemed expedient to enact certain legislation, the following Hidayat is promulgated within the whole of the Patiala State territories and it shall have effect from 15th January, 1932, 2nd Magh, 1938." It comprises 1-18 pages.
3. Sardar Sewa Singh Thikriwala was popularly known as Kirpan Bahadur.
4. The Home Minister, Patiala No. 5558-15-C dt. 8-5-43 p. 329.

In the year 1937, a meeting of the working committee of the Panjab Riyasti Parja Mandal was held under the Presidentship of L. Sant Ram Vakil of Phul, Nabha State at Bradlaugh Hall Lahore on March 9, 1937. It was resolved there to hold a Kisan Conference in the States and to carry its propaganda urging the Kisans (peasants) to join the said Conference in large numbers so that their rights might be protected, the election of the office-bearers of this conference was effected as under:—

1. Hari Singh Dhoot, Kapurthala—President
2. L. Sant Ram Vakil Nabha—General Secretary
3. Bhagwan Singh Longowalia—Secretary
4. Mansa Ram Dhihar—Secretary

The Kisan Conference was held at village Kamalpur, P.S. Jagraon, Ludhiana District under the presidentship of Master Kabul Singh, M.L.A., on the 1st and 2nd of January, 1938 in which the Zamidars were asked not to pay income-tax and land revenue etc. The question of forming Kisan Committees village-wise was also decided upon therein.

After this, the workers of the Panjab Kisan Committee began to tour actively through the Panjab States, distributing a large number of Urdu and Gurmukhi membership forms for purposes of enlisting Kisans as members of the committee. The forms contained the request to Patiala Darbar in reducing the land revenue and accede to some so-called agrarian demands.

Sardar Bhagat Singh Dhatogal, and a Parja Mandal worker and Mansa Ram Dhuri got themselves enlisted as the members of the Kisan Committees in the State. Wazir Singh Daftriwala, Jagir Singh Phaguwala, Harnam Singh Dharamgarh, Santa Singh Pandhi, Hazura Singh Mattran, Parja Mandalists, too, had begun efforts at the formation of Kisan Committees in the State, particularly in Sunam District. Gurmukhi posters regarding the formation of Kisan Committees were published by Partap Singh Nadampore, president, Parja Mandal, Tehsil Bhawanigarh.

The following also began to take active part to urge peasants and others to become the members of the Kisan Committees:

1. Sujjan Singh Bapiana, 2. Darbara Singh Khiwa Shahzada Singhwala, 3. Ram Singh Matti, 4. Dharam Singh Carpen-

ter Dalel Singhwala, 5. Mangal Singh Sangatpura, 6. Jang Singh Joga, 7. Giani Mohinder Singh Bhaiki Pashaur, 8. Lall Singh Longowala, 9. Ishar Singh Khokar, 10. Prem Singh Gujran and 11. Santa Singh "Pandhi" Dirbha.

At this time there were in all 866 members of Kisan Committee, who belonged in the following distritcs:

Patiala district	Sunam district	Barnala district
19	782	65

According to an article appearing under the caption "Kisan Day" in the Hindustan Times, Delhi, dated August 20, 1939, Professor N. G. Ranga, Vice-President of the All-India Kisan Sabha, in a statement to the press, appealed to all Kisan workers and Sabhas all over India to observe September 1st 1939 as the "Fourth All-India Kisan Day" and thus to strengthen the minimum demands of the Kisans. But this Kisan Day was not celebrated in the State.

In a Kisan Conference, which was held at village Garangam, near Kharar, Ambala District, on the 24th and 25th June, 1939, Sunder Lal Vakil of Bassi, a Parja Mandalist, describing the condition of peasants, exhorted the audience to send Jathas to participate in the Kisan Morcha at Lahore in that year.

Another Kisan conference was held at village Bopa Rai Khurd, near Raikot, Ludhiana District, on September 8, 1939. Dulla Singh Jalaldiwal, Barnala, who was then the detenus in the Panjab under Rule 129 of the Defence of India Rules, was the chairman of its ReceptionCommittee. Nearly 30 Kisans, who were residents of the State partcipated in it.[5]

Muzara Movement

In this connection the Muzara (tenant) movement was started and organised by the interested element among the Muzaras for the non-payment of Batai to Biswedars, particularly it had its origin in the Barnala District under the leadership of 1. Narain Singh Bhadaur, 2. Anokh Singh Jeondan, 3. Dharam Singh

5. The following being prominent: Lal Singh Jalaldiwal, Bachan Singh Sekha, Chanan Singh Bhadaur, Narain Singh, Ajmer Singh Tamkot, Bachitter Singh Jhaloor.

"Pakkar" Dalelsinghwaia, and 4. Kundha Singh of Anupgarh.

This movement was identical with the Kisan movement, its head office being at Budhlada, Hissar District.

Their main object was to incite the tenants against payment of Batai to the Biswedars. They voiced the alleged Muzara grievances against the Biswedars, by holding meetings outside the State at places, such as Budhlada, Hissar District. They formed a Muzara Committee, held at a meeting of the Muzara Committees, Patiala State at village Jethuke, Ludhiana District in April, 1939. It was resolved that the Maharaja of Patiala might be requested first through their deputations, to settle their old standing disputes with the Biswedars, that they would not pay "Batai" to the Biswedars and that in case no heed would be paid to their request by His Highness' Government Patiala, they should approach the Hon'ble the Resident, Panjab States Lahore at Simla by taking their Jathas in hundreds or so. The Muzaras of Bhadaur resisted the Police, who were deputed for effecting "Batai" operations. According to their plans, a Muzara Jatha,[6] started from Raikot, Ludhiana District on foot towards Simla on June 3, 1939, and marched through the British territory making halts in the Gurdwaras. It reached village Mansuran, Ludhiana District on the 5th of June, 1939. They reached Ludhiana the next day where Muni Lal Kalia, M.L.A. (Panjab) Advocate, Ludhiana and leaders of the Ludhiana Congress Committee made arrangements for their board, lodging procession and public meeting to give a wide publicity to their propaganda.

The leaders of this Jatha and Muni Lal Kalia were told by the Additional District Magistrate, Ludhiana that so many people could not be allowed to approach the Resident, Simla, hence they would elect five representatives for this purpose and the rest should wait at Ludhiana for the result.[7]

The Muzara representatives, however, were not allowed an interview by the Resident on the ground that no outsider like Muni Lal Kalia could be the member of their deputation and

6. Anokh Singh Jeonada, Chanan SinghBhadaur, Partap Singh Jewan Singhwala, Kundha Singh. Anupgarh, Sundar Singh Kishangarh.
7. They agreed to send the following as their representatives to Simla: Muni Lal Kalia, M.L.A., Ludhiana, Chanan Singh Bhadaur, Anokh Singh of Jeondan, Kundha Singh Anupgarh and Bishan Singh Jewan Singhwala.

that only the State subjects could have an interview. Thus the representatives of the Jatha came back and met their companions at Machiwara. The Jatha then marched onward on foot and reached Gurdwara Chamkaur Singh.

The members of this Jatha were told by the Ambala District Officers that only 5 of them could go to Simla. They paid no heed but quietly left Chamkaur Sahib towards Salimpore, P. S. Morinda, Ambala District. At Salimpore Ambala Police forced them to obey the orders of the District Magistrate, Rupar, Ambala District. They then selected 1. Anokh Singh Jeondan, 2. Chanan Singh Bhadaur, 3. Kartar Singh Jewansinghwala, 4. Kundha Singh Anupgarh, and 5. Sunder Singh Kisangarh to go to Simla to see the Resident of States.

This deputation had an interview with the Resident and placed their grievances before him, who promised to write His Highness' Government, Patiala for the settlement of their disputes.

The deputationists had also an interview with Raja Hari Kishan Kaul, the then Revenue Minister, Patiala, who assured them that their cause would be given due consideration.

On June 23, 1939, the members of this deputation reached Shehna and met the members of their Jatha. Consequently they returned to their respective home villages. In this behalf a commission of 1. M. N. Raina, Minister of Law, 2. S. D. K. Sen, Foreign Minister and 3. Lt.-Col. S. Harbans Singh, the then Revenue Commissioner, was appointed to enquire into disputes pending between occupancy tenants and Biswedars of the State.[8]

The Commission started its work but the ring leaders of the Muzara party did not allow the Muzaras, under their influence, to appear before the Commission, saying that no justice could be expected from such a commission on which there was no representative of member of the Muzara Committee.

Consequently agitation was started for the non-payment of Batai to Biswedars at all costs. Printed posters to this effect were freely distributed and the public meetings were held at various places in Ferozepore, Ludhiana, Hissar and Karnal District.

---

8. Vide Ijlas-i-Khas Order No. 23 dated 17-7-1939.

In view of their activities, some tenants of Dharamgarh and its neighbouring villages were proceeded against u/s 107/151 Cr. P.C. by the local police, to avoid an apprehension of a breach of the peace. When Harnam Singh of Dharamgarh and other active members of his party saw that they would be arrested, they urged upon the tenants to gather at Budhlada with a view to start in a Jatha to place their grievances before the Resident at Lahore. Accordingly a Muzara Jatha of about 75 persons started on November 11, 1939 by train for Railway Station Kasu Begu, Ferozepore District. From there they undertook the journey on foot, making demonstrations and speeches on the alleged grievances of the tenants. The number of the Jatha went on increasing on the way as other tenants from Patiala State continued to join them. When this Jatha reached Lahore on November 11, 1939 its number had risen to 125. On arrival of this Jatha the orders of District Magistrate, Lahore promulgated u/s 144 Cr. P.C. were notified to them if they went in batches of five or more on the Mall Road or towards the residence or the office of the Resident, they would be prosecuted against for defiance of the orders.

Under the circumstances they returned on July 12, 1939 to their villages after receiving a reply to their telegram from the Resident to the effect that no interview could be granted as long as their disputes were not settled by the Commission appointed by the Government of Patiala in this connection.

During the year 1940-41, the Muzaras held meetings at Budhlada, Takhtupura and Shehna, wherein a demand was made for the early publication of the report of enquiry by the Commission. A meeting was held at Takhtupura the 27th January, 1941 under the presidentship of both Ujaggar Singh Bhaur. of Thikriwala and Narain Singh of Bhadaur. He tried to revive and intensify the Muzara movement as he had done in a meeting held at village Jethuwal, Ferozepore District. He also published posters and submitted a declaration of the "Rayasti Dunia" in the court of District Magistrate, Ludhiana, for the purpose of propaganda of the Muzara Party. Some posters and articles were also published by him, for which he was prosecuted against u/s 38 of the Patiala Defence Rules. He also delivered many speeches against the Patiala State Administration.

Narain Singh of Bhadaur, President of the Muzara Committee also published several posters containing grievances of the Muzaras. He was also prosecuted under rule 38 of the Patiala Defence Rules.[9]

Narain Singh Bhadaur, President of the Muzara Committee, Patiala State, Ishar Singh Tamkot, Sadhu Singh Chukerian, Bharpoor Singh Dhiluana, Dharam Singh of Dalel Singhwala, Kishan Singh of Mohar Singhwala, Chand Singh, Kharak Singh of Kharak Singhwala and Kishan Singh Mangal, Muzaras of Barnala District took active part in making the Kisan Conference a success which was then to be held at Kortana, Ferozepore District in September, 1941 with a view to laying their grievances against the Biswedari system before the Resident, the Muzaras again wanted to approach the Resident.[10]

51 Muzaras with Gurdial Singh Kalal of Bhadaur and Phuman Singh Kishangarh, as their leaders reached Patiala with a view to lay their grievances before the Resident during his visit to Patiala in connection with the opening of the Industrial Exhibition at Patiala in 1942.

In another meeting held at Kalahri, Hissar District on February 7, 1940 the following were elected as office-bearers of the so called Kisan Committee, Tehsil Mansa.

On February 28, 1940, a meeting of Panjab Kisan Committee was held in the Jallianwala Bagh, Amritsar and of the Patiala State Kisan Committee, the following office-bearers were elected:

---

9. Darbara Singh of Khiwa Shesha Singhwala, Gurdial Singh Kalal and Chand Singh Jaijee of Bhadaur and Anokh Singh of Jeondan were its ring leaders. They were espousing the cause of Kisan Movement in the Panjab.

10. 1. A Jatha of 5 muzaras headed by Anokh Singh of Jeondan reached Simla.
    2. A Jatha of 27 Muzaras headed by Narain Singh of Bhadaur left for Lahore.
    3. A Jatha of 5 muzaras headed by Dharam Singh Dalel Singhwala left for Lahore from Budhlada.
    4. A Jatha of muzaras headed by Chanan Singh of Dialgarh left for Lahore from Takhtupura.
    5. Bhag Singh of Khilla, Jathedar.
    6. Dharam Singh of Dalel Singhwala, Secy.
    7. Joga Bapiana, Jathedar.
    8. Dalip Singh Khandal.

1. Bhagwan Singh Longowalia, 2. Harnam Singh Dharamgarh, 3. Waryam Singh Jaladiwal, 4. Dharam Singh Fakkar of Dalel Singhwala, 5. Jagir Singh Joga.

During the year 1940, the Panjab Kisan Committee issued circular letters to all District Kisan Committees instructing them to observe 9th July, 1940 as a "Protest Day" all over the Provinces against the wholesale arrests of Kisan leaders and socialists in the Panjab.

These circular letters were received in the State Governments of Panjab States took very strict measures to check these activities in their States and thus the Protest Day could not be held so successfully in the States, as elsewhere.

In the year 1941, a Kisan conference was convened at fatehgarh Kortana, Ferozepore District on December 20, 1941, but the State subjects were prohibited to take part in it. Jagir Singh Joga was convicted and sentenced in this connection and the conference was banned.

Gurmukhi posters containing advertisement of an anti-Fascist Kisan Conference which was to be held at village Ugrahan on the 5th and 6th September 1942 were published and distributed under the signatures of Hazura Singh Mattran and Ishar Singh Tamkot, the President and General Secretary respectively of the proposed conference.

Gurdial Singh Dhillon, the Inspector General of Police issued instructions to the Nazim and the Superintendents of Police, Sunam to serve notices on the organisers of the conference, directing them to refrain from holding it, failing which they would be tried under the Defence Rules.

Accordingly notices in connection with the banning of the Communist Conference at Ugrahan were issued by the District Magistrate, Sunam on Hazura Singh and Ishar Singh, which were posted on a common place of village Ugrahan. Other necessary preventive measures were also adopted by the District officers to prevent people from joining the conference on September 9, 1942. A large number of communists, majority of whom were the Muzaras of the Biswedari villages of the State, especially of vilagers Pharwahi, Tamkot, Dalel Singh Wala and Kishangarh, reached Railway Station Chhajli.

Achhra Singh Chhina, and Jagat Singh of Lyallpur, Propaganda Secretary and Assistant Propaganda Secretary respectively of the Panjab Kisan Committee arrived there. They were received by the congregation there with shouts of "Inqalab Zindabad" etc. When they were ready to set out towards Ugrahan some Lamberdars of Village Chhajli who were toadying told them that they would not allow the residents of the British territory, to enter the State territory in order to agitate.

Achhra Singh Chhina, leader of the party, replied that they had come for their sake, but they requested them to go back. Communists did not accede to their request and started towards Ugrahan, when they reached near village Ugrahan, the village Panchayat forbade them to enter the village in the first instance, as the majority of its inhabitants were opposed to the holding of the conference. Then the Tehsildar and S.H.O., Sunam served notices upon Achhara Singh Chhina and Jagjit Singh, Lyallpur, the latter refused to leave. Eventually the Communist party after exchanging some argument with the officers returned to Railway Station Chhajli, from where they left for their homes.

Communists took the banning of the conference seriously and decided to hold their conference in the British territory adjoining the borders of the State.

At the close of the Kisan School at Bhangali District Lahore, a meeting of the Panjab Kisan Committee was held there in camera on August 31, 1942, which was attended by all the prominent Kisan workers, who happened to be there on that day. It was decided in that meeting to resuscitate Kisan Committees in Panjab States. It was further decided to organise units of Communist Party side by side the Kisan Committees in every district, which would work under the instructions of Panjab Communist Party.

Punjab Kisan Committees tried their best to enlist Kisan members. Its activities were not confined to Patiala State only but were directed in all other States and Panjab Districts. Gurdev Singh Josh Khanal, Hazura Singh Mattran, Jagir Singh Joga, and Harnam Singh Dharmgarh enlisted members in Patiala State, Hira Singh and Hardit Singh Bhattal in Nabha State, Inder Singh, Wazir Singh and Gujjar Singh in Jind State, Sewa Singh Rapla and Mangal Singh in Malerkotla State.

The Kisan Committee was out to raise their strength as soon as possible by enlisting a sufficiently large number of people so that they could prove advantageous to the Kisans.

An evil consequence of the Kisan Committee which succeeded in raising its strength, was the Muzaras tried to get themselves declared as hereditary tenants and were trying to achieve their object since then. But it was a fact that as yet the Kisan Committee did not command such a large strength which could guarantee its success than by an unlawful action.

Do Hanjoo—October, 1941

Chanan Singh of Dalel Singh Wala, P. S. Dirbha distributed copies of the poster under the caption "Political Agent Sahab Riyast Patiala Muzarian da Deputation" by Anokh Singh Jeonda, President Kisan Muzara Committee Patiala State and a pamphlet entitled "Do Hanjoo'. In the poster it was mentioned that that the Enquiry Commission and His Highness did not do justice to them inspite of verbal assurances given to them from time to time. Instead of staying orders for execution of decrees pending result of the enquiry tenants were ejected.

They had, therefore, decided to approach the Resident in the form of a deputation. In the pamphlet "Do Janju", by Dharam Singh "Phakkar" Dalel Singhwala various methods just or unjust adopted by the Biswedars to acquire land were narrated. It was described how the Kisans were unjustly treated in the past Bandobasts (Settlements). The promises of Rulers of Patiala State and other officers for abolition of Batai system were repeated. In connection with tenants' refusal to pay Batai, the Police at the instigation of Jai Singh opened fire at Qila Hakiman which resulted in several casualties, injuries and convictions. His Highness' Government appointed an Enquiry Commission to appease tenants but their cases were decided though Captain Sardar M. N. Raina informed the Resident that the cases would be decided in two months. The following demands were made :

1. Abolition of Batai System.
2. Release of persons convicted in connection with the Kisan Movement and withdrawal of cases against others.
3. Restoration of confiscated property and stoppage of execution of decrees.
4. Recognising non-occupancy tenants as occupancy tenants and introducing the system of assessment in cash.

5. Realisation of land Revenue direct by the Tehsil authorities.

Kisan Conference At Village Rar

Kisan conference was organised by the Muzaras or the State in general and those or Tehsils Mansa and Sunam in particular at village Rar, Tehsil Mansa in league with the Communist Party of the Panjab whose leaders were Achhar Singh of Chhina, Amritsar District, Sohan Singh Josh M.L.A. etc. with a view to reviving the Muzara Movement.

In 1942, the Muzaras had summoned a Kisan Conference at village Ugranan near Sunam in which Achhar Singh of Chhina President-elect of the proposed Rar Conference and Jagjt Singh B.A., LL.B. of Lyallpore accompanied by some Muzaras of Tehsil Mansa were to participate but could not do so, on account of the Ugrahan Kisan Conference having been banned by the Patiala Government.

The object of the Communist party of the Panjab in organising the Kisan Conference at village Rar was two-fold i.e. on one hand they wanted to enlist the sympathies and enlist in their ranks the 'Muzaras' of the State to swell their following. On the other they wanted to regain their lost prestige which they had failed to achieve in the districts of Amritsar and Lahore inparticular and in the Malwa tract they came out of jail on giving an undertaking to help in the War efforts. Under this idea they wanted to start the "Muzara" movement enmass by registering the sympathies of the "Muzaras" of the state such as those of Tehsils Mansa and Sunam who had their grievances against the Biswedari system for the abolition of which they had been marching in Jathas to Lahore and Simla to wait upon the Resident for the Panjab States, Lahore in the years 1939, 1940 and 1941 backed by outsiders, such as Muni Lal Kalia of Ludhiana and Hari Singh of Gill, Ludhiana District.

In the year 1939 the "Muzaras" of Bhadaur took up a very defiant attitude. They started the agitation, preaching non-payment of Batai, as a result of which 32 Muzaras of Bhadaur were prosecuted for their unlawful activities. As the Muzaras appeared to harbour the fear seeing their cause weak. lost the findings

---

11. Case No. 830/C of 1939. Dated 14th & 15th of August, 1943, p. 335.

of the Commission should go against them, they, therefore, were all out to itensify their activities to achieve their ends.[11]

The Kisan Conference 1945

The Kisan Conference was held in village Sehna, District Ludhiana, on July 7, 1945 to protest against the pre-planned looting and beating of the Patiala State Mazaras by the State Officials and the Biswedars. This conference emphasised on the followsing points :

1. To approach the Patiala Government to stop action against Muzaras u/s 424 I. P., under which section the Patiala Government was arresting the Muzaras.
2. To stop looting of Muzaras by the State officials and Biswedars.
3. To stop Batai System. The conference expressed great resentment over the non-publication of the Muzara Commission's Report although it was in 1938.

Partap Singh of Jakhapal further supported the above noted resolution explaining that "in order to secure their rights from the Govt. the Muzaras must first organise themselves. In 1917 the Kisan of Russia extermunated once for all the Biswedars in Russia. Had the State Muzaras get themselves organised also protested against the use of Hadyat 1988 in the Phulkian States which he added, greatly restricted their civil liberties. Continuing he said that since the time this Red Flag had come out victoricus. Empires were being liquidated and the day was quite near when they (The Kisans) will see the Maharajas falling down for ever."[12]

The Central Zamindara League, Kapurthala

Zimindara agitation was started in Kapurthala State as early as in 1931, but it assumed a vehement form against Kapurthala State Administration under the leadership of Master Hari Singh Dhoot in early 1935. This agitation was mainly based on the following concepts:—

1. The unit of measurement of length in field survey that is pace or KARM, which was in vogue in the State was less com-

---

12. Proceedings of Kisan Conference held at village Shehna. District Ludhiana on 23 & 24.3.2002/7 & 8.7.1945.

pared as to the adjoining British territory.

2. The rates of land revenue assessment in the State were excessively higher as compared to those levied in the adjoining British Territory; and that keeping in view these two facts 50% reduction in the land revenue was demanded by the Zamindars.

3. The Begar cess known as "Haq-ul-Khidmat" was also very harsh and out-dated.

DIFFERENT MEASUREMENTS

The unit of the local measurement of length of land which was in vogue in the State was KARM equivalent to 54 inches. In different districts in the Panjab the Standard of land survey varied.

1. In Districts of Jullundur, Hoshiarpur and Shahpur Kandi (Gurdaspur District), one Karm was equal to 57.5 inches.

2. In Districts of Amritsar, Gurdaspur except Shakargarh Tehsil, Shahpur Kandi, and Chak Andoara, Pathankot Tahsil, Ferozepur (except Fazilka), Lahore (except northern part of Ravi), one Karm was equal to 60 inches.

3. In Chak Andhara Pathankot Tahsil (District Gurdaspur), northern part of Ravi (Lahore District), Fazilka Tahsil (Ferozepur District), one Karm was equal to 66 inches.

In several districts of the British Panjab land measurement in accordance with Ghamaun prevalent, generally the unit of measurement of length was Karm in this State. There was divergence in standard of measurement of land in several districts of Panjab during the British rule. The effect of this decrease in the unit of measurement of land as compared to the adjoining Districts of Jullundur during field survey was that one acre was equivalent to 211 marlas while in the Kapurthala State one acre was equal to 239 marlas. Thus the difference of 28 marlas (one Kanal eight marlas) in one acre or in other words difference of nineteen marlas in one Ghamoun, while one kanal comprised twenty marlas and one Ghamoun consisted of 8 kanals.

CONFERENCE AT KHAIRA

A conference of Kapurthala State Zamindars attended by 3,000 people was convened at village Khaira, District Jullundur on the 2nd February, 1935 and the following important resolutions were adopted:—

1. This conference welcomed Lieut. Col. Fisher on his assumption of the duties of the office of Chief Minister Kapurthala and it was earnestly hoped that during his tenure of office exploitation of the masses, which was a marked feature of the last regime would be replaced by a programme for their economic, social and educational uplift and politcial advancement, resulting in happiness, contentment and peace in the State, as preordained by Col. Wilberforce Bell, A.G.G. Panjab States, in his Banquest speech at Kapurthala on December 8, 1934. The new Chief Minister was requested at the Conference to move freely among the country folk in order to gain first-hand and accurate knowledge of their condition and grievances, definitely instructing the local officials not to stand in the way of the people, as they had been accustomed to approach him with their representations. He was assured of the Zimindars full support in all measures of drastic retrenchment and economic amelioration of the masses.

2. The Conference emphatically demanded that:—

Immediate steps might be taken to place the flagrantly unjust and crushing land revenue assessment on an equitable basis through an expert and impartial agency so as to reduce the rates at least to the level of those being charged in the adjacent British district.

3. The Central Zimindar League's Resolution of 19th January supported the Faman-i-Shahi the State Government and urged upon to implement the concepts of the League. Further the Conference expressed its full confidence in the lead given to the community by the Central Zimindara League.

4. The State Government was requested to discourage communalism effectively, which had already wrought havoc in the State and was still a potential danger to public peace and further appealed to the masses of all communities to unite for their common good and refuse to be exploited by selfish communal and separatist agencies.

5. It was demanded that a Legislative Assembly on the lines of the Central Zimindara League's Resolution of January 3, 1935, might be introduced at an early date:—

It was further demanded that election to the proposed assembly might take place on the basis of:

a) Joint electorates and vote for every tax-payer.

b) Single Member constituencies.

c) Separation of urban and rural areas.

At Conference, it was definitely and unequivocally made clear that the Zimindars opposed vehemently the introduction of communal representation, or cleavage on religious lines, in any form or shape what-so-ever, and would prefer to have no Reforms that would accentuate communalist.

6. The conference requested the new Chief Minister to lift the ban on political meetings, the imposition of which particularly in the rural areas, was quite unjustified, so that the people might have full constitutional liberty to ventilate their grievances, whose redress, it was presumed, was the special mission of Lieut. Col. Fisher.

7. The Conference expressed sorrow at the death of S. Sewa Singh Thikriwala in Patiala Jail and considered his martyrdom a clarion call to the States' People to start an earnest struggle to break off the shackles of unbridled autocracy in the States.

ZIMINDARA CONFERENCE AT MUSAPUR

A conference of the Zimindars of Phagwara Ilaqa in Kapurthala State, was attended by 3000 persons at the village of Musapur near Domeli, in District Jullundur, on February 25, 1935. The following resolutions among others were adopted:—

1. The Conference urgently demanded that the crushing land revenue assessment might be immediately revised and placed on an equitable basis, through an impartial and expert agency so as to assimilate it to the principles and rates of assessment prevalent in the adjoining British Districts, taking into due calculation the shortness of the measurement scale in the state. The reported proposals of a meagre reduction in the land revenue were highly disappointing and the conference desired to make it emphatically clear to all concerned than an unsatisfactory amount of reduction was bound only to intensify the prevalent discontent and drive the zimindar community to a state of despair. Any solution of the problem which fell short of reduction

to the level of the rates in the neighbouring British territory would prove only a temporary relief.

2. Full confidence was reposed in the lead given to the community by the Central Zimindara League and the masses were appealed to be on their guard against communal agencies which had already done them a lot of harm.

3. Introduction of a Legislative Assembly was demanded on the lines of the demand of the Central Zamindara League and it was made clear further that the Zamindars were opposed to the introduction of communal representation in any form.

4. This Conference, while expressing its sense of indignation at the forfeiture by the Kapurthala Government of pension of Jamadar Amar Singh for his participation in the constitutional agitation for reduction in land revenue congratulated the said Sardar on his cheerful sacrifice for the noble cause.

5. The State Government was urged upon to take immediate steps for the redress of the grievances of the peasants of Bohani and Thakarwal, Phagwara.

6. The state government was requested to construct bridges over the Sufaid Bain and Kail and to metal the Phagwara-Rahana Jattan Road in order to facilitate vehicular traffic and render access to market easier for the agriculturists of the Tehsil.

The Zamindara struggle continued and the workers had to suffer a lot from the cruel hands of the Kapurthala State officials. Meanwhile, the Revenue authorities began to make inquiries about the Zimindara League demands from the various quarters of the British Territory as well as from the other Panjab States.

It is evident from Sadr's order dated 29-1-35 that inquiries were made from the neighbouring States about their rates of land revenue, and temporary engagement of an E.A.C. from the Panjab was sanctioned. There was no such record in the State showing what were the revenue rates in adjoining districts, Jullundur, Hoshiarpur and Ferozepur. Without having the full knowledge of revenue rates in the adjoining districts of the British Panjab and those in the neighbouring States no comparison could be made by the State authorities.

On the net revenue the percentage of cesses which was

taken by the State was Rs. 14/1/- and was detailed as below:—

1. Patwar	Rs.	3.2	per cent
2. Chaukidara	Rs.	1.8	„
3. Education	Rs.	1.0	„
4. Localrate	Rs.	1.9	„
5. Haqul Khidmit	Rs.	3.10	„
6. Parkhai	Rs.	0.2	„
7. Malba	Rs.	3.2	„
Total:	Rs.	14.1	„

The Settlement Operations which were commenced in this State in about 1921, ended with the settlement of Tahsil Phagwara in 1931. With the exception of 116 villages of Kapurthala and Bholath Tehsil (formerly named as Tehsil Dhilan) and the whole of Sultanpur Tahsil, in all other parts of the State, in the present settlement assessment revenue rates of the previous settlement were not changed and were kept quite the same and no enhancement in revenue was made by revising the revenue rates. In spite of the fact that prices of agricultural produce were higher in those days as compared to these days but no consideration of high level of prices was made and the revenue rates were not revised. This method of assessment was adopted just in accordance with the approval of His Highness, the Maharaja of Kapurthala.

On the value of agricultural produce, was dependent the payment of the land revenue. According to the practice in the past no change was made in the land revenue during the period of settlement and that system worked satisfactorily as no big changes in prices did occur. But whenever there was a great economic depression and slump in prices, the revenue payers found it difficult to meet their dues. The Government in the British Panjab when the need arose came to their help by liberal relief at each harvest in the form of remission in revenue.

Enough time still remained in the next settlement and no one could say with any amount of certainty whether in future prices would fall or rise and there might be times when the prices were to be very high and when the prices were to be very low. If on the one hand at the time when the present settlement came into effect, as the prices were high the revenue payers felt no difficulty in paying the revenue, on the other hand it could not be overlooked that if the prevailing low scale prices were taken for the permanent remission of the revenue, it would not look fair for the future interests of the State.

In order to overcome this difficulty the Panjab Government evolved a new scheme of assessment of land revenue for the district of Lyallpur. According to this scheme, the remission of land revenue was based upon the principle of general level of prices of agricultural produce. By this system, the demand of revenue was made dependent on prices. By working out the figures of prices of last 20 years, the average prices for twenty years, the class of land and other factors, the average rate of revenue was determined. This average rate was considered the maximum which Government could take at any time during the currency of the settlement.

But the Government would only take this maximum rate of revenue when the prices were equally high or higher than prices represented by the schedule prepared at the time of assessment. In case in any year the prices were lower than that represented by the schedule the Government would make remission in the revenue rate which would be proportionate to the difference. This method was in the interest of land revenue payer. On these findings the Revenue Department recommended if the Kapurthala Darbar approved this principle of sliding scale of remission in land revenue, this method of assessment may be considered to see whether it could meet the demands of the zimindars. On the other hand, the zimindars, who were eager to get their demands acceded to, accelerated the agitation.

The State Government had to accept the demands of the zimindars, but the leaders, who were arrested, were not yet released. This act on the part of the State Government was much resented by the peasants. Master Hari Singh Jathedar, Amar Singh and Sardar Sadhu Singh, the heroes of this struggle were shut in dark cells of the Central Jail, Kapurthala. Harsh treatment was meted out to them. The soul of the movement Master Hari Singh Dhoot was separated from the rest of the prisoners. This cell was like a hell in which the Master was confined for 24 hours. In the severe heat of June, he was denied natural air in addition to undergoing other hardships of the Jail. He was given rotton food to eat. He was brought from Jail to the Kotwali lock-up, and was tortured by Police in order to compel him to render apology whereupon he went on hunger strike. On grounds of his bad health he was taken to hospital where he had a narrow escape.

Sadhu Singh, a brave leader who was accustomed to bear all hardships with a smiling face had been again brought to the Kotwali lockup. Children and wife of Sadhu Singh were made to cry before Sadhu Singh so that he might be compelled apology. Undaunted by these atrocities Sadhu Singh persisted in his demands.

Ultimately the Government acceded to the demands of zimindars and released their leaders. Thus ended the agitation, which received impetus from the concepts of the Central Zimindara League.

6

THE PANJAB CIVIL CODE

Early History

The history of the development of Civil Code in the Panjab under the British Rule was quite new in itself, because before these was no such separate department under this designation existing in this country. The attempt was a new one, and was striking success.

There were no regular courts of law and no separate department of Civil administration. Every Chief decided cases according to his own discretion and regarded justice as a source of income. There was no hierarchy of courts, and no written laws for the guidance of the judges. The same officer had to do the multifarious duties of collecting revenue, and of dispensing justice in his chiefdom. There was no uniform system of law for the country as a whole, and no common authority to enforce it.

The main concern of the Chieftain was to make money out of the whole transaction as long as it was consistent with the maintenance of peace. It was not his lookout to see to the merits of the case. The standpoint of the state is depicted in these words:— "He who gains his point pays his 'shukrana' or present of gratitude, and he who is lost pays his 'jurmana' or penalty."

If a Khura-Khoj or trace of footsteps was carried to the gate or the door of the village, the zamindars were to make good the loss or show atrack beyond their own village. On the commission of a "Daka" or burglary or highway robbery, the Chief within whose jurisdictions the act was perpetrated had recourse to the lextalionis or some other retaliatory measure. This summary method of inemnification was of absolute necessity as many of the chiefs and their zamindars harboured criminals and shared in their malpractices. Debtors and revenue defaulters often absconded and found shelter in some other Chief's territory and thus very easily evaded the payment of claims against them. A promise was made to pay their debts on security, when they had the means to do so.

Such was in short the state of the country at the advent of the British Rule. By the igenuity of the new officers of the British Government, and under their guidance the laws, hitherto altogether unwritten in this country, were reduced to writing and condified. Courts were established in various parts of the country, and people were made to take more interest in the dispensation of justice.

Dalhousie fully recognized the importance of upholding 'native institutions and practices as far as they were consistant with the distribution of justice to all classes', of maintaining village communities in all their integrity, and of improving and sonsolidating popular institutions".[1]

The Board Of Administration

Under the Board of Administration "the Commissioners were Superintendents of revenue and police, and exercised the civil appellate and the original criminal powers of Sessions Judges. The Deputy Commissioners were given subordinate civil, criminal and fiscal powers, combining in one person the different aspects of the administration and thereby much increasing its vigour".[2] "Whilst the Board was maturing civil, criminal, and revenue rules of general application, each Deputy Commissioner, subject to loosely defined limitations, had a free hand in shaping customs as to land tenures.

"Hitherto the strong man armed, whether community or individual, had acted as he listed, hence practices were in such a fluid state that, in most districts, the customary law was shaped and fixed in its original form in accordance with the views or right and expediency of their earliest Deputy Commissioners and Settlement Officers. In the making of the laws generally, for which the Board was responsible, the Province was fortu-

1. Selections from Papers on Indebtedness and Land Transfer, Panjab Settlement Manual — James Douie, p. 360.
2. Panjab Administration Report, p. 24.
3. Panjab under War & Peace—thorbun, pp. 166-167.

nate in the fact that no professional lawyers had a share".[4]

The proposed objects of the Board were "that substantial justice should be plainly dealt out to a simple people, unused to the intricacies of legal proceedings. Their aim was to avoid all technicality, circumlocution, and obsourity, to simplify and abridge every rule, procedure, and process. They endeavoured to form tribunals which would not be hedged in with forms unintelligible to the vulgar, and only to be interpreted by professional lawyers, but which would be open and accessible courts of justice, where every man pleading his own cause and confronted face to face with his opponents, might prosecute his own claim or conduct his own defence".[5]

The Arbitrators

In order to maintain the position of the village committees of elders, "judges were instructed to encourage litigants to refer the issues between them to arbitrators chosen for the purpose, the power of giving effect to or varying the award being retained by the Court. Until some years after the Mutiny of 1857, the system served its purpose well. Afterwards as the grip of the law became firmer, first village committees of elders—in other words, the voice of public opinion, ceased to have authority and next references to arbitration in law suits fell into disrepute.[6] The Board itself recognized the unfortunate effect of the new tendencies remarking "that they could hardly consider that civil justice had advanced as satisfactorily as the other branches of the administration. Indeed they were not sure that it would ever be successful. There was no part of the British system so difficult to popularise".[7]

Panjab Cviil Code-1853

Accordingly those rules which had already been current in the previously annexed Satluj divisions were extended to the Civil Courts throughout the Province after annexation, as they were calculated to ensure substantial justice unfettered by technicalities. In criminal law the code adopted during the Resi-

4. Panjab under War & Peace—Thorbun, pp. 166-167.
5. Panjab under War & Peace—Thorburn, p. 169.
6. Panjab under War & Peace—Thorburn, pp. 166-167.
7. Panjab Administration Report (1849-50), p. 153.

dency period[8] was maintained. But in order to temper the autocratic power of Deputy Commissioners "and secure reasonable uniformity in the dispensation of civil justice, a collection of rules, which soon acquired the name of the 'Panjab Cvil Code', was prepared in 1853 and circulated as a manual for information and guidance.

Being lucid, simple, and suited to the circumstances of the people, the Code soon acquired the force of law. In rural tracts it answered its purpose admirably", "though it failed to cover all the legal complexities arising from business transaction in expanding commercial centres".[9] We have the most open and liberal provisions for the admission of evidence. We have complete arrangements for reference to arbitration and for the ascertainment of local custom. We have a procedure without any pretension to exactitude; but a procedure which provides for the litigants and their respective witnesses being confronted in open court, for a decision being arrived at immediately, and for judgment being delivered to the parties then and there.[10] Suits for landed property were dealt with by Revenue Courts, i.e. Revenue Officers acting in a judicial instead of an executive capacity.[11]

Introduction Of The English Legal System

The power of legislation lay with the Panjab Government before 1861. "The orders of officers which it constantly issued were, to a certain extent, essentially of a legislative character, but then they were scarcely ever in a legislative form. It is not matter of surprise that this should have been so, for the authority prescribing the rule immediately modified or explained it, if it gave rise to any inconvenience, or was found to be ambiguous. But the system was destroyed by the Indian Councils' Act".[12] After that Act no legislative power existed in India which was not derived from this Statute; but to prevent a whole-

---

8. Land of The Five Rivers—Trevaskis, pp. 208-209.
9. Panjab Administration Report, p. 95.
   Mussalmans and Moneylenders in the Panjab—Thorburn, p. 11.
10. Stated John Lawrence, in 1856.
11. Land of The Five Rivers—Trevaskis, p. 287.
    Panjab Land Administration Manual—Douie, p. 792.
12. Village Communities in The East & West—Maine, pp. 391-92.

sale cancellation of essentially legislative rules the force of law was given to all rules made previously for non-Regulation provinces by or under the authority of the Government of India, or of a Lieutenant-Governor:—

"By this provision an enormous and most miscellaneous mass of rules, clothed to a great extent in general and popular language was suddenly established as law, and invested with solidity and unchangeableness to a degree which its authors had never contemplated".[13]

Chief Court

A fruitful field of legal activity was thus provided for the Chief Court which was in 1866 substituted for the Judicial Commissioner who had previously supervised judicial affairs in the Panjab. "It was constituted the final appellate authority in civil and criminal cases, with powers also of original crimial jurisdiction in cases where European British subjects were charged with various offences, and of original civil jusdiction in special cases".[14] In the same year the regulation code of Civil Procedure was extended to the Province, and lawyers were permitted to plead in all courts.[15]

The assimilation of the Panjab to the regulation pattern of law-ridden Provinces, like Bengal and the North-Western Provinces, was then forced on by the Legislative Department of the Government of India with hot-house celerity:—

"Justice, equity, and good conscience, the old desiderata by which the soundness of a judgment was measured by an appellate court, were no longer guides to a right decision. Their place was usurped by Regulations, Acts, Sections, Clauses, and the latest Rulings of that object of the poor man's dread and the District Officer's sarcasm—the Chief Court".

The new legal system thus introduced greatly strengthened

---

13. Panjab Administration Report, p. 143.
    Village Communities in the East & West—Maine, pp. 391-92.
    Panjab Settlement Maunal—James Douie, p. 562.
14. Panjab Administration Report, p. 97.
15. Panjab under War & Peace—Thorburn, p. 23.
    Panjab Peasant in Prosperity & Debt—Darling, p. 205.
    Village Communities in East & West—Maine, p. 395.
    Wealth & Welfare of the Panjab—Calvert, p. 125.

"the disposition to look on unlimited power of transfer as an essential feature of proprietary right and a necessity of economic progress".[16] The number of transfers of land rapidly increased, and the cosditions and circumstances of the poor agriculturists was a serious cause of unpopularity to the British Administration. "The Senior Judge of the Panjab, a broadminded English Lawyer, was strongly of opinion that the courts were becoming a burden and a disaster to the people of the Panjab:—[17]
"The Panjab Government itself was of the same opinion and repeatedly protested against innovations which were rapidly impowering the countryside". Some elasticity was indeed allowed in the frontier districts and the remote mountain canton of Kulu, which were declared territories for which special regulation might be made other than Acts of the Legislature.[18] Advantage was taken of this to retain some of their original powers for the Frontier Committees of elders.[19] But on the whole the state of things was such as to disappoint the hopes of the early administrators of the Provinces.

Panjab Laws Act—1872

The old plan of administration had been entirely reversed. The Panjab, whose efficient administration had saved India during the Mutiny, was fast sicking to the level of the rest of the law-ridden sub-continent:-[20]
With the passing of the Panjab Laws Act of 1872, the Panjab Civil Code ceased to have any binding force. But tht Act at the same time declared that 'In questions regarding inheritance, special property of females, betrothal, marriage, dowery, adoption, guardianship, minority bastardy, family relation, wills, legacies, gifts, partitions, or any religions usage or institution, the (primary) rule of decision' should be 'only custom of any body or class of persons, which is not contrary to justice, equity, and good conscience and has not been declared to be void by any competent authority'.[21]

16. Panjab Land Administration Manual—James Douie, p. 9.
17. Selection from Papers & Indebtedness and Land Transfer, pp. 61-62.
18. Panjab Administration Report, p. 142
19. Jirga.
20. Musalmans and Moneylenders in the Panjab—Thorburn, p. 117.
21. Panjab Settlement Manual—James Douie, p. 562.

Regular Civil Courts Established

In 1874-75 regular Civil Courts were established which took over from District Officers and their staffs the settlement of suits for debts against agriculturists[22] "Their establishment was regarded by the commercial classes as a further step in the promotion of their interests, by the rural masses as additional evidence of the ascendancy of the rule of the money-landers." The common belief was strengthened by the facts that the subordinate judicial staff was drawn from the trading and ministerial classes of the towns, that they were located as was, of course, reasonable-wherever money-lenders contragated, and had as was natural little intercourse except with men of their own caste.

As they were bound of the Civil Procedure Code, Evidence, Contract, and other acts, their local ignorance and unfamiliarity with village life generally lent point to the common sneer that a bond and a witness, however worthless, secured a decree. Thus, the new debt-registering and collecting agency was hated by the people, and gave a further impetus to petty litigation. Within a decade the number of suits disposed of in the year rose to over a quarter of a million, so that in that year alone on the average each wider kindered[23] had a civil suit "a carnival of litigation remunerative to Government and the pleaders but ruinous to the peasantry".[24]

With the introduction of regular Courts and trained lawyers the delicate adjustment became impossible. Every administrative act was questioned that could not be shown to be in accordance with some Act of the Legislature; and the Indian Councils Act,[25] the Panjab Laws Act,[26] and the First Forest,[27] Land Reve-

---

22. Panjab Administration Report, p. 95.
23. This Act was passed in 1861.
24. The Panjab Laws Act of 1872.
25. In 1855 John Lawrence, as Chief Commissioner, authorised Deputy Commissioners to mark off areas specially adopted for the growth of timber or fuel, from which the owners would only be allowed to take their essential requirements for agricultural or domestic purposes; and in the hill areas north of Rawalpindi the mistake made in Kangra was not repeated, and all waste lands were definitely declared to be the property of Government (Punjab Administration Report) p. 571.
26. To remedy this defect the first Land Revenue Act was passed in 1871 supplemented by rules having the force of law under the Act (The

nue and Tenancy Acts represent the attempt to prevent the complete paralysis of the administration under the new conditions.

The Administrators were compelled to lie, the interpretation of the Acts being left to Courts, which had little knowledge of the circumstances to which the Act applied, and were prevented by the very assence of their being from paying other than incidental regard to consideration of expediency.[28] When an Act was round quite unworkable recourse was had to further legislation, soon itself to be overlaid with a mass of interpretations, conveyed in the rulings of the Courts. In some cases elasticity was obtained by conferring on subordinate authorities the power of making rules under the Act. This admirable procedure, which to a certain extent provided for the exercise of discretionary authority under a legal form might have been more widely used with advantage.

Sun Dried Bureaucrats.

As a matter of fact, it did little to temper the rigidity of the legal system, which was only rendered workable by the scant heed paid by many Deputy Commissioners to legal rules. Even these holder spirits were, gradually restrained, till a dull soulless uniformity settled on the whole administration earning for those was conducted it the nickname of sun-dried bureaucrats.[29] Of the enactments enibread in the Panjab "those connected with revents, excise, rent, tenant-right, forests, village officers, and the like having been gradually evolved to meet local circumstances and being chiefly rules and practices already in force compressed into codified forms to which jurisdiction under then was confined, their working" was generally simple smooth and inexpensive.

Land System of British India Vol. II pp. 75)

27. Under Prinsep, while a few of the recorded occupancy tenants were proprietors, the majority lost their rights, thought in some cases they were protected against rent-enhancement for limited periods. It was as a result of the controversy engendered by these changes that the first Panjab Tenancy Act was passed in 1868. at a period also characterised by a passion for legislation on every possible subject
Panjab Settlement Manual—James Douie, pp. 200-227.
28. Village Community in East & West—Maine. p. 394
29. Village Community in East & West—Maine, pp. 394-397

Hence lawyers, when permitted to plead seldom made use of the privilege. "Such was not the case in the vast field of economic and social relations, over disputes in which the Chief Court and subordinate judiciary exercised exclusive jurisdiction. Throughout that field the laws in force were conceived, shaped, and carried through Council by English Lawyers ignorant of India. As a consequence, successive legal members of Council treated India, with her diverse nationalities and conditions, as if the whole continent were inhabited by a homogenous and highly educated commercial people, all anxious that their inter-relations should be regulated by uniform up-to-date Western laws".

Hardly any such Act, passed between 1870-1884, was comprehensible to laymen. Until the introduction of what Lord Curzon described as the "complex paraphernalia of the Chief Court," every peasant was competent to conduct his legal affairs himself without recourse to the assistance of that intellectual mercenary-the lawyer. This was no longer possible after the passing of the Specific Relief and Easements Acts which permitted the interference of the Civil Courts in the social life of Panjab.

The Easement Act

Under the Easement Act, a villager who found the familiar pathway closed to his ancestral field, could sue the "dominant owner for a release of the servient heritage' under Chapters IV and V of the Easements Act. Even in English the words were hardly intelligible, so a man who wished to fight and meant to win must perforce put his case into the hands of a lawyer with the ultimate result of having to mortgage land to meet his law expenses. A man of simpler tastes would remove the obstruction, hazarding an assault or riot, with consequent complications, all involving expenditure.

Of an entirely different character were measures like the Specific Relief and Easements Act, which defined existed to be remedied, and where there was no pretence that the measure would remedy it, if it had existed.[32] "The gradual return of the

---

31. Selections from Papers on Indebtedness & Land Transfer, p. 60.
32. Musalmans and Moneylenders in the Panjab-Thorburn p. 189.

Government of India to sober-mindedness was the result of a combination of course, the exhaustion of raw material; the insistence of district officers, and to a small extent of unofficial English opinion, that the growing evils in the body politic were largely but to excessive and unsuitable legislation; and latterly, the wise relegation of parochial subjects to the newly created provincial legislative councils. So long as the Indian masses were alone the "Corpus Vile" the torrent of new enactments attracted little notice, but as soon as the comparatively wealthy classes, and particularly the small European Community, became directly affected, the proceedings of the Government began to be subjected to scrutiny, and legislation caused charge.[33]

Exageration of These Acts in The Lower Courts

The atmosphere of unreality which was introduced into juridical relations by these Acts was exaggerated in the lower courts. Conscious of his inability to understand them, the amateur Judge, whose work was still often mainly executive, endeavoured to elaborate something which bore a faint resemblance to a professional judgment, hoping thus to impress his superiors with a sense of his legal capacity.

The professional Bar, with a sense of his legal capacity more versed in technicalities than the amateur Bench, was generally in a position to browheat the titular Judge. Cases were generally regarded not as enquities into matters of fact or even of law, but the battles between renowned champions of the Bar. There was no limit to the sum which it was worth while to pay them for any one who wished to escape a hanging or to ruin so enemy.[34]

Dictatorship of the Bar.

Such a notable victory was gained when the "Chief Court," on the revision side, quashed a decision arrived at after lengthy and costly proceedings, on the technical ground that as the officer giving the decision had signed himself "Magistrate of the District," instead of 'Deputy Commissioner' he had acted ultra vires.[35] 'Many Judges, aghast at the costly protraction of litiga-

---

33. Panjab under War & Peace—Thorburn, p. 244.
34. Musalmans and Moneylenders in the Panjab—Thorburn, p. 187.
35. Panjab under War & Peace-Thorburn, p. 249.

tion and the juridical chaos produced by against the dictatorship of the Bar. Such man rode rough-shed over lawyers' quibbles, deciding their cases on the real merits in judgements remarkable for blunt common sense, and the omission of vaxatious refrences to Acts, Section, or Rulings. If their judgements reached the Chief Court on appeal or revision, that Court generally to uphold the lower Court's decision. But being bound to interpret the law as it was, its innate common sense cramped by the arguments of watchful pleaders, that Court was often reduced to the necessity of justifying its conclusions on technical grounds, setting aside the clear direction of the law by special pleading.

It was "not however on every occasion that the Chief Court allowed its judgments and instructions to be governed by a healthy sympathy for that was reasonable or desirable. In the case of Barrister-Judges, who had themselves practised at the Bar, the instincts of the old Advocate sometimes operated to cause the evolution of subtle distinctions which, becoming rulings, were often prospective of far-reaching consequence of evil,"[36] when the law as declared was contrary to previous practice, costum, or popular sentiment.[37]

Gave Birth to Cheap Practitioners.

The system gave birth to an annually increasing number of low class legal practitioners, a large number of whom were legal quacks, depending on the credulity of foolish litigants, and impeding, rather than assisting, the administration of justice.[38] "To have to enter a Court as principal in a civil case was a real misfortune for a Panjab peasant. It was an education in evil. "However honest and unsophisticated he might have been when he first breathed the contaminating atmosphere of the law, by the time his case was over. On entering the precincts of the Court, he soon became bewildered by the perversions his simple plaint or reply underwent when reduced to writing by a petition-writer, who would either personally coach him in the still more demoralising suggestions of the judicial tout.

This latter classes of practitioner either did business on his

---

36. Musalmans and Moneylenders in the Panjab-Thorburn, pp. 119-120, 191-195.
37. Panjab under War & Peace-Thorburn, p. 249.
38. Musalmans and Moneylenders in the Panjab-Thorburn, p. 134.

own account by coaching witnesses or explaining the "Law" to litigants, or else acted as a jackal to inferior pleaders.[39] Even if a winner, the litigant was often eventually ruined, the lawyer seeing to it that little of the sum, decreed him by the Court, ever actually reached his pocket. Litigation was, in fact, potent means for the benefit of the urban literati, and a frequent cause of indebtedness.

The Executive and the Judicial

The doctrinaire system which pervaded the law Courts, was not entirely without influence over the executive, being especially powerful in the Secretariat. Staffed mainly by brainy men, selected early in their service for a life of comparative ease in Lahore and Simla, despising the dust and heat of district life, the Secretariat became a fitting seedbed for the doctrines of 'laisses faire", the economic man, the survival of the fittest, the sanctity of contract, and the inherent right of every free man to be free to alienate his land, the Secretary was clever enough to confute the illogical rejoinders of protesting Deputy Commissioners every time.

The Economic Man.

They were economic men, competing with each other for things that had a cash value. Religions faith, family honour, and other similar relics of the past were gradually disappearing through education. The nearest approach to this economic ideal was to be found in the urban Hindu, whose single-minded pursuit to monetary values led him far under the new system. The peasant was more conservative. But there was nevertheless to be found in each village a number of economic men sufficient to break the old prestige of the committees of elders and to resolve the organic unity of the village community into that confused medley of warning atoms so believed of the doctrinaire.

Custom and the British Civil Code

Primitive custom had taught the peasant the wickedness of lying to his fellow villagers, but enlightened self-interest dis-

39. Musalmans and Moneylenders in the Panjab-Thorburn, pp. 130-131. The Panjab Peasant in Prosperity and Debt-Darling, pp. 76-78.

covered that a truthful case had no chance of success in the British Court. Judges of a later day, who compared about a cloud of false witnesses, complained bitterly of the lack of public spirit shown in the law Courts, did not always realise that was a direct result of the doctrinaire teachings of the nineteenth century. It was the system, not individuals that were to blame. The lawyer who, having taken a large fee from his client, deliberately delayed the case in order to extract more fees, was merely economic man aiming at the acquisition of wealth, by methods of enlightened self-interest.

The judge, who disregarded common sense on technical grounds, or who overrode the law in the interest of justice by special pleading was only trying to make the best of legal system, preserved in England by Wig politicians for political ends and then trasplanted to entirely alien surroundings at the other end of the globe.[40]

Punjab Customary Law

In the Panjab, the English legal system was seen at its worst in its interpretation of the local customary law. Even in the more Brahminised provinces large bodies of indigenous custom had grown up independently of the codified law as expounded in Man and commentators.[41] In the pre-British Panjab, custom prevailed in agricultural areas, Hindu & Muslim codified law being only followed in the towns; and the Panjab Law Act definitely laid down that in social relations the binding rule of decision should be custom.[42] What the custom actually might be was left to the Courts to determine. The underlying principles of tribal custom were simple enough. Succession to hereditary property followed the agnatic rule within the wider kindred but in default of agnatic within the wider hindered any one with a show of right, e.g. a daughter, a place of an adopted son might inherit.

Provision was also made for the maintenance of helpless dependents, such as widows, children, and unmarried daughters. There were slight local or tribal modifications due to the influence of the religious codes or local customs, e.g. Muslims tended

40. Commonsense in Law—Vinogradoff, p. 138.
41. Land of the Five-Rivers-Trevaskis, pp. 13-14, 23-27.
42. Doctor of Muslim jurisprudence.

to favour daughters and Hindus adopted sons. But generally speaking the custom was such that a Roman Proctor, an imperial jurisprudent, a Muslim Qazi, or one of Napoleon's legal commissioners wold have found no difficulty in smoothing on the rugged edges and presenting the world with something which could be understood by an ordinary men of intelligence but the Punjab Chief Court not only emphasised and exaggerated all the distinctions which already existed, but gave the sanctity of rulings to purely adventitious and fortuitous differences:

"There is no doubt" (quoth one Judge) "a general tendency of the stronger to override the weak. In such cases the Court must be careful and refuse to uphold rights which have ceased to exist."[43] As a result chaos reigned supreme. A strong son-in-law armed with an unscrupulous counsel and a brazened batch of false withnesses might get a ruling that a daughter could succeed against near collaterals, and such a ruling might form a basis of further rulings encroaching on the agnatic principle. A further element of uncertainty was introduced by the susceptible personal equation of certain Judges who were known to favour daughters.

Eventually it became as impossible to forecast whether the agnatic principle would, or would not, be followed in a particular case, as to predict the result of a horse race. A similar uncertainty grew up as to when tribal custom was be followed instead of Hindu or Muslim law. In one instance a large estate[44] went to rack and ruin for nearly fifty year (1872-1921) while the Chief Court were deciding whether its owners followed the Muslim law or agricultural custom, it not being worth any one's while to keep the buildings in repair till the question of ownership was decided.

The paralysing effects of the uncertainty incidental to English legal method was pointed out a century earlier by the utilitarian Bentham. "On the question what the law is, so long as the rule of action is kept in the state of common, alias unwritten,

---

43. Panjab Administration Report of 1893. Quoted in Elis's Notes on Panjab Custom (Lahore, Civil and Military Gazette Press p. 54.)
44. Kharkhauda, in the Rohtak District. The family, which dated from Mughal times, possessed many old historic buildings, all of which fell into ruins during the litigation. The case is described in the Lahore Civil and Military Gazette of 10th November, 1921.

alias imaginary law, authority is everything. The question is what on a given occasion a (the Judge) is likely to think; wait till your fortune has been spent in the inquiry, and you will know; but for as much as it is naturally a man's wish to be able to give a guess as to what the result will eventually be, before he has spent his fortune, he applies, through the medium of B(an attorney) for an opinion to C(a counsel) who, considering what D(a former Judge) has said or been supposed to say, deduces there from his guess as to what when the time comes, judge A, he thinks, will say.[45] "The same vagueness is characteristic of most English law books, where the mass of information conveyed is so great that "frequently the wood cannot be seen for the trees".[46]

Mystification is the peculiar characteristic of English law as distinguished from the legal systems of the Continent, which derived from the logical Roman system, are readily comprehensible to a man of ordinary intelligence.[47] But even in England efforts were made to limit the element of uncertainty as far as possible, it being recognised "that it is not only important to find the right solution of legal problems, but also to keep to solutions once obtained in order not to confuse the public and the legal profession. Indeed it has been said with some exaggeration that in law certainty is more important than justice."[48] Thus in England before a custom could have validity it had to be shown to be both certain and continuous; and besides these elementary requirements, it must have had on existence from immemorial times.[49]

But in the Panjab Custom ,as interpreted in the Courts, "need not necessarily be ancient or invariable. As the legal convictions of the community change, those changes "must from time to time be recognised and recorded in the courts".[50] No reliance could be placed on the Courts upholding previous rulings if false witnesses could prove that custom had changed.

---

45. Bentham, VIII, p. 397
46. Lord Riddell in John o' London's Weekly, 15th March, 1924.
47. Village Communities in East & West-Maine, pp. 59-60.
48. Commonsense in Law—Vinogradoff, pp. 176-77.
49. Commonsense in Law-Vinogradoff. p. 154
50. Notes on Panjab Custom, Lahore, Civil and Military Gazette Press Ellis, pp. 5-6

Matrimonial Cases

This uncertainty was particularly unfortunate in its application to the marriage relations of a people with tribal notions of family honour. "For thirty years subsequent to annexation the rule of the Panjab Courts was, that, until consummation, the breach of marriage" contract between infants entered into by guardians entitled the aggrieved party to compensation only, as in the case of a breach of betrothal.

In 1879 the legality of the practice was challenged and fought up to the Chief Court, which ruled on the "principle, that an infant marriage was binding until lawful divorce by the husband on attaining his majority". This new departure was the cause of widespread demoralisation, as the following instance will show. "In 1876 a boy of ten was 'married' to a young woman, who soon after induced her boy-husband's mother—his surviving guardian—to give her a divorce, whereupon the girl married her lover and had a family by him. In 1884 the original boy-husband, now a man, informed of the ruling of 1872, sued for restitution of conjugal rights, and obtained a decree. As the woman declined to live with him, he sought to execute his decree by imprisoning her for refusing, and charged her illegal husband, the father of her children, with adultery. In all his proceedings, the law was with him, both father and mother of the children had been guilty of aultery, and the children were bastards. Thus, by the ruling of 1870 not only was an approved practice of lang standing upset, but confusion was created in family relations all over the province."

"Again in 1884 a young Muslim lady was married to a suitable husband, also a Muslim. A few months afterwards she verted to Christianity, and refused to live with her husband. The subordinate courts decreed him what is called restitution of conjugal rights, but the Chief Court ruled that as by verting she had 'DE FACTO' apostatised and quasi-balasphemed the Prophet, she had therefore ceased to be a wife from the day she had changed her faith.

Comments

Comment on the absurdity of such a decision is hardly need-

51. Panjab under War & Peace-Thorburn, pp. 250-51.

ed, especially when it is remembered that the prophet licensed the marriages of the faithful with Jews and Christians, and that under the Muslim law blasphemers were put to death by storing.[52] "The consequence of a criminal ruling were even more disastrous to domestic relationships. "The Chief Court held that in cases of offences against married women, such as adultery and abduction, unless marriage were preliminary admitted or proved the charge could not be sustained. Thenceforth, as the accused, when sophisticated, or defended by a lawyer, invariably denied the fact of marriage, and proof, when possible was a costly and lengthy affairs, aggrieved husbands, failing to obtain justice from the Courts, were forced to take the law into their own hands a proceeding prolific in offences of violence, and at the root of a large percentage of the cases of murder, arson and other mischief in the Province."[53]

Records of Custom Prepared by Revenue Authorities

In the meantime the revenue authorities made a partially successful attempt to straighten out the middle by preparing records of local and tribal custom. These were started in 1864 by Prinsep who "also requested his Settlement Officers to draw up tehsil records embodying the 'LEXLOCI' on certain important matters connected with agriculture, such, as the planting and cutting of trees and the rights and privileges of new cultivators".

His object was two-fold, to lighten the settlement record by setting forth finally for whole tribes and for wide tracts of country customs which had hit her to been entered in the record for each estate, and to collect information which would be of use to the Courts in the administration of justice.[54]

With the suppression of the Panjab Civil Code increased attention was paid to the compilation of records of tribal custom at the time of settlement. It was "provided that where the customs regulating particular relations were common to the whole tribe or to a group of villages, they might be collected into

---

52. Musalmans and Moneylenders in the Panjab-Thorburn, p. 120.
53. Musalmans & Moneylenders in the Panjab, Thorburn, p. 121.
Panjab under War & Peace—Thorburn, pp. 248-249.
54. Panjab Settlement Manual—James Douie, p. 561.

tribal" statements. Two sets of questions were drawn up, one dealing with tribal customs, regulating social relations, and the other with local agrarian customs.[55] Unfortunately no presumption of truth attached to such a record of custom. "But if the record of tribal custom had evidently been prepared after careful enquiry ,and especially if the answers were fortified by the quotation of precedents, Courts of Justice might be expected to treat the replied recorded as valuable evidence.[56] "Unfortunately, however, the weight actually attached to these records was not sufficient to give any apreciable measure of stability or certainty to Panjab customary law.[57]

55. Rivaj-i-Am.
56. Settlement Manual-James Douie-p. 566.
57. The Land of the Five Rivers—Trevaskis, pp. 290-306.

7

PANJAB DURING 1932-1941

1. Sikandar Hayat Khan-1932

Sikandar Hayat Khan was born on June 5, 1892 and was educated at M.A.O. College Aligarh. He further joined University College, London. He got his Commission in the Indian Army and was posted to 2/67th Punjabis, later known as 1/2nd Punjabis. He first served on the North-West Frontier Province and then in the Third Afghan War. He was appointed to the Brigade Headquarters and was the First Indian to Command a Company on active service. He also served as Recruiting Officer.

He returned to the Panjab Legislature Council by land holders constituency. He was taken as non-official member of Police Enquiry Commission in 1926 and Personal Assistance to Mela Officer during Prince of Wales' visit. He was elected by the Panjab Council to the Provincial Simon Commission, which elected him as its Chairman. He was connected with the Board of 11 Companies including Messers Owin Roberts, the Panjab Portland Cement Co.; Wah Stone and Lime Company; North India Constitutions-1 Engineers and the Frontier Mining Syndicates.

He was appointed the Revenue Member of the Panjab Government, in 1929 for three months and became permanent Revenue Member in 1930. He was appointed as Acting-Governor of the Panjab from July to October, 1932. He was awared the title of M.B.E., in 1920, and E.B.E. in 1933.

2. Sir G.F. De Montmorency—1932-33.

Account of his life and works has already been given in Capter No. XI.

3. Sir H.W. Emerson—1933-1938.

Sir Harbert William Emerson, was born on June 1, 1881. He was educated in the Calday Grange Grammar School, and Magdalne College Cambridge. He entered the Indian Civil Service in 1905 and acted as the Manager of the Panjab in 1917. After this, he was appoointed Secretary to Government Finance Department in 1926; Chief Secretary to Panjab Government from 1927 to 1928; Secretary to Government of India, Home Department from 1930-32. He assumed charge as the Governor of the Panjab on April 13, 1933 and was awarded titles of G.C.I.E.; K.C.; S.I. C.B.E. He governed this province from 1934 to 1938.

4. Sir H. D. Craik 1938-1941

Sir Henry Duffield Craik was born on January 2, 1876 and was educated at Eton and Oembroke College, Oxford. He entered the Indian Civil Service as Settlement Officer in the Panjab in 1899. He acted as Sessions Judge and Secretary to the Governor-General of India; Home Department from 1919 to 1922. He was appointed the Chief Secretary of the Panjab from 1922 to 1927 and was appointed the Commissioner in 1927. He was appointed Member of the Panjab Executive Council in 1934, where he worked as such till 1934. After this, he was appointed Home Member of the Governor-General, Executive Council from 1934 to 1938. He assumed the charge of the Governor of the Panjab in April 1938 till 1941. He was awarded the title of Bart; K.C.S.I.

Government of India Act, 1935

During the Thirties of the twentieth century many radical changes occurred in the general set-up of the Panjab history. Under the Government of India Act, 1919, partial responsibility was introduced in the Provinces. The Act of 1935 made a clear advance in this direction. The whole of the Provincial Executive was now made responsible to or removable by the Legislative Assembly of the Province. The difference between the reserved and the transferred subjects was dropped. All Provincial subjects were placed under the charge of popular Ministers.

Provincial Autonomy Crippled

However, this did not mean that the Provincial Autonomy, as actually granted by the Act, was genuine or complete. It was crippled by many limitations. There were many things which the Provincial Legislature could not do. The Governors were given an imposing set of powers, which were inconsistent with the spirit of the Provincal Autonomy. In fact the framers of the Act intended the Provincial Autonomy to work in collusion with the Autonomy of the Governors, which was impossible as a practical proposition.

The Provincial List

Those subjects which were of common interest for the whole of India and demanded a uniform treatment were included in the Federal List, which contained 59 items. Subjects which were mostly of Provincial interest and about which uniformity of treatment throughout India was not essential were placed in the Provincial List, which included 54 items, out of which the important ones were:—

"Public order, justice and courts, police, prisons, public debt of the province, provincial public services, public health and sanitation, education, communications, water supply, irrigation and canals, agriculture, land tenures, agricultural loans, forests, mines and fisheries in the province, unemployment and poor relief, co-operative societies, land revenue, taxes on agrcultural income, taxes on profession and trades and stamps duties."

The Concurrent List

A third list was also drawn, which contained items which though primarily of provincial interest, yet could require a uniform treatment or policy throughout India. This was called the Concurrent List. It contained 36 subjects, some of which were: criminal law and criminal procedure, civil procedure, evidence and oaths, marriage and divorce, adoption, wills, intestacy and succession, registration of deeds and documents, trusts, contracts, arbitration, bankruptcy, newspapers, books and printing presses, prevention of cruelty to animals, jurisdiction and powers of courts in these matters, factories and labour welfare, old age pensions, unemployment insurance, trade unions, industrial and labour disputes, animals and plants and electricity.

Discretion of the Governor

Ministers were appointed by the Governor in his discretion. He could also dismiss them. But, in practice, he was bound to call the leader of the majority party in the legislative assembly to become the Chief Minister and to name the remaining Ministers. Hence this power of appointment or the dismissal of Ministers was more or less formal. The appointment and dismissal of Ministers followed the usual parliamentary method, except in extraordinary cases. The Governor was given the power to preside over the Provincial Cabinet in his discretion. The Ministers, and especially the Secretaries, were expected to keep the Governor informed regarding the course of the administration especially in those matters where a special responsibility was placed on the Governor.

Powers With Regard To Police Department

The Governor was given special powers to control the Police Department in the Province. This was deemed necessary in the interest of law and order. The Governor was to approve all Police Regulations in his individual judgment. He was also given the power to lay down that Police secrets would not be disclosed except in a manner and to the authority decided by him.

Powers With Regard To Services

It was a special responsibility of the Governor to safeguard the legitimate interests of the Services. They were to be protected against any injustice done to them. No action against a member of Superior Services could be taken, except with the approval of the Governor, which he was to give in his individual judgment. The postings and transfers of keymen, like the Deputy Commissioners, were to be decided in his individual judgment.

Legislative Powers

The Governor had the power to summon and to prorogue the Legislative Houses of Provinces. He could dissolve the Lower House in his discretion. His assent was necessary to every Bill before it became a Law. He could send a Bill for reconsideration. He could reserve it for the consideration of the Governor-General and his Majesty's Government. He could stop the discussion of any Bill, Resolution, Adjournment Motion or an answer to a question, if he considered such a course necessary for the proper discharge of his special responsibilities. He could call a joint sitting of the Houses to iron out differences between them. Most of these powers were to be exercised in his discretion.

Failure Of The Constitutional Machinery

Section 93 of the Act gave the Governors the power to declare the Failure of the Constitutional machinery, in the Provinces. It was provided that whenever the Governor was satisfied that a situation had arisen in which the Government of the Province could not be carried on in accordance with the provisions of the Act of 1935, he might, by proclamation, declare that his functions would, to such an extent, as might be specified in the proclamation, be exercised by him in his discretion and assume to himself all or any of the powers vested or exercisable by any Provincial body or authority. Any such proclamation might contain such incidental and consequential provisions, as might appear to him necessary for giving effect to the object of the proclamation. He could not, however, assume to himself any of the powers of the High Court of the Province. nor he could suspend any provision of the Act relating to the High Court.

Such a proclamation required to be communicated to the Secreary of State and was to be laid before both the Houses of the Parliament. Its operation was limited to six months, unless approved by resolutions of both the Houses of the Parliament; in which case it would continue for a further period of twelve months from the date it would have ceased to operate. But such a proclamation could, in no case, remain in force for more than three years. Such a proclamation was to be made by the Governor in his discretion and with the concurrence of the Governor-General.

The Repercussions

The Indian National Congress rejected the Government of India Act of 1935, because of the powers of intervention given to Governors in the provinces and the Diarchy in the Centre. It resolved to capture power and then destroy the constitution. The Muslim League followed suit but reserved the right to try out the provincial scheme "for what it was worth". The princes who had shown much alacrity in accepting federation got cold feet when they realised it would mean surrendering some of their "sovereignty". Sikh political parties had already condemned the communal award; they added their voice to the chorus of denunciation. For all practical purposes, the Government of India Act of 1935 was a still-born child.

Allocation Of Seats

According to the Act 1935, the Panjab Legislative Assembly was allotted 175 seats with the following allocation:—

General Seats	42
Seats reserved for Scheduled Castes	8
Sikh	31
Muslims	84
Anglo-Indians	1
Europeans	1
Indian Christians	2
Commerce, Industry, Mining, Planting	1
Landholders	5
Universities	1
Labour	3

Seats for women:

General	1
Sikh	1
Muslim	2

First Panjab Elections

The first elections under the new Act were held in the winter of 1936-37. The Sikhs had the choice of backing either the Congress or the Unionists. They rejected both; the Congress because of its predominantly anti-Sikh Arya Samaj leadership; the Unionists because, despite of their championing the cause of an the agriculturists,[1] their primary interest was the Musalman Jat; the Sikh and Hindu Jat was of secondary importance They could have formed alliances with one or the other political party, but none of the leaders had the foresight or the following to do so. Instead they split their forces into the Akali and the anti-Akali group (known as the Khalsa National Party), both

1. Which found favour in the eyes of Sikh Agriculturists.

of minor importance in provincial affairs and of none whatsoever on the national scene.

The Congress Lost Majority In The Panjab

In all provinces except Bengal, Sindh and the Panjab, the Indian National Congress swept the polls. Its poorest performance was in the Panjab, where it got a bare 10 per cent of the vote. Out of the total of 175 seats, the Unonists won 96 and the Khalsa Nationalist Party won 20, the rest were shared by the Congress, Muslim League, Communists, and Independents[2].

The Unionist Ministry—1937

Sir Sikandar Hayat Khan was called out by the Governor to form his ministry, which consisted of the following members:—

Panjab Ministry—1937-44

1. Sir Sikandar Hayat Khan—Premier
1. Sir Sunder Singh Majithia—Revenue Minister
3. Sir Chhotu Ram—Development Minister
4. Mr. Manohar Lal—Finance Minister
5. Major Khizar Hayat Khan Tiwana—Public Works Minister
6. Mian Abdul Haye—Education Minister

Principal Officers Of the Panjab Legislative Assembly

1. Chaudhari Shihab-ud-Din—Speaker
2. Sardar Dasondha Singh—Deputy Speaker
3. Sardar Bahadur Abnasha Singh—Secretary
4. Khan Sahib Hakim Ahmad Shuja—Asstt. Secretary

Sir Sikandar Hayat Khan chose his cabinet of three Muslims, two Hindus, and one Sikh. The rural-Jat majority was in evidence as before; of the six Ministers only one of the Hindus Mr. Manohar Lal was an urban non-agriculturist.[3] In 1937 Sardar Bahadur Sardar Buta Singh was replaced by Sardar Dasondha Singh.

The Unionist Ministry did not have an easy time. War with Hitlerite Germany and the increased tempo of the Nationalist

2. The Partition of India—Philips, p. 417.
3. Pioneer, October 15 and 17, 1937.

Movement indicated a change in the political barometer. People knew India would soon be free; but who woud be master of the Panjab whether the Muslims, the Sikhs or the Hindus.

Rapproachement Between Jinnah and Sikander

Jinnah wanted to oust Sir Sikander Hayat Khan from the Panjab but the other Muslim leaders told Mr. Jinnah to have cordial relations with the Panjab Muslim Chief Minister. Ahmad Yar Khan Daultana was one of such leaders who wanted to establish good relations between Mr. Jinnah and the Premier of the Panjab, Sir Sikandar Hayat Khna. Even the Secretary of the Unionist Party, Ahmad Yar Khan Daultana, who called himself one of the 'ardent Jinnahites' tried to bring about a settlement and submitted to Jinnah a list of members to be elected on the League Council adding: "All these are your men against the whole world." After the failure of the League-Unionist negotiations, Ahmad Yar Khan Daultana, once again approached Jinnah, as 'You have millions of admirers in this world but I can assure you that few will come up to my standard of devoted loyalty and profound admiration.'

Daultanà assured Jinnah that like himself, Sir Sikandar Hayat Khan was also 'a great admirer of his leadership, statesmanship and his other unique qualities.' "I feel it will be very unfortunate if there is any hostility between two parties in which you and Sir Muhammad Iqbal are on one side and Sir Sikandar Hayat Khan and myself on the other. I am writing to Sir Sikandar Hayat Khan to have talk with you and to try to come to a working settlement. Let us have minor difference of opinion but it should be far from hostility or ill-will to each other."

Sikandar's Efforts To Reconcile Jinnah

The Unionist group in the Panjab led by Sir Sikandar Hayat Khan joined the League. Immediately after his return from Lucknow, Sikandar wrote to Jinnah: 'You will be glad to learn that enrolment of the League members is going apace and we hope to be able to set ùp district Leagues throughout the province in a short space of time.

"I have instructed all the Unionist Muslim Members to start enrolling Muslims in their ilaqas and I am receiving very promising and satisfactory reports from the various parts of the province. On the whole, the development at Lucknow which brought about the solidarity of the Muslims throughout India was welcomed by the Muslim masses......The Lucknow session gave fresh strength to the League and the unity which Jinnah aspired to was partly achieved within about a year of his launching the programme.[4]

The British Government Backed The Unionists

Particularly in an area like the Panjab the British Government were in no mood to allow an urban politician like Jinnah to disturb the countryside from where they had drawn a major portion of their army. In order to maintain support in these areas, the British had relied heavily on the influence of the landed gentry and the power of the Deputy Commissioners. As stated earlier, in 1932 Jinnah complained of those 'spineless' Muslim leaders who would consult the Deputy Commissioner before extending their support to him.

The British had given support to Unionist leaders like Sir Fazl-i-Hussain to consolidate their position in the Panjab. Instead of dividing the people of Panjab into rival groups of Hindus, Muslims and Sikhs, the British had viewed with favour the emergence of the Unionist Party which had brought within its fold Hindu, Muslim and Sikh peasants and landowners beloinging to the Jat and Rajput tribes. Panjabi soldiers, who constituted half of the British Indian army, came from these rural classes.

Thus, one could see that the British disliked the idea of these classes being drawn into the maelstorm of either Indian agitational politics or the purely communal pull of the Muslim League. When Jinnah started reorganising the Muslim League in early 1935, Fazl-i-Husain sent word to him that he should keep 'his finger out of the Panjab pie'.[5] The pro-British Aga Khan, leader of the Khoja Community in India, lent his financial support to the Unionist Party and not to Jinnah's Muslim League.

---

4. Pioneer, October 15 and 17, 1937.
5. Azim Husain, Fazl-i-Husain (1946), p. 309.

Mian Sir Fazl-i-Husain

Sir Fazl-i-Husain was the greatest Unionist who wanted to unite all the communities of the Panjab. He was much above the communal bias. As long as he remained alive Muhammad Ali Jinnah could not catch any strength, whatsoever, in this province. He was so dynamic personality among the people, that the communal bodies always suffered a set-back in the Panjab. A brief sketch of his works and achievements is given below:—

Sir Fazl-i-Husain's death on the 9th July, 1936 had shocked the whole of the Panjab. Several meetings in the Panjab and elsewhere were held to give expression to the sense of sorrow that had prevailed. The most notable of these occasions was the memorial meeting in Simla held on July 14, 1936, at whcih His Excellency, the Governor, paid an eloquent tribute to the memory of the late statesman.

Sir Fazl-i-Husain became a member of the Council of the Governor-General of India and was at the time of his death a Minister of the Crown in the Panjab. He was a Minister in the Panjab and later a member of Council.

His colleagues had many opportunities of gaining an insight into his great capacity for affairs, his skill in debate and in the handling of men, his tireless industry and above all his whole-hearted devotion to his country. With this devotion he had very marked characteristics of an active sympathy with the more backward classes of the population. He was an impartial observer. He found his co-religionists backward in education, he set himself to improve their opportunities. He found the Zamindars of the province subject to a land revenue law which set no limit to the assessment that could be placed upon their lands.

He succeeded in getting fixed in the Panjab Land Revenue Amendment Act of 1928, a limit which was half the previous nominal limit. This Act was the most conspucious of his achievements in the Legislative Council. Another of his conspicuous achievement was the Panchayat Act which was believed to be the ideal one. Another instance of his achievement in the uplift of his own cuntrymen was the proposal to start model villages with educated youngmen with the object of raising the standard of life in the villages generally.

This proposal crystallized in what were known as the "educated chaks" in the extension of the Lower Chenab Canal Colony. Further development of this policy occurred when a start was made with the selection of 60 graduates with the object of putting them upon the land. It was originally to Sir Fazl-i-Husain that we owe the idea of these educated chaks or of putting graduates upon the land with the object of raising the village life of the province generally.

However ,there is no time to dilate upon the details of his achievements. As was said in the Press at the time of his death, his was a dynamic personality which dominated the Panjab for more than fifteen years, and while he was a Minister and later member of the Government, none of the acts of legislature or of Government failed to bear traces of his strong personality. Before concluding it should be referred to his great courage which enabled him to work longer hours and with greater vigour than most other men in spite of severe handicap of a delicate constitution and practically constant ill-health.

It was this lion-hearted courage coupled with his strong sense of public duty that led him to accept the Governor's invitation to take up the portfolio of education shortly before his death, when his health must have been failing and spirit must have been longing for rest. As His Excellency said it was a tragedy that he should not have been spared to help India along the next stage of constitutional Government.

Sir Fazl-i-Husain left us at a time when his great capacity for managing men, his clear insight into the essentials of a problem, his great influence over the people of the province were most needed. Mian Sir Fazl-i-Hussain's death at that critical juncture in the history of the province was indeed a great calamity. The people lost in him a great parliamentarian, a far-sighted administrator and a forceful leader. As leader of the House and as a Minister and a member of the Panjab Government, he had left permanent land marks of progress and policy and so long as Panjab continued to honour its great men and patriots, Sir Fazl-i-Husain's name will live for ever in the Panjab and his country.[6]

The Muslim League's performance in Panjab as already

6. Panjab Legislative Council, Dated October 20, 1936, p. 6.

narrated n the provincial.elections for 1937 was extremely poor. But Jinnah succeeded in making the best of these adverse circumstances. Sir Sikandar Hyat Khan, the Unionist Premier, joined the Muslim League and a pact known as the Sikandar-Jinnah pact was concluded between the two parties. When some Muslim League members complained that this alliance had damaged the prestige of the Muslim League in the Panjab, Jinnah was reported to have assured them that while agreeing with his objective of building Muslim solidarity, he had to devise the best possible means in the short-run to achieve the long term objective. Jinnah wrote, "I want to pull them (Muslim) up step by step and before making them run I want to be sure that they are capable of standing on their own legs."[7]

Sikander's Nominal Allegiance to the League

Sir Sikandar Hyat Khan owed nominal allegiance to Mr. Jinnah but by and large he followed the policies of the Unionist party established by Sir Mian Fazl-i-Hussain and Chaudhuri Chhotu Ram as a joint front of rural interests against the Congress, the Muslim League and the Urban Intelligensia.

To summarise the whole affair it can be mentioned that in 1938, Sir Sikandar Hyat Khan speaking at a dinner in honour of Sir Henry Craik, Governor of the Panjab, offered to place service of the martial classes of the Panjab at the disposal of Britain in case she was involved in a war. On the 4th of December, 1938, All-India Muslim League had laid down that no responsible member of the Muslim League shall make any pronouncement on this question. But although Sir Sikandar Hyat Khan was present in that meeting, so lately as 25th August, 1939, barely two or three days before the meeting of the Council of the All-India Muslim League Council at Delhi, Sir Sikandar Hyat had reiterated the same offer only in a stronger form.

Sayyed Muhammad Ali Rishidi's resolution, therefore, recounted all these facts and asked the Council in these circumstances to place on record its sense of regret at "Sir Sikandar Hyat Khan's statement on the question relating to war does in no way represent the views of the Muslims of India. Sir Raza Ali moved an amendment to this resolution which stated "that the opinion

---

7. Dawn, December 25, 1955.

and sentiments expressed by Sir Sikandar Hyat Khan in his statement to the press on August 25, 1939 in no way represent the views of the Muslims of India."[8]

Khan Bahadur Ahmad Yar Khan Daultana and other Unionist Muslim members voted against the amendment but the amendment was passed as a substantial resoultion, because Syyed Ali Muhammad Rishidi withdrew his own resolution and Mr. Fazal-ul-Haq supported the amendment.[9] In this way the Jinnah Muslim League began to grow day by day, while Sir Sikandar Hyat's League began to dwindle. But he was so capable and popular leader that during his time the Muslim League, opposed to Sir Sikandar Hyat Khan could not establish its hold on the Panjab politics.

Sir Sikandar Hyat Khan, however, was forming his counter Muslim League. He was a liberal Muslim who wanted to accommodate the interests of all the communities of the Panjab. But the validity of the new Muslim League with Sir Sikandar Hyat Khan, as President, formed at his house, was questioned Malik Barkat Ali. The question of the affiliation of the League came up before the working committee of the Jinnah Muslim League which was then meeting at Delhi in February, 1940. Apart from other things Malik Barkat Ali raised the legal question of the validity of the new League at Delhi on August 29, 1939, adopted a resolution to the affect that "if the Panjab Muslim League was not organised by November, 15, 1939, the organising committee of the Panjab Muslim League shall stand automatically dissolved."

Malik Barkat Ali pointed out that the organising committee failed to organise the provincial Muslim League by November 14, and the Committee was dissolved. The formation of the new Muslim League and the election of office-bearers on January 10, 1940 was, therefore, illegal. Mr. Barkat Ali in a long letter to Mr. Jinnah appealed to him not to tender further to the ambition

---

8. A correspondent in the Statesman pointed out that in his appeal at the recent meeting of the Muslim League at Bombay Sir Sikandar Hyat Khan had urged his co-religionists to unite and thus win over the rule of India as their forefathers had done. This had created amusement in some and irritation in others. (The Daily Tribune, Lahore, July 20, 1939).
9. The Daily Tribune, Lahore, September 4, 1939.

of Sir Sikandar Hyat Khan and thus wreck the Muslim League in the Panjab. The question was serious because the next session of the Muslim League was to come off at Lahore in March next. And it was inadvisable to have two rival parties of the League in the Provinces where the Annual session was being held.[10]

The Sikhs and the Muslim League

The Sikhs were also making vigorous efforts in the Western Districts of the United Provinces at organising their forces and establishing Sikh Centres. On April 16, 1940, two or three subsequent days they held the first U.P. Sikh Conference. Master Tara Singh, President Shiromani Gurdwara Prabandhak Committee, Amritsar presided. In the course of his presidential address he also referred to the Pakistan scheme of the Muslim League and said that the Sikhs were greatly agitated over it. "If we are opposed to the English rule", he said, "we shall certainly oppose the Muslim rule".

Master Tara Singh made it clear that none should except the Sikhs to meekly yield to such a wild demand. He regretted that in opposing the Pakistan scheme some Sikhs have lost their heads and were preaching the establishment of Sikh rule, such a step would simply add to the confusion that had already been created by the Muslim League.

Whatever the Muslim League might say they had dealt a blow at their aspirations for Swaraj. It was the country's misfortune. He had, however, hoped that the Muslims of India would repudiate the decisions of the Muslim League. But if the Muslims agreed with the Pakistan, resolution of the League, it would be the beginning of a declaration of Civil War. He will call the proposal as being nothing short of madness. Speaking for the Sikhs he said they wanted Swaraj and nothing but Swaraj. They did not want Sikh rule. They would oppose every form of communal or foreign rule. "If the Muslims of the Muslim League mentality will make an effort to establish their rule, they will have to cross an ocean of the Sikh Blood.[11] He appealed to every Muslim not to be carried away by the 'fantastic dreams of their

---

10. The Daily Tribune, Lahore, February 2, 1940.
11. Chikha Sare Sikhan di Ravi te pahlan Jalegee,
Pher Jinnah had teri Pakistan banegee.

impractical leaders and play the role of enemies of Swaraj at the very moment when Swaraj appears to be in sight".[12]

Referring to the Sikh States, he regretted that the British Government was now installing upon the Nabha 'Gaddi' a 'patit'. The Sikhs were now feeling the revival of religious sentiments amongst themselves. They had now made up their mind to make another effort to save the Sikh States. They did not know why a Sikh Prince could not be deposed "When be becomes 'Patit' by cutting his sacred hairs."

Master Tara Singh also appealed for recognition of the Sikh community's rights as a minority community in the U.P. where not a single seat had been allotted to them. He pointed out that the number of Sikhs in United Provinces had "substantially increased" during the past four years and was daily increasing. In conclusion he referred to the great changes that were imminent in the world and they might be called upon any moment to serve the cause of humanity. This they would only be able to do it. "This strength can be acquired only by following the dictates of our religion. Become Sikhs and devout Sikhs, and the Guru will bless you with strength which our forefathers possessed".

The Khalistan Scheme

As a counter-blast to the Muslim League Pakistan scheme some Sikh leaders had put forward what they called "The Khalistan Scheme". A representative meeting of Sikhs was held at Amritsar on Sunday, May 20, 1940 attended by about 125 leading Sikhs. This meeting was independent of Master Tara Singh's Akali Party. The meeting decided to establish Guru Raj Khalsa Darbar in order to give practical shape to the Khalistan scheme. The chief object of the new organisation was to strive to establish an independent Sikh State from Jamna to Jamrud, to establish two other independent Sikh States in Takht Sri Hazur Sahib (Hyderabad State) and Takht Sri Patna Sahib to protect the Sikh shrines, to secure the return of Maharaja Gurcharan Singh to the throne of Nabha, and to reform the management of Sikh trust properties under the Sikh rule. They claimed to rule the whole of the Panjab from the Jamuna to the Jamrud and in support of this claim they said that it was from the Sikhs that the British

12. The Daily Tribune, Lahore, April 16, 1940.

took over the Panjab at the time of the Annexation in 1849. A meeting of the Raj-Khalsa Board was held on Wednesday night May 23, 1940 under the Presidentship of Sardar Gopal Singh Gargaj. At this meeting certain questions connected with the scheme of pushing forward the Khalistan project and setting up of "an Independent Sikh State" were discussed. A Working Committee of the Board consisting of half a dozen men was formed with the object of framing constitution of the Raj Khalsa Darbar Board, establishing its branches in various places and securing the support of different Sikh parties for the Khalistan scheme. It was also decided that the members of this party should participate in the All-India Akali and All-India Sikh Conferences[13] to be held in Lahore, as well as to fix the dates of the Raj Khalsa Conference to be held at Amritsar with the object of giving practical shape to the Khalistan scheme.

The Second World War—1939-1945

Five M.L.A's, it is pointed out, had already been in Jail on charges of sedition, and one, namely Sohan Singh Josh, for waging war against the King in the well-known Meerut conspiracy case, while Harjan Singh had been a prisoner, under regulation III of 1918. It was much to be regretted that in thus rounding up "the Reds", the Unionist Ministry was bringing these men into prominence which would certainly, enhance their claim to the leadership of masses. The Panjab Government claimed that in making these arrests they were inspired by the determination not to let subversive activities endanger the internal securities of the provinces. Abdullah Safder was one of those arrested on Thursday, the 27th June, 1940, that he managed to escape from the Dwelmandi thana. Mr. Ram Chandra was another of the arrested persons.

Even the student community had not been spared Mr Rajbans Krishan, prominent member of the Lahore students Union, was also taken into custody. The student community took prompt action to enter a vigorous protest against the arrest of their comrade, whose only fault was, so far as one could see, that he was one of the most farward from amongst the student community in organising processions and meetings of students.

---

13. The Daily Tribune, Lahore, May 22, 1940.

Political Unrest

The Lahore students organised a protect meeting with Nawabzada Mazhar Ali, a nephew of the Panjab Premier himself, in the Chair. Chaudhri Krishan Gopal Dutt, Dr. Satyapal observed that was the most opportune moment for creating a delicate situation for the Panjab Government. He laid particular stress on the necessity of cutting a political programme before the masses of the Panjab. He was of the-opinion that "Charkha" alone would not succeed in dethroning Sir Sikandar Hyat Khan from the ministerial Gaddi. The main resolution was moved from the Chair. In moving this resolution, Mr. Mazhar Ali entered a strong protest against the arrest of Mr. Rajbans Krishan, which he characterised as a wanton unprovoked attack on the Students Movement. He declared that the student community would accept the challenge. The following is the full text of the resolution.

"The meeting of the Lahore Student Union and the Panjab Students' Federation registers his services condemnation of Government for the arrest under the Defence of India Act of one of our leading student workers Rajbans Krishan. We consider this to be a wanton and unprovoked attack of the student movement. The fact that no charge is being made, shows that there is no proof in possession of the Government against our comrade. We demand from the Government that Rajbans Krishan be released forthwith or he be charged in open court."

This meeting wishes to draw the attention of the student Community in the province to the growing repression in the country and the attack on the academic and civil liberties of students launched by the Government Over 100 arrests of student leaders have been made all over the country in order to terrorise us and crush the movement.

"But to-day we stand united and determined to resist any onslaught of imperialism on our movement. We warn the Government that we will not tolerate this policy of vindictiveness and repression and no amount of terrorism will break our ranks. We stand united, firm and resolute for the achievement of our objective-freedom, peace, progress."

Two Tragic Events

Soon after followed two tragic events which changed the

complexion of the Panjab politics. The sudden death of Sir Sikandar Hyat Khan and the ghastly murder of Umar Allah Bakhsh removed two of Jinnah's strongest opponents.

A Mystery

Sir Sikandar was a force for sobriety and moderation and had successfully resisted Jinnah's attempts to capture the mind of the Muslim masses in the Panjab.

After the death of Sir Sikandar Hyat Khan, Khizar Hyat Khan assumed the office of Chief Minister. He made no major changes in the Council of Ministers of his predecessor. In 1944, two more ministers namely Sir Muhammad Jamal Khan Leghari and Nawab Ashiq Hussain assumed the charge of portfolios of Public Work and dismissal of Sardar Shauqat Hyat Khan Public Works Minister and letter newly created ministry.

Khizar Hyat Khan broadly followed his policies but lacked Sir Sikandar's experience and standing. Sir Sikandar had kept the bureaucracy under strict control and did not allow the civil servants, whether British or India, to meddle with politics. After Sir Sikandar's death, some members of the Indian Civil Service began to show an undue preference for the policy of the Muslim League. It had sometimes been said that the Muslim members of the Indian Civil Service did more to strengthen the League than any politician except Jinnah. This may be an exaggeration, but there is little doubt that these officers did play a role in securing Government support for the Muslim League in diverse ways. Their motives were often mixed. Some smarted from a sense of inferiority vis-a-vis some of their British and Hindu colleagues. Others felt that a Muslim state like Pakistan would be their domination, as most of them regarded themselves intellectually and morally superior to the politicians. Khizar Hyat Khan did his best to check these tendencies but he was only partially successful.

The murder of Allah Bakhsh had more serious consequences. The mystery of his death was never known. Many thought that his murder was due to a personal vendetta. Some attributed it to Allah Bakhsh, strong measures against the Hurs. Others thought that communal elements in Sind were disturbed by his growing strength and popularity. Nothing certain can be said as investigations were carried out in half-hearted manner even before the partition of the country. After the establishment of Pakistan, the matter gradually went out of the public mind. His assassination was in many case a great loss to the national forces of the Panjab. He had emerged as a bold and able leader from a Muslim majority province and many thought that he had the making of an all India leader who could have challenged Jinnah. The death in quick succession of Sir Sikandar Hyat Khan and Allah Bakhsh left the field open seemed to favour him.

During the tenure of the Unionist Ministry, the following Bills were passed.

1. The Panjab Unemployment Insurance Bill (Disallowed).
2. The Panjab Hours of Work Bill
3. The Panjab Health Insurance Bill
4. The Panjab District Boards (Amendment) bill
5. The Panjab Removal of Beggary Bill
6. The Panjab Land Revenue (Amendment) Bill
7. The Panjab Fixation of Minimum Rates of Wages Bill
8. The Panjab Anti-Phooka Bill
9. The Panjab and Small Towns Patrol (Amendment) Bill
10. The Panjab Municipal (Amendment) Bill
11. The Panjab Muslim Wuqaf Bill

THE KHAKSAR MOVEMENT

Invasion of Lahore

About five thousand Khaksars had surreptitiously arrived in Lahore from the North-West Frontier Province and the general public did not know the reason for their arrival." As happened immediately after the ban by the Panjab Government on quasi-military organisations in the province the incident lent itself to the belief that Allama-Mashriqi was in all probability going to defy the restrictive orders, as he did in the United Provinces some time previously.

The Muslim Press was practically unanimous of the view that the Khaksars will alienate their sympathies if they launch a campaign of civil disobedience.

The Khaksars intended to concentrate their forces on three fronts, namely, Lahore, Ambala and Attock. They did not follow the Congress method of non-violence in their civlī disobedience, but freely used the spade as their offensive and defensive weapon. A Khaksar leader was reported to have said to the representative of the Civil & Military Gazette, Lahore. "It will be a severe encounter and we are looking forward to it."[14]

Allama Mashriqi

Inayat Ullah Khan, notably known as Allama Mashriqi, the founder leader of Khaksar movement, was born on August 25, 1888 at Amritsar. After matriculating in 1902 he joined the Forman Christian College, Lahore, where he graduated in 1906. Next year he took his M.A. degree. He went to England and joined Cambridge University. Passing tripos examination in Mathematics from the University, with distinction, he passed another tripos examination in Persian and Arabic. He then took his B.Sc degree in Physics and a degree in mechanical science. He went to Paris and did also some distinguished work there.

Vice-Principal Islamia College, Peshawar

Returning to India in 1913, he was appointed the Vice-Principal of Islamia College at Peshawar. After some years his services were transferred to the Government of India as Under-Secretary in the Education Department. Reverting to his post in the Frontier Province he resigned in 1924. At Peshawar the Allama as he subsequently wished to be called came itno contact with Maulvi Muhammad Muslim Earuqi. Both were dynamic personalities and both were great admirers of the great pan-Islamic leader Maulana Sayyed Jamal-ud-Din Afghani.

Influenced by Jamal-Ud-Din Afghani

Allama Mashriqi was influenced by the writtings of Jamal-ud-Din Afghani. When the Khilafat agitation and the Hijrat movement were in full swing, Inayat Ullah was very much agitated. It was at this time that he wrote his book the 'Tazkira' which is a sort of commentary on Islam in the spirit of a modern enthusiastic Pan-Islamist. It presented the Quran in a new light and attracted a good deal of attraction far and wide.

Influenced by Hitler

In 1926 Inayat Ullah was invited to take part in the Khilafat

---

14. The Daily Tribune, Lahore, March 17, 1940.

Conference held in Egypt. He met Hitler in 1929. Hitler was at this time planning a revolution in Germany. It is not improbable that from the German revolutionary leader, Inayat Ullah imbibed revolutionary ideas. After his return from Europe in 1930, he started the Khaksar movement for bringing about a revolution in India in the interest of Pan-Islamism. His writings show that he regarded Islam as a military religion guided and controlled by a military dictator."

Object of the Movement

He propounded that Prophet Muhammad and his successors. the Caliphs intended:-

1. To establish Muslim soverignty over the whole world and to convert the Muslim community into a ruling class in the different countries. "The Khaksar movement was, ,therefore, intended as an instrument for building up the world domination of Islam on the "five pillars of Namaz, Roza, Zakat, Haj, and Kamla."
2. "In short ,you should be united. You should dominate. You must again become conquerors and masters of the world. This is the true teaching of the Quaran and it was for this that Musalmans had become the masters of the world in the early stage of Islam" Allama Mashriqi thus exhorted the Muslims.
3. "We are making through military life the whole nation a fighting nation," he preached.
4. According to the Allama military life come out of Namaz. Roza, Zakat, Haj and Kalma.
5. The old Musalman considered Roza, Namaj, Haj and Zakat as weapons to wage war against the world. He had before him the sovereignty of the whole world. This was the lesson which was given directly by the Prophet of Islam to the Muslims. The Quran had proclaimed in unequivocal, words to the world that the Prophet was sent with the true religion and definite instructions that he should make all other religions subservient to this religions regardless if this domination of the world caused affiction to the Kafirs.
6. He regarded Islam and Military life as synonymous words and, therefore, the giving up of military life was tenantamount to the giving up of Islam.

Conclusion

The great object of the Khaksar movement, founded by the

Allama, was, therefore, to make the Muslims again into a military body so that they may once again dominate the world. It may be mentioned here that the Allama, had laid out his plans after considerable deliberation. He proposed to have any Bait-ul-Mal,[15] which will include cash, as well as, tents, guns, horses and lands. In his preachings he gave details of the provision he would like to be made and explained how he would train his men and how he would maintain his army.

Construction of the Khaksars

The Allama divided the Khaksars into three classes. The "Mujahids", "Janbaz" and "Muavins". The Mujahids were the regular body, the Janbaz were the men who pledged to sacrifice their all, including life itself. The Janbaz required to give a pledge of implicit obedience, written in his own blood, to the effect that his all, his life and property would be at the back and call of his commander.

The Head Office, had for some years been established at Ichhra, near Lahore. It was called Adara-i-Aliya.[16]

Organisation

The Khaksar movement maintained a weekly paper Al-Islah. All power was rested in the Allama who was regarded as the dictator or the Amir. The Adara-i-Aliya was entirely under his control. The smaller units of the Khaksar organization were under an officer called by the name of Salar-i-Mulla. Minute details were laid down for their discipline and training. Over every three Salari-i-Mualla was a Sir Salar, who was himself controlled by Salar-i-Ilaqa. Above the district officer was Salar-i-Khas, who was in charge of the whole province. The officer immediately below the Allama himself was called Nazim-i-Ala" who controlled two provinces . The discipline of the organisation was maintained by means of secret discipline of the organisation officers in plain clothes who were called Khufia Salar-i-Zabat. They were appointed by the dictator himself. Nor should we omit to mention the "Jallad" another officer attached to every Khaksar organization. It was he who struck those who may be sentenced

15. A Central Treasury.
16. The Supreme Institution.

punishment with long and heavy leather lash.

Symbol of the Movement

Like Hitler in his earlier revolutionary days the Khaksars carried a spade or a Belcha as a symbol of the movement. It was said that Prophet Muhammad himself at the battle of Badr used such a weapon, both for offence and defence.[17]

Lahore Attacked, March 20, 1940

Panjab Ban on Quasi-Military Parades Defied.

Allama Mashiriqui's gruesome orders to his followers "to lay a bed of corpses" in Lahore were carried out on 19th March, 1940 when two groups of armed Khaksars clashed with the police near the Tibbi Police Station. It is stated that 26 men received fatal injuries. Among the police officers injured were Mr. D. Gamsford, Senior Superintendent of Police and Mr. P.C.D. Beatly, Deputy Superintendent of Police. Their condition was grave. More than fifty Khaksars were injured

K.S. Mir Afzal, City Inspector of Police, in describing the happenings said:-

"We talked to them politey, and pleaded with them to disperse quietly." "In a second somebody signalled to them and raising their spades they made a most sudden and unprovoked attack on the police party. It was an unequal fight because they numbered about 160 and we were only a score, Mr. Bourne (C.D.) Mr. Gamsford, and Mr. Beatly and myself were injured."

Encounter with the Police

A second party of Khaksars emerged from a nearby mosque to reinforce their comrades, who had concealed themselves in the adjoining houses. They, however, did not find the police unprepared.

Additional Police was requisitioned. A large number of police lorries arrived in a short time. Another warning was given to the Khaksars to disperse, but in view of the violent attitude the police had to open fire in order to disperse them.

As many as 248 Khaksars were on trial in Lahore on April 17, 1940. The trial took place in the Central Jail Lahore before

---

17. The Daily Tribune, Lahore, April 3, 1940.

Mr. A. Iser, Special Magistrate, deputed by the Government to try those cases.

Game of Hide and Seek

The game of hide and seek between the Khaksars and the police continued on April 17, 1940. A squad of Khaksars suddenly appeared from a mosque in Anarkali and soon Mr. E.W.C. Wace, D.I.G. Police, Mr. F.C. Bourne, District Magistrate, Khan Abdul Samad Khan, City Magistrate, K.B. Syed Ahmad Shah, Superintendent of Police, C.I.D., and the Senior Superintendent of Police, Lahore arrived on the spot with a Tear Gas Squad. One of the Khaksars broke the musket of the police. Eventually the Khaksars over-powered with tear gass and arrested.

Settlement with the Khaksars

Informed circles lost all hope of a settlement with the Khaksar leaders on May 17, 1940. The political correspondent of a local and Anglo-Indian Daily believed that "the Khaksar menace in Lahore with the help of 'local' encouragement was becoming more formidable and whatever hopes of a settlement were entertained were fast dwindling circles declared that "since the blockade of the mosques was lifted, the Khaksars assumed the role of heroes and there was no fear of a shortage of good food for them while they remained in their sanctuaries. They were assured of free and good in the mosques and this fact had indeed attracted "all sorts of persons and recruits to the ranks of the Khaksars. They were feasted for some days and at the end of it they did not mind going to jail where again food of some sort was assured to them". More recruits were coming in than the number of Khaksars arrested from day to day. The correspondent reported that "among the recruits there was a large proportion of boys in their teens."

It was being felt that unless the Government was determined to handle the situation with a firm hand it may become out of control. Since the sympathy of the local Muslims with the Khaksars was steadiy growing, this also showed by the fact that the Muslim students of the local Islamia College held a meeting as a mark of sympathy with the Khaksars they abstained themselves from the college for one day. Most of the students carried out this resolution.

Khaksars in Patiala

The Khaksars Movement first came to the notice of State Government at Bassi in 1939, but could not spread rather became somewhat unpopular with the local Muslims in consequence of some criticisms levelled against its parent body and its originator, in Muslim circles outside the State. The local promoters ordered to have their society one of the Bassi Pathana, who had a fire-wood shop in Patiala, tried to revive it in Patiala city. A Khaksar flag was put up on one tailor's shop and the one Muhammad Sadiq was appointed its "Salar".

Muhammad Sadiq arrested

They had a few parades when Muhammad Sadiq was arrested in connection with the Hindu-Muslim clash which occured at Patiala on 24th May, 1939. He subsequently turned an approver and was ousted by the local Khaksars. At the same time open parades were stopped. An order was issued that the Khaksars should either suspend their activities or register themselves under the 1988 Hadyat. As a result of this, their Belcha Parades were suspended for some time and some correspondence started between the local Khaksar enthusiasts and their leader Alama Mashriqi.

Just at this time, the Khaksars got into some trouble in Lucknow and at some other places in the U.P. where they launched Civil Disobedience. Their leader was arrested, got out of jail on giving an understanding, which was subsequently repudiated by him. A heated controversy, as to whether he had given the understanding or it had been forged, as alleged by him, led to his re-entry into U.P. against orders promulugated under Sec: 144 and resulted in his arrest and conviction.

Khaksar Jathas from many parts in British India, particularly the Panjab, the North West Frontier Province and Sind provinces, established some camps on the borders of the U.P. and tried to invade it at some places. Clashes occurred between the Police and the Khaksars and in Bulandshahar the Military had to be used and some firing had to be resorted to, resulting in about a dozen Khaksar casualities. The U.P. incidents and clashes focussed public attention on the Khaksar movement and gave it a great impetus. A few Patiala State subjects had also gone to various camps on the borders of the U.P., but that they did not go in any formation from Bassi or Patiala but to camps concerned with other Khaksars.[18]

Their strength in Patiala State

The strength of the Khaksars in Patiala State range between 150 and 200, but their correct number coud not be ascertained, because they did not show their record saying that no register was mantained by them.

Their work was confined to social service no doubt but they were secretly organising themselves and were holding parades in a military formation. Although they did not interfere in any way or contravene State regulations in particular yet they secretly continued their work against the provisions of Hidayat 1988.[19] Following in the wake of excitement and interest caused by the U.P. incidents they began to revive their activities in the State in contraventon of Ijlas-i-Khas orders.

After these orders were served upon them, they could not take part in any way in this movement but they continued to function and act upon Allama Mashiriqui's programme. They were expressing their sympathies to and offering prayers for his release in different mosques. The local Khaksars of British territory. They were reported to be participating in khaksar meetings held at Ambala.

Just after the declaration by the Government of India declaring this body to be unlawful arrests of Khaksars were made at different places in the British territory. Articles appeared in different papers regarding the attitude of the Khaksars, who challenged rather threatened the Govt. of India to disturb the machinery of the Govt.

All of them tendered unconditional written apologies and gave undertaking for remaining faithful to His Highness' person and throne and not to take part in any activity of the khaksars and that they had severed their connection from the Khaksar organisation.

Thereupon, on the recommendation of the district authori-

---

18. Khaksar Movement in Patiala State. Case No. 1012/c of 1939. A.D. dated 9. 12. 39, p. 24.
19. The law of the land regarding the registration of socities.

ties and the Inspector General of Police, the Home Minister. His Highness' Government, Patiala recommended the case for Ijlas-i-Khas sanction for the acceptance of appologies and the withdrawal of cases against them. The required sanction was accorded on 10.8.41 and the cases were withdrawn.[20]

Other communities were alerted

As a reaction to the Khaksar movement and specially as the result of these revelation as to the purpose of the movement the Sikhs in particular, and other communities in general, were greatly alerted and the Akali Dal was organising arrangements for strengthening Akali militia.

The Akali Sena

An important meeting of the Jathedars or Commanders of the Akali Military popularly known as the Akali Sena Fauj, was held at Amritsar (May 14, 1940) at the office of the Shromani Akali Dal. Jathedars from all over the province were present. Master Tara Singh presided. The meeting discussed the Panjab Government's ban on parades of quasi-military organisation. The general trend of opinion was that the Sikhs had no desire to defy the ban or unduly embarass the authorities. At the same time there was wide agreement that the Akali Dal should be strengthened by fresh recruitment and properly exercised, particularly in Gatka and other sports. It was further decided to set up regular divisions of the militia and the work of proper organisation was entrusted to Jathedar Mohan Sngh. The Akali Sena was over ten thousand volunteers throughout the Panjab.[21]

20. Dated 14.7.1943 vide case No. 1012/c of 1939 pp. 107-110 Case No. 1012/c of 1941 p. 20.
21. The Daily Tribune, Lahore, dated 11.5.40.

8

PANJAB DURING 1941-1947

1. Sir B. J. Glancy 1941-1946

Sir Bertrand James Glancy was born on December 3, 1882 and was educated at Clifton Manmouth, Eter College Oxford. He was the son of Colonel T. Glancy R.E. He was married in 1914 to Grace Steel. He entered Indian Civil Service in 1905 and served in the Panjab as Assistant Commissioner and Political Assistant, temporary Under-Secretary to Governor General of India, Foreign Department from March to November, 1913. He was appointed Agent to the Governor General in Rajputana in March, 1915; First Assistant to Resident in Kashmir in December, 1918, Deputy Secretary to Governor General of India in June, 1919; Political Department, in October, 1921; and again in April, 1927. He was further appointed officiating Agent to Governor General, Panjab States in April, 1929; in Foreign and Political Department in July, 1932 and again in July, 1933: Member, Council of State from July, 1933; Secretary Chamber of Princes in October, 1934 and Political Advisor to H.E., the Crown Representative, in 1938. He assumed charge of the Governor of the Panjab on the 17th of April, 1941.

2. Sir E. M. Jenkins 1946-1947

Sir Evan Meredith Jenkins was born on February 2, 1896. He was educated at Rugby Balliol College Oxford. He joined Indian Civil Service in 1920 and various responsible posts in the Panjab and in the Central Secretriat until 1937. He was appointed the Chief Commissioner of Delhi in 1937, Secretary to the Government of India, Department of Supply in July, 1940, Private Secretary to His Excellency, the Viceroy and Secretary to the Governor-General (personal) in 1943. He was made K.C.I.E. in 1944 K.C.S.I. in 1946. He was appointed the Governor of the Panjab on April 8, 1946.

PARTITION OF THE PANJAB

Birth of Pakistan

Congress had long stood for the unity of India. They had fought the general election of 1937 on this platform. Pakistan grew out of the two-nation theory of the Muslim League, which since 1930 had been synonymous with its permanent president, the late Muhammad Ali Jinnah, called by the Muslims Qaid-i-Azam.[1] The Career of Qaidi-i-Azam Jinnah indicated a curious and ironic development from being the apostle of Hindi-Muslim Unity, as he was called by admiring Congressmen, to be the chief exponent, advocate and creator of Pakistan—a state based upon the thesis that the Muslims of India were a separate nation, and as such needed a homeland and State for themselves, separate from Hindu-Land.

The background

Dr Muhammad Iqbal in his presidential address at the Annual Muslim League Session held at Allahabad in 1930, advocated the establishment of a separate Muslim State or Federation in India on the basis of the Muslims' separate political identity, in these words: "The Muslim demand for the creation of Muslim India within India is, therefore, perfactly justified..............I would like to see the Panjab North-West Frontier Province, Sind and Bluchistan amalgamated into a single state. Self Government within the British Empire, or without the British Empire, the information of a consolidated North-West Indian Muslim State appears to me to be the final destiny of the Muslims at least of North-West-India."[2]

This was the first thing thrown into the atmosphere of Indian politics of a separate Muslim State or Federation. But the thing at this stage was a vague aspiration, the desire towards a separate State was not formed in anybody's mind as a concrete programme-symptomatic nevertheless of a dangerous way of thinking and an explosive kind of mentality.

---

1. The Supreme Leader.
2. Indian Annual Registrar, 1930 Vol. II, N.N. Mitra, p. 339.

Dr. Muhammad Iqbal's doctrine did not immediately find much support among the Indian Muslims. At the Round Table Conference which was held in London soon after, the Muslim delegates talked in terms only of safeguards and the proportions of seats the Muslims might get in the various legislatures of India in addition to plea for the creation of a new Muslim-majority province, namely Sind. The official policy of the Muslim League in those years continued to be very much the same—any thought of setting up a separate state being regarded as the vision of an idealist, a poet, but in no way of a practical politician.

Muslim students at Cambridge

But Dr Muhammad Iqbal was by no means the only Muslim who thought in terms of a separate Muslim State in India. In January, 1933 appeared, on behalf of certain Indian Muslim students at Cambridge, headed by Chaudhri Rahmat Ali, a pamphlet entitled 'Now or Never'. This pamphlet advocated a complete break away of the Muslims of North-Western Zones of India from the rest of the Indian nation. "India" it said, "is not the name of single country, nor the home of one single nation. It is in fact, the designation of a state created for the first time in history by the British."

The Muslims were shown in this pamphlet to be altogether separate in their way of life from the other people of India, and hence the unmistakable conclusion was suggested that they must have a separate state of their own.[3]

It is necessary here to point out that the essence of this last argument given above had been repeated ever since 1940 by all Muslim Leaguers. Differences and cleavages had been emhpasised and the doctrine of hate and the animosity had been preached. Muslim separatism had been bolstered up. All attempts made in the past-comparatively remote and recent-by far-sighted Hindus and Muslims. Poet-lauriates, founders of faiths and others had been sought to be written off. This exaggerated account of the cleavage between the Muslim, the Hindu and Sikh way of life led, when factors favourable to such a consummation had developed fully, to the orgy of rioting in Bengal, the N.W.F. Province, the Panjab and Sind. As a matter of fact, it would have been

3. Muslim League Attack on the Sikhs & Hindus—p. 5.

surprising if after the gospel of hate which the Muslim League had been preaching to the Indian Muslims for so many years, these riots and their accompanying horrors and devastation had not occurred.

Pakistan

The word "Pakistan"[4] which so powerfully caught the imagination of the Muslims of India, and which pinned the vague flating idealism of sacants like Dr. Muhammad Iqbal to a concrete objective and programme, is a coinage of Chaudrari Rehmat Ali. He was hailed among the Muslims as the founder of Pakistan Natoinal Movement. The coinage is said to have been formed from initial letters of the names of the Provinces designed to compose the original Pakistan, "the North-Western zone". These provinces were: Panjab Afghanistan, N.W. Frontier Province, Kashmir and Baluchistan. Apart from this genesis of the name, which perhaps was an after thought, the name is Persian compound formation; and an offensive challenge to the non-Muslims, extremely defiant and provoking, is inherent in it.

Pakistan, as has been told above, was originally conceived to comprise cnly he North-Western areas of the Panjab, Sind, Kashmir, the N.W. Frontier Province and Baluchistan. But in a latter concept of the thing, issued in the form of a revised version of the original scheme, it was devised to comprise, besides the areas originally ear-marked for it, also Assam and Bengal in the East, and Hederabad and Malabar in the South.

All this mentioned above was elaborated by Rehmat Ali, in 1940, the year in which his concept had been so far successful that the Lahore Session of the Muslim League passed the famous Pakistan Resolution, adopting the achievement of an independent "Muslim State" out of the United India of British formation, as the immediate goal of the Muslim League policy. Even the then famous Lahore resolution of March 23, 1940 not only contemplated such as situation but on the contrary it spelt out two sovereign Muslim states, one in the West and the other in the East. This would stand out crystal clear if we carefully study the working of the introductory para of this resolution which

4. A persian compound—Pak means pure and sitan means—Abode of pure.

says, "Resolved that it is the cnosidered view of this session of the All India Muslim League that no constitutional plan would be workable in this country or acceptable to Muslims unless it is designed in the following basic principles, viz, that geographically contiguous units were demarcated into regions which would be so constituted, with such territorial re-adjustment as may be necessary, that the areas in which the Muslims werenumerically in a majority as in the North-Western and Eastern Zones of India should be grouped to constitute "Independent State in which the constituent unit shall be unanimous sovereign[5]."

The Fatal Flaw in the Creation of Pakistan

The seeds of Pakistan's inevitable disintegration were sown right at the time of its birth. The fatal flaw lay in yoking its two desperate wings separated from each other, by more than 100 miles of Indian territory. While the Western zone was dry, the Eastern one was a sheet of water. The former was rugged and relatively empty and the later desperately over-populated. The West spoke Urdu, the East Bengali, Their culture and outlook, by and large, were radically divergent. The Eastern zone had higher literacy rate than the Western. Their economic structure was totally different. Even their food and dress were not the same.

The people of the two wings had antithetical character. The Panjabi was robust and aggressive whereas the Bengali Muslims still felt passionately Bengali, so much so that they protested furiously when in 1905 Lord Curzon tried to divide the province into East and West Bengal. It was one of the rare occasion when a Viceroy had to renounce a pet project. Pakistan as created was thus a geographical monstrosity with no modern precedent in history. The two wheels of Pakistan stood unevenly structed at the time of common religion.[6]

The Muslim League Army

At this period the Muslim League was preparing, for a large scale struggle against Hindu India, and in the Panjab inevitably against the Sikhs and Hindus. The Muslim League had been

5. Pakistan Political System in Crisis—Varma, p. 12.
6. Pakistan Political System in Crisis—Varma, p. 11.

gathering a private army of its own, to which training was being imparted in fighting, stabbing and assaults. Arms were being collected, and demobilized Muslim personnel of the Indian Army were freely enlisted in the Muslim League army.

The Muslim League Volunteer Corps

This army, began about the year 1938, continued to expand and grow better equipped.

It had two famous organisations; one was the Muslim League voulnteer Corps, which was parallel to the Congress Seva Dal. But there was a great difference between the Congress body and this League Offshoot. The congress adopted and followed its creed of non-violence. The Congress volunteers were forbidden even under the gravest provocation to retaliate with physical force. They were to regulate crowds ,to organize picketing, anti-Government processions, to arrange protest strikes, but in no way to fight. But the Muslim League creed was non-violent. Every town with any Muslim inhabitants who could be counted only as rabble and who very often with the connivance of the black sheep among the police force lived on crime. Such elements were thefvaourite recruiting ground for the Muslim League volunteer corps. Any hooligan with the badge and uniform of a political organisation, which was day in and day out preaching the gospel of hatred against other communities, would be formidable in a well-organised group which could back him up and direct him to secret and violent action.

2. The Muslim National Guards

The Muslim National Guards did not owe any formal allegiance to the Muslim League, though it had the same flag as the Muslim League had. The National Guards was the secret arm of Muslim League. Its membership was secret and had its own centres and headquarters, where its members received military training and such instructions as would make them effective in times of rioting, such as using the lathi, the spear and the knife.

The Salar

The Unit Commander of the Muslim National Guards was known as Salar, over whom were higher officers, but all functioning secretly and with clearly such instructions as would make them formidable in rioting against non-Muslim population.[7] The National Guards had their own jeeps and lorries, which helped them in swift mobility for attack on Hindu and Sikh localities, in sniping and stabbing lonely passers-by and in carrying away loot.

One of the articles the Muslim National Guards prized and stored was petrol, which was to be used as a means of incendiarism on a large and devastating scale. The Muslims of the Panjab, and earlier of Bengal made use of it very thoroughly and effectively, and hundreds of burnt town and villages in the two provinces bore tragic evidence of how thorough the preparations of the Muslim League had been for its war on Hindus and Sikhs.

Regular tests were held of the Muslim National Guards in feats of fighting and attack. Marks were given and certificates were issued. The facsimile of one such certificates from Jullundur, dated November 3, 1946 are still in possession of some people of the Panjab. This is only one of the thousands of such certificates which were given at the various centres and headquarters of the Guards in the Panjab and elsewhere. The Muslims had a widespread and well-trained semi-military organisations to back up its programme and policy.

A Great Danger to the Breach of the Peace

So alarming was the rise of the Muslim National Guards that the Panjab Government took serious notice of this development, which proved to be dangerous for the peace of the Province. But the entire machinery of the Government being pre-Muslim, nothing serious was done about the Muslim National Guards. "The necessity for recruitment and reorganisation of the Muslim League National Guards is occupying the at entire of the Provincial Salar. An increase of 5,630 Guards has been reported and accelerated activity has been noticeable in the western and north-western Panjab. In the eastern Panjab, active training has been confined mainly in Simla, Ambala Cantt, Panipat, where Guards have been exercising secretly in Lathi Fighting and in the Central Panjab and in Jullundur District, where

7. When in January, 1947 the Lahore office of the Muslim National Guards was raided by the Panjab Police a good deal of Military equipment including steel helmets and badges were recovered.

Khaksars have undertaken their training. Open activity has been confined to warning Muslims to destroy looted property and refrain from giving evidence in connection with the recent disturbances."

"There are already indications that the Guards are being used as secret messengers, and their general activities are becoming less open, and in some places, they are active in arming the community.[8] It has been reported that financial aid from the Centre has been promised, particularly for the Western Districts which are to act as recruiting grounds for the entire Province. Enlistment in the Rawalpindi and Camphellpore Districts has been particularly brisk and efforts have been made to colist the services of ex-soldiers. The increase in membership is noticeable in all districts, however, and it is estimated that the number of Muslim League National Guards in the Province now is in the neighbourhood of 39,000."[9]

Two Pronged Thrust

The Muslim League, therefore, had this two-pronged thrust to make in its assault on the non-Muslims of the Muslim majority areas.

1. In the first place it was preaching its two-nation theory and its uncompromising opposition to the Hindus, and in the Panjab to the Sikhs as well. It tried to write off all such things as common Indian Culture and an Indian Nationhood. In the name of self-determination for the Muslims of India, it inculcated in them the creed of intolerance, arrogance and hate. All this made any compromise with Hindu India an impossibility for the Muslims, they must fight against the Hindus to enforce their extreme demands. This fight came in 1946 when the Muslim League gave its Direct Action call on the 27th July of that year.
2. The Muslim League had been preparing the Muslims physically and militarily for such a fight which when it came, the Hindus and Sikhs were caught unawarded, and suffered heavily, in women abducted and dishonoured, in property looted and houses and religious and educational places burnt. Retaliation by

8. Muslims
9. Wrote Mr. Akhtar Hussain, the Chief Secretary to the Governor of the Panjab in April, 1947.

the Hindus and Sikhs was only belated, and after the Muslim onslaught was becoming continuous and a threat to their very existence. Before August, 1947 such retaliatory measures even served the purpose of the Muslim League, for it created that atmosphere of civil war in India, which the Muslim League found necessary for the furtherance of its programme and policy. It could trot out atrocity stories and incite Muslims elsewhere to fall upon Hindus and Sikhs, as they actually did in the North-West Frontier province in December, 1946 and January, 1947. Such were the aims and methods of the Muslim League.

In the Panjab arms were easily obtainable, and it was rumoured that the Sikhs had collected stocks of firearms in the Gurdwaras of Amritsar, in addition to an armoury of rifles and revolvers which they had amassed in Patiala State. An unconfirmed report stated that an ex-I.N.A. officer was training a group of ex-I.N.A. Sikhs.

Three Demands of Mr. Jinnah

1. Jinnah's first demand—The recognition of the 'two nations' theory there was absolute unanimity in Congress circles that it should not and could not be conceded. It ran counter to the creed of the Congress and to the facts of Indian life. It was mischievous and potentially dangerous. It would give Pakistan a handle to interfere in the affairs of India, undermine the basis of India's existence and encourage other groups and communities in the country to emulate the Muslim League. The future state of independent India could not stand on the theory of disintegration and, whatever its enemies might say, the Congress had no ambition to establish a Hindu State.

2. Jinnah's second demand—the inclusion in Pakistan of almost the entire area convered by six Muslim majority provinces. Congress leaders became determined that if Jinnah had Pakistan it should not be Pakistan with those districts of Assam and Bengal and of the Panjab in which the population was predominantly non-Muslim. They decided to hoist Jinnah with his own patard. Every argument that could be used in favour of Pakistan could equally be used in favour of the seclusion of the non-Muslim areas from Pakistan.

Moreover, Jinnah had already compromised his position on this point. The Lahore resolution of the Muslim League had spoken only of the demarcation of 'geographically' contiguous units' and admitted the necessity of 'territorial re-adjustments'.[10] The non-Muslim majority districts of Assam and Bengal and of the Panjab were equally contiguous to the rest of India and with popular feeling there being strong against their inclusion within Pakistan, the Congress was in a formidable bargaining position vis-a-vis the Muslim League.

3. Jinnah's third demand, namely, the total separation of Pakistan from the rest of India and the elimination of a common centre in any form, the Congress had already gone a long way in meeting it. In fact, Gandhi in his talks and correspondence with Jinnah in 1944 had studiously avoided mentioning the term 'central government' and he instead suggested 'a Board of Representatives of both the States' or any other 'authority acceptable to both the parties' whose effectiveness would largely or solely depend upon mutual goodwill.[11]

Jinnah had insisted 'first on complete partition as between two nations, and then an agreement between them as on Foreign Affairs, etc. He would not agree to anything simultaneous.'[12] Congress leaders, therefore, did not need to make any further material concession in order to meet Jinnah's third demand in full. All that they were required to do was to reconcile themselves and their followers—to the painful prospect of the complete separation of Pakistan from the rest of India. It was, however, by no means any easy task.

First Trial for Strength

The 1946 elections in the Panjab provided to the Muslim League the first opportunity for a trial of strength in the Panjab. The Panjab, called corner stone of Pakistan was the one province in which the Muslim League had not been able to form a Ministry. It was not on the ground that the Muslim did not have in this province what was called 'Pakistan in action'. But that was not enough. The Panjab must go to Muslim League, in name as

10. Speeches and Documents on the Indian Constitution—Gwyer & Appadorai, Vol. II, p. 443.
11. Speeches and Documents on the Indian Constitution—Gwyer & Appadorai, Vol. II, pp. 554-55.
12. Speeches and Documents on the Indian Constitution—Gwyer & Appadori, Vol. II, p. 443.

well as in action in order to make Mr. Jinnah's edifice of Pakistan complete.

For this purpose it was necessary that an overwhelmingly large number of Muslim seats must be won by the League in the Panjab. A more majority of Muslim seats would not do for in the Panjab. Out of its 175 seats, as many as about 87 worked out to be non-Muslim, as some of the special constituencies like the University, Lahore, Commerce and Landlords went to non-Muslims. The League, therefore, must win all or almost all Muslim seats, for which purpose it must defeat the Unionist Party of which Sir Khizar Hyat Khan, Premier of the Panjab, successor to Sir Sikandar Hyat Khan, was the leader.

The Unionist Party

As the Unionist leader, detesting the methods of Muslim League and regarding the path of the partition of the country harmful for the Muslims themselves, was bent upon giving a fight to the League, the contest was expected to be very bitter, as it actually turned out to be. The Muslim League fought on the programme of Pakistan which it placed before the Muslim masses. The Unionist Muslim realizing the over whelming force of the Pakistan appeal to Muslim Masses, did not oppose Pakistan but they argued, more wisely perhaps than the Leaguers from the Muslims point of view, that to press for a separate state of Pakistan would inevitably entail cuttaing off of Hindu and Sikh area from the Panjab and would be detrimental to economic interest of the Muslims themselves. But so deeply had the Pakistan poisón seeped into the Muslim mind that the Unionist fought everywhere a narrowly defensive battle.

The Muslims appeared to have gone thoroughly Muslim League by this time. The officials and the police everywhere helped the Muslim League candidates by the usual methods of threats and cajolery employed on the electorate. The Most violent and vituperative abuse was employed against the Unionists. As the Muslim League plank was Pakistan, so naturally the Congress and the Sikhs came in for extensive and violent abuse.

Death Blow to the Unionists

The untimely demise of Sir Sikander Hyat Khan in 1944, under the tragic circumstances and the death of Rai Bahadur

Chaudhari Sir Chhotu Ram in 1945 gave a death blow to the Unionist Party. Though Sir Khizar Hyat Khan and his other colleagues were equally strong, united and enthusiastic, yet Sir Khizar Hyat Khan, the successor of the late Premier of the Panjab lacked the shrewdness and intelligence to cope with the political situation which ultimately led to the partition of the Panjab. Brief sketches of both the stewart Unionists are given below for the general interest of the readers:-

Major Sir Sikandar Hyat Khan, K.B.E. 1892-1944

Sir Sikandar Hyat Khan's sudden and untimely death on December 26, 1944, under extremely tragic circumstances shook the country from one end to the other and moved the hearts of his friends and foes. No body could imagine when the people were enjoying the brilliant function given by him to celebrate the marriages of his two sons that his end was so near.

Sir Sikandar Hyat Khan was a gentleman of unique qualities of head and heart. He was a brave soldier, a shrewd politician, a far-seeing statesman, an experienced and great administrator, and above all a great leader of men and a true patriot.

Sir Sikandar Hyat Khan started career first in the Army. He was a Recruiting Officer during the First World War. For his good work he was given a Commission and attached to one of the Panjabi regiments. In the Third Afghan War he commanded a company on active service, being the first Indian to have exercised command. After that he returned to civil life and entered politics. It was in this sphere that unique success awaited him. In a short space of time he rose to the highest offices which had been given to very few men and filled them with distinction. He first returned to the old Legislative Council in 1923 and made his mark in the old Council by hard-work, clear thinking and ability, and when the late Mian Sir Fazl-i-Husain went to the Government of India he was chosen to fill the temporary vacancy. His success in that temporary vacancy ensured his appointment later as Revenue Member, a post which he filled with great distinction it was during his tenure of office as Revenue Member that he twice officiated as Governor of this Province, the highest office to which an Indian can aspire under the constitution, and was universally acclaimed a success. On the termination of his office as Revenue Member he was selected as Deputy Governor of the Reserve Bank of India, a post carrying very high salary and no worries. But this heart was always in the Panjab, with the poor and the backward in the Panjab to serve them was his life's mission.

Accordingly, on the demise of Sir Fazl-i-Hussain, he sacrificed his high salary and life of ease, and came back to the rough and stormy life and uncertainties of politics. His work was recent history and was well known to all. It will be for the future historian to record his verdict, but it could be claimed without any fear of contradiction that he was the most successful Premier under the new constitution, and that the future generations of the Panjab would look forward with gratitude and pride to his work in the sphere. He was a great man, and the loss of such a man would be felt at any time but it was very difficult to repair it during those critical days, and the breach caused by his death was not filled.

Two things were uppermost in his mind during the last two or three years and they were communal harmony and war efforts. He believed that his motherland could not achieve automony without communal harmony and unless the country was made from aggression by the victory of the United Nations which stood for freedom. In furtherence of these objects he never spared himself, and in spite of his ill health he undertook two journeys to Iraq and Egypt to attend to the needs of the soldiers. It was a pity that the victory was in sight and the victorious armies were soon to return to India, but he was not there to greet them. It was the loss of such man that the people were so much shocked.[13]

Rao Bahadur Chaudhri Sir Chhotu Ram. 1881-1944

As to Chaudhri Sir Chhotu Ram's life, his later life was known to each and every one, even to the very children in the villages and cities. He was born in 1881 in a peasant home and Garhi Sample, in Rohtak District, the village and the district which he made famous by his subsequent public service. He had to face many difficulties and surmount obstacles during the earlier portion of his life but with his usual perservance, ability and

13. Panjab Legislative Assembly, Dated March 4, 1943, pp. 2-3.

zeal, he got over all of them and graduated in law.

First of all he practised as a lawyer at Agra and then shifted to his home district of Rohtak in 1912. He soon found that legal work was not the only thing which interested him and he began to take up interest in wider affairs of local politics and education. He started founding schools and many of them exist to day to his great memory. Later on he became popular figure in the local District Board and he started party on non-communal and economic lines. He did very well in the District Board and gained popularity all over the district.

Later, his chance came when he was returned to the old Legislative Council and he was appointed a Minister in 1924. His work was such that his ability and his zeal and enthusiasm won him the recognition of all those who came in contact with him. He made his voice felt in the wider provincial field and he was soon found to be the popular defender of the rights of the Zamindars.

He was the co-founder of the Unionist party with the Sir Fazl-i-Husain and worked as his first lieutenant and right-hand man till Mian Sahib left to join the Central Government. Sir Chhotu Ram then became the factor and de jure leader of the Unionist Party for a long time in the old Legislative Council. His stand for his ideals was so strong that at one time he had only one Hindu follower left. But still he stuck to his guns and he had the unique distinction of being the only Hindu leading the party with a majority of Muslims.

Before he was returned to power in 1936 it is well known that ministership was offered to hm many times. It is also well known that he could have been the leader of certain other sections which were ready to have him as their leader. But he said, 'No I will not have anything to do either with the ministership or leadership' unless it is on Unionist lines and according to the programme that he had in view. His chance came in 1937 when the party of which he had been the leader was returned to power. He was then appointed Minister of Development and later as Minister of Revenue which office he held till the day of his death.

His work in the interests of the poor of all classes, and particularly the zimindars, is well known. The part he plays in getting the agrarian legislation through is well known. He did all this under those difficult circumstances for communal harmony. If people of the various communities and classes could be welded together, the comenting factors were the great personalities of Sir Fazl-i-Hussain and the Honourable Rao Bahadur Chaudhri Sir Chhotu Ram. His work in the interests of communal harmony will never be forgotten. His work for the uplift of the poor will never be forgotten and it is well known that he travelled day and night, motoring hundreds of miles, to see the poor and redress their grievances. It was that, which mostly affected his health. Doctors advised him to take rest, but he would not. He went on making journeys all in the interests of the cause so dear to his heart and in the interests of the poor. He saved nothing, as was well known to all. All he earned went to the furtherence of the cause he believed in, or as stipends to the poor. His eloquence was such that thousands came to hear him from great distances, walking on foot. He lectured for hours and kept the audience spell bound.

He was a statesman with a dynamic personality. His contribution to the life of the province will be long remembered. He passed away but the ideals and the work he had done shall remain for ever. In him the province had lost a great Panjabi. His loss was all the greater when his constructive brain was needed for the service of his country. Future generations of Panjabis will always remember the life work and the services rendered by him to the cause of the Panjab.

The late Sir Fazl-i-Hussain could never have succeeded in forming the Unionist Party if he had not got a convert and an ally of the type of Sir Chhotu Ram, who had strong convictions. He had the courage and wisdom of creating unity on economic basis and he was the heart and soul of that movement. He believed that the true foundation of unity of the Panjab and even of unity of the whole of India was only possible if it were based on economic factors. His zeal and selflessness during the years he was in the Opposition carried his Muslim friends with him and as a leader he got their full support. It was not an easy matter for a Hindu to lead a party the majority of whom were Muslims. They followed him steadfastly because they had great respect for his selflessness and convictions.[14]

14. Panjab Legislative Assembly, Dated February 19, 1945, p. 6.

Hindus and Sikhs Stood by the Unionists Party

The League won as many as 76 seats (they claimed to have 78) in the Panjab Assembly. They were undoubtedly the largest single party in the Legislature. They hoped to form a ministry with the help of a few defections from among the Muslim Unionist, some Indian Christians, Anglo-Indians and Europeans. 88 in a House of 175 would give either party a working majority. But the Hindus and Sikhs, having already experienced the 'Pakistan in action' of the Muslim—dominated Unionist Ministry, many of whose erstwhile support not to be ruled over by a party which stood frankly and nakedly for Muslim rule and for the partition of India and the subjugation of the Hindus and Sikhs for the greater glory of Islam, as had been preached by Rahmat Ali, Dr. Muhammad Iqbal and by the Muslim League propagandists and press in general.

The Coalition Ministry

In the negotiations for ministry-making which went over, not a single Hindu or Sikh member of the Provincial Legislature was willing to walk into the Muslim League camp. The Indian Christians preferred to stand with the Congress with its ideal of a tolerant, secular state in India, rather than with the Muslim League. So, by a majority of nearly 100 members in the provincial Legislature, with Sir Khizar Hayat Khan as Premier, the Congress, the Panthic Party and the Unionist Party in coalition formed the Coalition Ministry in Mar 1946.

The Muslim League Intensified the Campaign

The Muslim League began to make brisk preparations for attack on Hindus and equally well on Sikhs. The Muslim League private army, the Muslim National Guards, began to expand. All kinds of Muslim rabble disbanded members of the Civic Guards, and such other elements were the favourite recruiting ground for this body. The Police, which in several provinces was overwhelmingly Muslim, helped in this recruitment, which was not so much of a secret, and in the collection of arms, equipment and petrol. Jeeps and lorries were possessed by the National Guard in the larger towns; they had stocks of steel helmets purchased from the Disposal Department.[15] Besides, large numbers of lethal weapons, such as knives daggers, swords and spears were made stocked by the Muslim National Guards. Well-to-do Muslim firms and individuals were reported in the months of August and September, 1946 to have distributed daggers and knives among Muslims of Lahore and Amritsar, Sword-making as an industry made rapid progress among Muslims in the Panjab, where for several years last restrictions on the possession and carrying about of the sword had been removed.[16]

Collection of Arms

Besides lethal weapons, there were fairly large quantities of fire-arms and means of incendiarism in the possession of Muslims. In the Panjab, besides smuggling arms fromIndia with the help and connivance of the Muslim Police, the Muslims with the same facility to hand could do successful gun-running from the tribal areas in the North-West. While a Hindu or Sikh carrying illegal weapons on him would be hauled up under the Arms Act, Muslims comparatively safe in doing so, unless they happened to be detected by some non-Muslim police officer.

The Communal Riots

Soon before the Direct Action Day, there had been an attack by Muslims on Sikhs and Hindus at Abbotabad, in the North-West Frontier Province. An account of the incident is as follows:

Abbotabad Non Muslims Attached-July 28, 1946

On July 28, 1946 Muslims held a public meeting in a garden near Gurdwara Singh Sabha. The District Magistrate and the Superinaendent of Police were present near the meeting place, but no precautions were taken. Stones and brickbats were exchanged between a few Sikhs i nthe Gurdwara and the Muslim mob outside.

---

15. This article was recovered in large numbers in the search of the Muslim National Guards office at Lahore in January, 1947.
16. Parcels of knives were frequently intercepted by the Railway Police in the Provinces of Bombay, Central Provinces, Bihar and the United Provinces while in transit from Wazirabad and Sialkot Centres of the Cutlery Industry in the Panjab, to the Muslim Leaguers of those Provinces.

"Muslims made repeated attempt to set fire to Gurdwara shops. These fires were put out by the Military fire-brigade. The Muslim mob divided into groups and began to loot and set on fire Hindu and Sikh shops. More than two dozen shops were looted."

"The Muslim mob met no resistance except at two places, where a gun was fired by a Sikh shopkeeper and a Gurkha Chaukidar. Sikhs were being harassed by Muslim policemen.[17]

This was only foretaste of Direct Action and the Pakistan to come. Abbotabad and adjoining area witnessed large scale murder and looting of Sikh and Hindus no long after this in December, 1946, and January, 1947. And then came March, 1947 with the succeeding terrible months.

Provocative Slogans

Sikh leaders publicly protested against the pro-Islam and provocative slogans of the Muslim League, such as 'Khoon se lenge Pakistan' 'Dena hoga Pakistan' and 'Leke rahenge Pakistan'; etc. On February 15, 1947 and February 21, 1947, on which tension among the communities was mounting high, the Muslim League was adopting a bullying menacing and hooligan character. The police merely watched Muslim mobs often thousand or more going about, threatening to disturb the intercommunal atmosphere with their provocative movement.

That the Muslim League agitation grew more and more violent after the middle of February, way shown by a number of incidents. There were several train hold-ups at Amritsar, Ludhiana, Gujranwala and other places. Lawlessness was on the increase, and the police took no more than the minimum, and in this case, wholly insufficient steps to meet the situation.

Very Violent Day

The 24th February, which was one month from the launching of the agitation, was a very violent day indeed and it incidentally revealed the League agitation in its true colours, as the fore-runner of the March, 1947 war on the Hindu and Sikh minorities. The Civil & Military Gazette report of the day is

17. The Daily *Tribune*, Lahore, July 29, 1946.

as under:—

"The Muslim League agitation assumed dangerous proportions in Amritsar where the police had to open fire on several occasions on February 24, 1947.

"A Sikh constable was beaten to death by a wild mob in the civil lines, the Additional District Magistrate was brutally assaulted......and a murderous attack was made on a sub-inspector by a demonstrator who was killed by police fire.[18]

This incident amply proved that Sikh in particular and Hindus and Sikhs in general, were in for trouble at the hands of Muslims. This dangerous charactor of the situation drew to statements on February 26, 1946, from important Sikh sources one from the Assembly Panthic Party and the other from Master Tara Singh.

Sir Khizar Hayat Khan, Premier of the Punjab coalition Ministry, although had survived the League agitation had but received such a drubbing at the hands of the Muslim League which made his heart sick. The foulest and filthiest abuse was uttered daily in all places where the League agitation was conducted, for Sir Khizar and his Muslim Colleagues, while the non-Muslim ministers came in for severe castigation minus the abuse. Probably Sir Khizar's relations situation in which he had falled foul of the majority of his coreligionists.

The statement of His Majesty's Government quoted above must have made him to ponder and to think of relinquishing office and his ministry naturally came to an end. Sir Khizar took this step, as he said he thought it incumbent to leave the field clear for the Muslim League to come to some arrangement with the other parties. On the next day, that is the 3rd March, 1947 the Governor of the Punjab invited the leaders of the Muslim League Assembly Party to form a ministry. But by that date a strong wave of protest against and opposition to the formation of a Muslim League Ministry, committed to the division of India and the establishment of Pakistan in the Punjab, arose among Hindus and Sikhs.

Procession of The Hindu-Sikh Students

The Hindu and Sikh students of Lahore took out a big

---

18. Civil and Military Gazette, Lahore, February 25, 1947.

procession to demonstrate their resolve not to tolerate a Muslim League Ministry. This perfectly non-violent procession was fired on by the Muslim police, which had stood hooliganism and law-breaking from Muslim mobs for over a month in the Province. Meetings, demonstrations and procession of Hindus and Sikhs continued in Lahore and Amritsar and some other towns. The situation was growing serious. Opposition to the Muslim League was rising with the result that in its effects at Ministry-making the Muslim League assembly party did not get a single Hindu or Sikh supporter.

The League Lost the Hindu-Sikh Confidence

The Governor found that he could not allow a purely Muslim Legaue ministry, without any support whatever from Hindus & Sikhs ,to be formed in the Punjab. The Muslim League having lost the confidence of Hindus and Sikhs due to its past conduct of several years and its creed of hate and violence, got no support from them. The Governor suspended the constitution and the Punjab from March, 1947 was to be governed directly by the Governor under section 93 of the Government of India Act.

A few factors prevalent in the Punjab situation in early March, 1947, were as under:—

1. The Muslim League agitation had as its aim the overthrow of the Coalition ministry, and clearing the way for the achievement of Pakistan.

2. H.M.C. Statement of February 20, 1947 declaring that power would be transferred in India, in default of the Central Governments, made it imperative for the League to capture power and to establish its own Government in the Punjab at all costs so that such a Government should be able to receive powers independently of a Central Government of India.

3. The "Victory Day" of March 2, 1947 was used by the League for marking provocative speaches. and whipping up the passions of the Muslim masses against all who might oppose Pakistan:

4. Not being able to get the cooperation of a single Hindu or Sikh inside Provincial Assembly, the Muslim League decided upon capturing power by waging a war on the minorities in the Punjab.

5. For this purpose the Riots of March, 1947 were started, which occurred simultaneously in Lahore, Amritsar, Jullundur, Multan, Rawalpindi, Campbellpur and other Districts, the aggressors in all places being Muslims;

6. Those riots were no ordinary riots, but were a war of subjugafion and conquest in which the Muslim people, the Muslim police and Muslim officials worked in perfect unison, and brought wide spread death, destructinn and uprooting to Hindus and Sikhs in a dozen districts killing many thousands and uprooting about a million, before the month was out.[19]

So, from the 5th March, 1947 onwards the constitutional game was up, and for the Hindus and Sikhs it became a struggle for sheer life against a fierce and well-planned Muslim onslaught-wall.

The fate of Lahore still lay in the hands of the non-Muslim legislators, who were to meet on June 23, 1947 to decide on the partition on otherwise of the Punjab, and later in the hands of the Boundary Commission. But the Muslim Leaguers wanted to drive all Hindus and Sikhs from a good riddance and action according to plan it. Hindus and Sikhs for generations in this magnificent city would fall into the hands of Muslims. If Lahore by any chance was allotted to India, it would have been a good thing to have destroyed this fiñe city and to make a present of heaps of ashes and cinder to the new rulers of India on August 15, 1947.

In Lahore, the Unionists, at first under Sikandar Hayat Khan and later their lender Khizar Hayat Khan, were offered every kind of support by the Punjab Hindus and Sikhs to form a strong bulwark against the Muslim League. But in spite of all these efforts in the Punjab League returned 78 Muslim members in a house of 175 during the elections to provincial assembly at the end of 1945. The total Muslim seats in the assembly were 90. But Khizar Hayat Khan, reviving the old Unionist Party with a strength of 13 Muslim members, joined hands with the Congress and Akali Sikhs in Lahore. He formed a Coalition Ministry with the support of 95 members, thus becoming the Premier of the province himself.

---

19. Muslim League Attack on the Sikhs and Hindus—p. 70.

Opposition Of The Muslim League

The Muslim masses protested that there was no justification for the Coalition ministry to continue in offices. As a step against the growing League popularity in the province, the Khizar Ministry took up strong repressive measures against the League. On January 24, 1947, seven members of the Punjab Muslim League High Command, voz., Iftikhar Husain Khan of Mamdot, Mumtaz Daultana, Iftikbarud Din, Begam Shah, Nawaz, Shaukat Hayat Khan, Flrozkhan Neon and Amir Husain Shah, were arrested in Lahore following their opposition to police which had come to search the League office in Lahore. On January 25, 1947, the League campaign against the Unionist Ministry became more pronounced among the masses. In Lahore 63 persons, including 16 League Members of he Legislative Assembly were arrested on that day. Tear gas and lathis were used by the police over rowdy processionists resulting in some casualties, particularly.

Set Back To The Unionist Ministry

The Khizar Congress Coalition was shaken to its foundation by the first impact of the League's Movement, for on the next day all League leaders were released by the government. On January 27, 1947, the League leaders again addressed a gathering outside the Mochi Gate to show their determination to fight for the ministry with all their resources. The police, thereupon arrested at midnight all top ranking Lague leaders including the Khan of Mamdot, Firozkhan Noon, Mumtaz Dultana, Iftikharud Din, Shaukat Hayat, Begam Shah Nawaz, Ghulam Mohi-ud-Din Qasuri, Dr. Oman Hayat Malik, Nurullah and Amirud Din.

The League campaign had spread like wild fire over the province. Muslim masses struggled against the Coalition ministry ceaselessly for a period of 34 days in Lahore and other places, until at last on February 25, 1947, the Punjab Government was compelled to make peace with the Muslim League. On February 26, 1947 the League leaders were released from different jails in the Punjab.

Declaration Of The Government

In the meantime the British Government had declared that

power will be transferred in some areas to the provincial Governments or in some such other way as may seem most reasonable. After months of hard work by the Cabinet Mission a great measure of agreement was obtained as to the method by which a constitution should be worked out. This was embodied in their statements of May last. His Majesty's Government thereby agreed to recommend to Parliament a constitution worked out in accordance with the proposals made therein by a fully representative Constituent Assembly.

But if it should appear that such a constitution will not have been worked out by a fully representative Assembly before the time mentioned n paragraph 7, His Majesty's Government will have to consider to whom the powers of the Central Government in British India should be handed over on due date, whether as a whole to some form of Central Government for British India, or in some areas to the existing Provincial Governments, or in such other way as may seem most responsible and in the best interests of the Indian people.[20]"

This declaration while on one side gave further impetus to the determination of the Punjab League to wrest power from the Khizar-Congress-Coalition, on the other side it inflamed the Sikhs with a passion to press for a homeland in the Punjab. Master Tara Singh, one of the leaders of the Sikhs, remarked, 'We Sikhs cannot co-operate with the League unless we are assured that there will be proper safeguards for the minorities. Unless there is an equitable settlement, we will proceed with the idea of partition of the Punjab. Our minimum demand is that in the Punjab, as it stands today, the Sikhs and Hindus should each be given 30 per cent representation in the Legislatures and in the services. Forty percent should go to the Muslims.'

With the declaration of the British Government that the power would be transferred to India by June, 1948 at the latest, things started moving very swiftly in Lahore. The League campaign grew more intense and the Sikhs began organising regiments of their own. The Hindustan Times, a Congress organ issued from Delhi, revealed, 'Before the fateful June of 1947 comes and the British pack up and go, the Punjab will have private armies ready to take the present controversy bet-

20. Statement of His Majesty's Govt., dated February 20, 1947.

ween the various "stands" (i.e. proposed independent sovereign states) to the arbitration of arms.[21]. While the Sikhs organised their Akali Fauj the Hindus strengthened their secret organisation, the Rashtriya Swayam Sevek Sangh. The Sangh had 3,200 regular and 8,000 temporary members in the Punjab. It had 10 paid propogandists and Jammu was their centre for the Punjab. They planned to launch attacks on the life and property of the Muslims say as soon as they got an opportunity.[22]

Fall Of The Coalition Ministry

Finding, at last, that Khizar Hayat Khan had lost all hold over the Muslim masses and that it was well nigh impossible for him to have a hold over the ministry against the onslaughts of the League, Khizar Hayat Khan tendered the resignation of his cabinet to the governor on March 2, 1947. This action further infuriated the Sikhs and Master Tara Singh isssued a statement next day in Lahore saying:

"Let the Khalsa Panth now realise the gravity of the situation. I expect every Sikh to do his duty. We shall live or die, but not submit to Muslim domination. On march Khalsa, rise andgird up your loins. The momentous hour has approached May God be our guide and guard us.,, On March 4, 1947 he came out of the Assembly Party Meeting Room, shouting 'Pakistan Murdabad' (Death unto Pakistan), and 'Sat Sri Akal' (Long Live Sikhism), and brandished his sword on the steps of the Assembly Chamber. He also declared:—

"The time has come when the might of the sword alone shall rule. The Sikhs are ready. We have to bring the Muslims to their senses.'

---

21. The Hindustan Times, February 23, 1947.
22. The following were the Hindu Government officials of the Panjab who organised the movement in Lahore:
    K.— from the Government Printing Press, Panjab, Lahore.
    M.— from the N.W. Railway Loco Workshops Mughalpura, Lahore
    K.L.K.— from the Government Telegraph Office, Lahore.
    R.R.S.K.— from the Controller, Military Accounts, Lahore.
    B.D.— from the Military Accounts Officers, Revenue Section.
    I.K.— from the General Post Office, Lahore (Extracts from a Secret Report of the Panjab Government Criminal Intelligence Department, published in the Dawn, Delhi, January 29, 1947. Initials of the name are only reported by the press).

'This day the Crusade starts. One hundred years from to-day our yellow flags were flying on the Fort of Lahore. The same flag shall fly again. Our battle-axe shall decide if the Muslims shall rule. Sikhs shall never disgrace the name of Guru Gobind Singh[23]

'I am a Jat, and the Jats embraced the Sikh cult to put an end to Muslim rule, and the same Jats will once again fight with their lives.[24]

'During these days, stage such demonstrations that the renegades amongst us may find it impossible to reach settlement whatever with the Muslim League.[25]

Murder & Arson Started

As a result of this Hindus and Sikhs suddenly burst forth into violent incendarism. Disturbances started in Lahore and spread all over the province. On March 5, 1947 in Lahore alone 18 persons were killed and injured. The trouble in Lahore originated with the taking out by Hindus and Sikhs of a procession through Anarkali bazar at 10 A.M. Some 200 or 300 Hindus and Sikhs walked through the bazar shouting 'Pakistan Murdabad' and forcibly hauling down Muslim League flags from Muslim shops. Thus when the Muslims of Lahore were driven to the well they also started paying the Hindus and Sikhs in their own coins. Large scale murder and arson started, as a result of which many lives were lost and property was destroyed. Lahore became a city of murders and flames. Out of the 82,000 houses in the Lahore Corporation area 6,000 houses were burnt down during these disturbances.[26] Lahore's fires were still smouldering when the last British Governor-General of India, Lord Louis Mountbatten, announced the plan of the transfer of power to Indians, on June, 3, 1947.

The British Government passed the Indian Independence Act on July 18, 1947 to make provision for the setting up in India of two Independent Dominions and August 15, 1947 was fixed as the last date for setting up these Dominions.

---

23. Gyani Kartar Singh.
24. Chaudhari Lahari Singh
25. Gopi Chand Bhargav.
26. The Civil & Military Gazette, Lahore's report dated the 17th February 1950.

Section 4, Sub-Section 1:

As from the appointed day (a) the province of the Panjab, as constituted under the Government of India Act of 1935, shall ecase to exist; and (b) there shall be constituted two new provinces, to be known respectively as West Panjab and East Panjab.

Sub-Section 2:

The boundaries of the said new provinces shall be such as may be determined, whether before or after the appointed day, by awards of Boundary Commissions appointed or to be appointed by the Governor-General in that behalf but until the boundaries are so determine(a) the districts specified in the second schedule to this Act shall be treated as the territories to be comprised in the new province of West Panjab and (b) the remainder of the territories comprised at the date of passing of this Act in the province of the Panjab shall be treated as the territories which are to be comprised in the new province of East Panjab. Thus the historic partition of the Panjab came into being on August 15, 1947.

BIBLIOGRAPHY

Aggarwal, R.N.: *National Movement and Constitutional Development of India.* Metropolitan Book Co. (P) Ltd., Delhi.

Aitchison, Sir Charles: *A Collection of Treaties Engagements and Sanads Relating to India and Neighbouring Countries.* Calcutta 1892.

Aitchison, Sir Charles: *Lord Lawrence.* Rulers of India Series, Oxford, 1894.

Ahluwalia, M.M.: *Kuka—The Freedom Fighters of the Punjab.* Allied Publishers (P) Ltd., Bombay-1.

Arnold, Edwin: *The Marquis of Dalhousie's Administration of British India, Vol. I and II.* London, 1862.

Baden Powell: *The Origin and Growth of Village Communities in India.* London, 1899.

Baden Powell: *The Land Systems of British India, Vol. I, II and III.* At the Clarendon Press, Oxford, 1892.

Baird, J.G.: *Private Letters of the Marquis of Dalhousie,* London, 1911.

Baqir, Muhammad: *Lahore—Past and Present.* Panjab University, Lahore, 1952.

Bosworth Smith, R.: *Life of Lord Lawrence, Vols. I and II.* Smith Elder & Co., London, 1883.

Calvert, H.: *The Wealth and Welfare of the Panjab.* The Civil & Military Gazette, Lahore, 1936.

Chaman Lal, Dewan: *Sixty Years of Congress.* The Lion Press, Lahore, 1936.

Charles, Sir Raikes: *Notes on the Revolt in the N.W. Province of India,* London, 1858.

Cooper, F.H.: *Crisis in the Punjab.* Lahore, 1858.

Darling, Edward: *The Punjab Peasant in Prosperity and Debt* Oxford University Press, Bombay, 1928.

Deol, G.S.; *The Role of the Ghadar Party in the National Movement.* Sterling Publishers, New Delhi-16.

Diaries: *Lahore Political Diaries*, Panjab Govt., Lahore.

Dictionary: *The Dictionary of National Biography Vols. XIII.* Oxford University Press, London, 1917.

Dodwell, H.H.: *The Cambridge History of India, Vol. VI.* The University Press, Cambridge, 1932.

Douie, Sir James: *The Panjab North-West Frontier Province and Kashmir.* The University Press, Cambridge, 1916.

Douie, Sir James: *Settlement Manual.* Civil & Military Gazette Press, Lahore.

Diver, Maud: *Honoraria Lawrence*, London, 1936.

Edwardes, Sir Herbert and Merivate Herman: *Life of Sir Henry Lawrence.* London, 1892.

Emma, Lady: *Memorials of the Life and Letters of Sir H. Edwardes.* London. 1886.

Evans, Bell Major: *The Annexation of the Punjab and the Maharaja Daleep Singh.* Department of Languages, Panjab 1970.

Farooqi, Mian Bashir Ahmed: *British Relations with the Cis-Sutlej States 1809-1823.* Panjab Govt. Record Office Publications. 1941.

Farquhar, J.N.: *Modern Religious Movements*, Munshiram Manoharlal, Delhi-6.

Fauja Singh Bajwa: *Kuka Movement.* Moti Lal Banarsi Das, Delhi, 1965.

Fitcheat, W.H.: *The Tale of the Great Mutiny*, London, 1907.

Ganda Singh, Dr.: *Patiala and East Panjab States Union.* Patiala Archives Publication No. 1, Patiala, 1951.

Ganda Singh, Dr.: *A Bibliography of the Pepsu.* Patiala Archives Publication No. 6, Patiala, 1954.

Garret, H.L.O.: *A Brief History of Police Battalions.* Department of History, Panjab University.

Gazetteer: *The Imperial Gazetteer of India, Vol. XII.* At the Clarendon Press, Oxford, 1908.

Gazetteer: *North-West Frontier Province.* Supdt., Govt. Printing

Press, Calcutta, 1908.

Gazetteer: *Panjab Provincial Series*. Supdt., Govt. Printing Press, Calcutta. 1908.

Gazetteer: *Afghanistan and Nepal*. Supdt., Govt. Printing Press. Calcutta, 1908.

Gazetteer: *The Gazetteer of India, Vol. I*. Publications Division Ministry of Information and Broadcasting.

Government Gazette: *Government Gazette Panjab and Its Dependencies*. Lahore, Oct. 25, 1900.

Gupta, Hari Ram: *Panjab on the Eve of First Sikh War*. Department of History, Panjab University.

Harbans Singh: *The Heritage of the Sikhs*. Asia Publishing House, Bombay-1, 1964.

Hardinge, Viscount: *Viscount Hardinge and Advance of the British Dominions into the Panjab*. Oxford, 1900.

Hasrat, B.J. Dr.: *Anglo-Sikh Relations 1799-1849*. V.V. Research Institute Book Agency, Hoshiarpur, 1968.

Hunter, W.W.: *The Marquees of Dalhousie*. Clarendon Press, Oxford, 1895.

Innes, A.D.: *A Short History of British India*. Methew, London, 1923.

Journal: *Asiatic Quarterly, 1894*. Indian Historical Commission Proceeding Part II, 1958.

Kay, Sir John William: *History of the Sepoy War Vol. I*, London, 1889.

Kay, Sir John William: *History of the Administration of the East India Company*. London, 1889.

Khilnani, N.M.: *The Panjab Under the Lawrences*. Panjab Government, Simla, 1951.

Khushwant Singh: *A History of the Sikhs, Vol. II*. Princeton University Press, London, 1966.

Latif, Muhammad: *History of the Panjab*. The Calcutta Central Press Company Ltd., Calcutta, 1891.

Login, E. /Dalhousie: *Lady Login's Recollections*. Language Deptt., Panjab, Patiala.

Lyall, Alfred: *The Rise of the British Dominion in the India.* John Murray, London, 1902.

Majumdar, R.C.: *History of the Freedom Movement in India, Vol. III.* Firma K. L. Mukhopadhyay, Calcutta, 1963.

Malleson, Col. G.E.: *Deceive Battles in India.* London, 1883.

Malleson, Col. G.E.: *Recreations of an Indian Official.* London, 1872.

Marriot, J.A.R.: *English in India.* Oxford University Press, 1932.

Marshman, J.C.: *The History of India, Vols. I, II and III*, London, 1874.

Memorandum: *Memorandum of the Disturbances in the Panjab, April, 1919.* Superintendent, Govt. Printing Press, Lahore, 1920.

Memorandum: *Memorandum on the Restriction of the Power to Alienation Interests in Land.* Superintendent, Govt. Printing Press, Calcutta, 1923.

Menon, V.P.: *The Transfer of Power in India.* Orient Longmans, New Delhi-1, 1947.

Morrison, J.L.: *Lawrence of Lucknow.* London, 1934.

Nalan, E.H.: *The Illustrated History of British Empire in India and East, Vols. I to VIII.* James S. Virtue, New York.

Obhrai, Dewan Chand: *The Revolution of North-West Province.* The London Book Co. (India) Ltd., Peshawar, 1938.

O'Dwyer, Sir Michael: *India As I Knew It 1885-1925.* Constable & Co. Ltd., Central Library.

P.A.R.: *Panjab Administration Reports, 1920-1922.* Panjab Government Press, Lahore.

Panikkar, K.M.: *The Indian Princes in Council.* Oxford University Press, London, 1936.

Pioneer: *The Rising on the North-West Frontier.* Pioneer Press, Allahabad, 1898.

Records: *Patiala and the Great War.* Soceity Ltd., London, 1915.

Records: *File No. P/206/B Case No. W.B. 28/A-1998 BK (1536).* Regarding War Effort of the Patiala State.

Records: *His Highness' Private Correspondence Chamber of*

Princes, Case No. V.D. 365, 1939.

Records: *Indian Princes and the War*. 5th September, 1940 to 1st May, 1941.

Records Indian Govt.: *Panjab Report, Vol. IV for the year 1851-52* Thos. Jones, Calcutta Gazette Office.

Records Indian Govt.: *Panjab Report, Vol. IV For the Year 1854-56*. J.F. Williams, Panjab Press.

Records Indian Govt.: *A History of the Development of the Police in the Panjab, 1849-1905*. Keeper of Records of the Govt. of Panjab.

Reports: *General Report on the Administration of Punjab Territories*. For the Year 1865-1866.

Reports: *General Report on the Administration of Panjab Territories*. For the Year 1862-1863.

Reports: *Major Inglis' Report on Plague in Jullundur and Hoshiarpur, 1897-1898*. Panjab Government.

Reports: *Mutiny Reports, Vol. VIII*. Panjab Government Records Office.

Reports: *Report of the Commission Appointed by the Panjab Sub-Committee of the Indian National Congress, Vols. I & II*. 1919-1920 K. Santhanam, Secretary to the Commission, Lahore.

Roberts, P.E.: *History of British India*. Oxford University Press, London, 1952.

Selections: *Selection from Papers on Indebtedness and Land Transfer*. Superintendent, Govt. Printing Press, Calcutta, 1895.

Satyapal: *Sixty Years of Congress*. The Lion Press, Lahore, 1946.

Sethi, R.R.: *John Lawrence as Commissioner of Jullundur Doab*. Panjab Monograph No. 10, Lahore, 1930.

S.G.P.C.: *Muslim League Attack on Sikhs and Hindus in the Panjab, 1947*. S.G.P.C., Amritsar, 1950.

Sharma, Sri Ram: *Panjab in Ferment*. S. Chand & Co. (Pvt) Ltd., New Delhi-1.

Spate, O.H.K.: *India and Pakistan*. Methew & Co. Ltd., London, 1964.

Stephen, Leslie, & Sidney Lee: *The Dictionary of National*

Biography, Oxford University Press, London, 1917.

Temple, Sir Richard: *Lord Lawrence*. Action Series, London. 1890.

Temple, Sir Richard: *Men and Events of My Times in India*. London, 1882.

Thomson & Garratt: *Rise and Fulfilment of British Rule in India*. London, 1935.

Thompson, W.P.: *Panjab Irrigation*. Civil & Military Gazette Press, Lahore, 1925.

Thorburn, S.S.: *Musalmans and Money Lenders in the Panjab*. Blackwood & Sons, 1886.

Thorburn, S.S.: *Panjab Under War and Peace*. Mahendra College, 5384, 5385 (777 p), Geography Section.

Times of India: *Ruling Princes and Chiefs of India*. The Times of India Press, Bombay, 1930.

Trevaskis, H. Kennedy: *The Panjab of Today, Vol. I & II*. The Civil & Military Gazette, Lahore, 1931-32.

Trevaskis, H. Kennedy: *The Land of Five Rivers*. Oxford University Press, London, 1928.

Trotter: *The Earl of Auckland*. Oxford. 1893.

Trotter, L.J.: *History of India, Vols. I and II*. W.H. Allen & Co., Pall Mall. S.W.

Varma, S.P.: *Pakistan Political System in Crisis*. South Asia Studies Centre, Department of Political Science, University of Rajasthan, Jaipur.

Vongradoss, Paul: *Common Sense in Law*, Williams & Norgate Home University Library.

INDEX